D0705758

Morality and the Environmental Crisis

The environmental crisis creates an unprecedented moral predicament: how to be a good person when our collective and individual actions contribute to immeasurable devastation and suffering. Drawing on an extraordinary range of sources from philosophy, political theory, global religion, ecology, and contemporary spirituality, Roger S. Gottlieb explores the ethical ambiguities, challenges, and opportunities we face. Engagingly written, intellectually rigorous, and forcefully argued, this volume explores the moral value of nature; the possibility of an "ecological" democracy; how we treat animals; the demands and limits of individual responsibility and collective political change; contemporary ambiguities of rationality; and how to face environmental despair. In *Morality and the Environmental Crisis*, Gottlieb combines compassion for the difficulties of contemporary moral life with an unflinching ethical commitment to awareness and action.

ROGER S. GOTTLIEB is Professor of Philosophy at Worcester Polytechnic Institute, and the Nautilus Book Award winning author or editor of twenty books of ethics, political theory, religious studies, and contemporary spirituality. He is internationally known as a leading analyst of religious environmentalism and for his original accounts of spirituality in an age of environmental crisis and the role of religion in a democratic society.

Cambridge Studies in Religion, Philosophy, and Society

Series Editors

Paul Moser, *Loyola University Chicago*
Chad Meister, *Bethel College*

This is a series of interdisciplinary texts devoted to major-level courses in religion, philosophy, and related fields. It includes original, current, and wide-spanning contributions by leading scholars from various disciplines that (a) focus on the central academic topics in religion and philosophy, (b) are seminal and up-to-date regarding recent developments in scholarship on the various key topics, and (c) incorporate, with needed precision and depth, the major differing perspectives and backgrounds – the central voices on the major religions and the religious, philosophical, and sociological viewpoints that cover the intellectual landscape today. Cambridge Studies in Religion, Philosophy, and Society is a direct response to this recent and widespread interest and need.

Recent Books in the Series

Roger Trigg
Religious Diversity: Philosophical and Political Dimensions

John Cottingham
Philosophy of Religion: Towards a More Humane Approach

William J. Wainwright
Reason, Revelation, and Devotion: Inference and Argument in Religion

Gordon Graham
Philosophy, Art, and Religion: Understanding Faith and Creativity

Keith Ward
The Christian Idea of God: A Philosophical Foundation for Faith

Timothy Samuel Shah and Jack Friedman
Homo Religiosus? Exploring the Roots of Religion and Religious Freedom in Human Experience

Sylvia Walsh
Kierkegaard and Religion: Personality, Character, and Virtue

Morality and the Environmental Crisis

ROGER S. GOTTLIEB

Worcester Polytechnic Institute

CAMBRIDGE
UNIVERSITY PRESS

CAMBRIDGE
UNIVERSITY PRESS

University Printing House, Cambridge CB2 8BS, United Kingdom

One Liberty Plaza, 20th Floor, New York, NY 10006, USA

477 Williamstown Road, Port Melbourne, VIC 3207, Australia

314–321, 3rd Floor, Plot 3, Splendor Forum, Jasola District Centre,
New Delhi – 110025, India

79 Anson Road, #06–04/06, Singapore 079906

Cambridge University Press is part of the University of Cambridge.

It furthers the University's mission by disseminating knowledge in the pursuit of
education, learning, and research at the highest international levels of excellence.

www.cambridge.org
Information on this title: www.cambridge.org/9781107140738
DOI: 10.1017/9781316493083

© Roger S. Gottlieb 2019

This publication is in copyright. Subject to statutory exception
and to the provisions of relevant collective licensing agreements,
no reproduction of any part may take place without the written
permission of Cambridge University Press.

First published 2019
Reprinted 2019

Printed in the United Kingdom by TJ International Ltd. Padstow Cornwall

A catalogue record for this publication is available from the British Library.

Library of Congress Cataloging-in-Publication Data
NAMES: Gottlieb, Roger S., author.
TITLE: Morality and the environmental crisis / Roger S. Gottlieb.
DESCRIPTION: Cambridge ; New York, NY : Cambridge University Press, 2019. |
SERIES: Cambridge studies in religion, philosophy, and society | Includes index.
IDENTIFIERS: LCCN 2018042077 | ISBN 9781107140738 (hardback : alk. paper) |
ISBN 9781316506127 (pbk. : alk. paper)
SUBJECTS: LCSH: Environmental ethics. | Environmental responsibility. |
Environmentalism–Philosophy.
Classification: LCC GE42 .G67 2019 | DDC 179/.1–dc23
LC record available at https://lccn.loc.gov/2018042077

ISBN 978-1-107-14073-8 Hardback
ISBN 978-1-316-50612-7 Paperback

Cambridge University Press has no responsibility for the persistence or accuracy
of URLs for external or third-party internet websites referred to in this publication
and does not guarantee that any content on such websites is, or will remain,
accurate or appropriate.

Once Again
FOR
AND TO
LIFE

Contents

Contents

Acknowledgments

My gratitude:

- To the students of my environmental philosophy courses at Worcester Polytechnic Institute – for listening, thinking, and asking tough questions.
- To Jeremy Bendik-Keymer, Nicholas Kratovil, David Kidner, and John Sanbonmatsu – for thoughtful criticisms and kind words.
- To fellow academics of environmental studies – for creating theory that really matters.
- To countless journalists and researchers – for providing essential information about the state of the world.
- To environmental activists – for providing inspiring examples of moral lives in a time of crisis.
- To life on earth – for allowing me to be part of the show.

Introduction

What is the right thing to do? Answers might come in the form of responses to particular ethical controversies – abortion, capital punishment, what to do about world hunger. Or they might focus on whether ethical judgements are rooted in universal principles, compassionate interpersonal connection, attempts to create the most happiness and least suffering, obedience to God, or the pursuit of spiritual enlightenment.

In the context of the environmental crisis, this book will address both particular questions (e.g., How responsible are ordinary people for pollution?) and the more general concerns of whether and how environmental ethics are rooted in rights, emotional connection, concern for suffering, or the development of environment benefiting virtues like gratitude and compassion.

Yet there are already many fine books that cover such issues. Why write – or read – this one?

Because what is too often ignored or taken for granted in these discussions is a more fundamental question: Can historical situations arise in which basic preconditions of moral action either do not exist or are significantly weakened? When it is very hard or even close to impossible to be – as almost all of us want to be – morally good? Before we decide what we ought to do, what our obligations are, or how a virtuous person would act, we must believe that we can answer these questions reasonably and act on what we know.

My first concern in this book, and one that will run through all the particular discussions, is with a general, widespread moral malaise that afflicts, in varying degrees, all of us – whether we realize it or not. It is the effect of the environmental crisis on our capacity to think and act morally:

to trust in our own ability be good people. And this is not just a question about each of us as individuals. Clearly many environmental issues – energy policy, laws governing pollutants, how children are educated about the moral meaning of nature – require collective responses. It is not only our personal morality that is at stake, but also the ethical meaning of our society, our culture, our entire civilization.

And that is why much of what I will offer here will be questions, dilemmas, and difficult choices. Of one thing only I am sure: Moral life in the face of environmental crisis offers few, if any, easy answers.

I

Environmental Crisis and Moral Life

1 A CRISIS OF THE BODY AND THE WORLD

In this Internet age the facts are not hard to find. They are, however, emotionally very difficult to take in.

So let us begin with a few typical environmental facts, just to set the emotional tone and create a context for what I am saying about moral life today.

- 2017 was the twenty-first consecutive warmer-than-average year since 1997. During the fall of 2016, the Arctic recorded temperatures 30 degrees higher than normal.[1]
- In a 2004 St. Louis study of newborns, the average baby was found with 187 toxic substances in their blood.[2]
- The World Health Organization recently estimated that three to six million deaths per year are attributable in whole or part to air pollution.
- A precipitous drop in insect populations, estimated to be as high as 75 percent, indicates potentially catastrophic effects on human agriculture in particular and plant species life in general.

[1] "Assessing the U.S. Climate in 2017," National Centers for Environmental Information Website. Accessed January 16, 2018, www.ncei.noaa.gov/news/national-climate-201712.
[2] "Body Burden: The Pollution in Newborns," Environmental Working Group Website. Accessed December 15, 2017, www.ewg.org/research/body-burden-pollution-newborns#.WjQJJ1WnGpo.

- In the United States 40–50 percent of rivers and lakes cannot support life.[3]
- Oceanic dead or low-oxygen zones now cover areas larger than North America, have dramatically increased over the last 50 years, and seriously threaten the ocean's ability to sustain life.[4]
- Human activity is leading to the fastest and largest die-off of species in seventy million years – approximately one species every 11 minutes.
- In August 2017, during Hurricane Harvey, some towns received 5 feet of water in less than 48 hours.
- Noise pollution, outstripping population growth, has many negative physical and psychological effects on people and animals. Significantly worse in minority and poor communicates, such pollution can lessen children's ability to learn, worsen high blood pressure, increase risk of strokes, and degrade people's emotional states.[5]
- Rainforests, overburdened by what we have done to the atmosphere, are now giving off rather than absorbing CO_2.
- Somewhere between 700 million and a billion people live in densely packed urban slums that are part of the megacities resulting from global urbanization. While racial minorities in the United States suffer from unjustly environmental ills, conditions in developing countries in Latin America, Africa, and Asia can be staggeringly bad. Examples are shanty towns literally built on or immediately next to gargantuan toxic facilities, so little sanitation that excrement is an immediate presence of daily life, people charged a significant percentage of their meager daily income for clean water or a toilet, housing sites in areas weakened by overdevelopment and correspondingly liable to flood or landslide. In short, there is an immediate and overwhelming level of human-generated pollution in the daily lives of somewhere between 10 and 20 percent of the human race.[6]

---

[3] Water Benefits Health Website. Accessed December 15, 2017, www.waterbenefitshealth .com/water-pollution-facts.html.

[4] Denise Breitberg, et al., "Declining Oxygen in the Global Ocean and Coastal Waters," *Science* Magazine Website. Accessed January 30, 2018, http://science.sciencemag.org/content/359/6371/eaam7240.

[5] Florence Williams, "Sound Effects," *Mother Jones*, January/February 2017. Stephan Stansfield, "How Noise Pollution Affects Your Health," Independent Website. Accessed October 9, 2017, www.independent.co.uk/life-style/health-and-families/features/how-noise-pollution-can-affect-your-health-a6853746.html.

[6] Mike Davis, *Planet of Slums* (London: Verso, 2007).

These facts, and many more, signal a transformation of both the planet and our own bodies. Or, we might say: it is a decisive transformation of the world, and because our bodies are part of that world, of our bodies as well.

These facts tell us is that the world is neither stable nor safe. The trees and birds, the water and the fish, may be poisoned, or contain poisons. Our own breasts and prostrates, afflicted with carcinogens, may cause our deaths. And so much grace that we've loved – the previously crystal clear ocean polluted with oil, the mountaintop littered with broken glass – has been destroyed, wounded, or threatened.

These reflections make us anxious, so let's have a nice glass of water to help us calm down.

But is there lead in our drinking water – like there was discovered in Flint, Michigan, and which some estimate is common in 10 percent of American communities?[7] The old pipes could be dangerous, better not risk it. And whom can you really trust to tell you the truth about those pipes? Authorities in Michigan knew for years that the Flint water was not safe but didn't inform the public.

Let's have a nice long drink from a water bottle instead – either the flimsy plastic ones that hold mass distributed "spring" water or the sturdier ones we carry around ourselves and fill with filtered water. But wait a minute, it seems that the plastic bottles may contain BPA, a carcinogen that leaches into the water from the plastic. So much for Poland Springs or Fiji Water. But our REI super-duper water bottle promises to be BPA free. Is it? How could we know? Keep in mind that for years no one knew that BPA was dangerous. Could there be something else they are missing in the water bottle, the one from which we just drank?

Forget the water. It's a nice day, let's go outside and relax, and sit under this beautiful maple tree. It's so hot. Unusually hot. But the shade is great. But, wait a second, what are all these black spots on the maple tree's leaves? They don't look too healthy. Could they come from the drought we've been having? Will the tree make it through the weather that is warmer from climate change? Will it succumb to one of the

---

[7] Grennan Millikan, "Lead Contaminated Water Is Much More Common Than You Think," Motherboard Website. Accessed December 15, 2017, https://motherboard.vice.com/en_us/article/yp3kg5/lead-contaminated-drinking-water-is-much-more-prevalent-than-you-think.

increasingly powerful storms? Should we worry about all the trees of childhood, the ones we sheltered under on hot days, climbed when we got older and stronger, whose leaves we raked after admiring their brilliant colors – how long will they resist illnesses to which they are made more vulnerable by global warming?

Why do we cough so much in summer? What lingers in the hazy air that is labeled in weather reports as "unhealthy"?

What is the sticky black substance that sticks to our feet at the beach (it is oil, from oil spills). What must it be like, around the Cape of Good Hope off extreme Southern Africa, where overloaded oil tankers routinely deal with bad weather by dumping excess oil into the oceans?

When the doctor looks at the x-ray a second time, clears his throat, and tells us we have to talk, do we think back to what might have been in the water, the air, the food?

When our child is diagnosed with autism, or attention deficit hyper-activity disorder (ADHD), or neurological deficits, or intellectual delay, or cancer – do we wonder what was in the toys/crib/carpet/wood panels that might have affected her genes or lungs or brain? Especially, that is, if we are aware that "Trillions of pounds of tens of thousands of toxic chemicals pour into the environment and into the products in our homes, workplaces, and schools ... no child can escape exposure ... no matter how wealthy their parents, how large their homes, how exclusive their schools."[8]

2 WHAT'S CHANGED?

It is not that human destructiveness toward the natural world, with dire consequences for nature and people alike, is unprecedented. The ancient Babylonians decimated their fields by overirrigation. In the *Critias,* Plato described how poor farming practices turned once-thriving agricultural land into barren wastes and ravines. Thousands of years ago Native Americans overhunted many large mammal species to extinction.[9] Antici-pating suburban sprawl by two millennia, a biblical prophet criticized

[8] Philip Shabecoff and Alice Shabecoff, *Poisoned for Profit: How Toxins Are Making Our Children Chronically Ill* (White River Junction, VT: Chelsea Green Publishing, 2010), p. 14.
[9] On Native Americans, see N. Scott Momaday, "A First American Views His Land," in David Landis Barnhill, ed., *At Home on the Earth* (Berkeley, CA: University of California Press, 1991), pp. 19–29.

those "who join house to house, who add field to field, until there is room
for no one but you" (Isaiah 5:18).

But this present environmental threat, moving at an accelerated pace
and caused by us, is something new and terrifying. We have done what no
human power, no matter how powerful, could do. The chemical balance
of the oceans was set by forces far beyond human control – until now,
when the excess of human-produced CO_2 has made the oceans 30 percent
more acidic. We are making mother's milk unsafe to drink because of
pollutants in the mother's body.

The extent of this change can be indicated by noting a few instances of
what we used to think of the natural world. In the Hebrew Bible, it was a
sign of God's unlimited power to fashion forms of life and an earth on
which they would dwell; and a marker of how much humans could
neither control nor understand them. In response to a critical question
about why he, a just man, was suffering, God puts Job in his place by
asking some obviously rhetorical questions:

> Can you pull in Leviathan with a fishhook
>   or tie down its tongue with a rope?
> Can you put a cord through its nose
>   or pierce its jaw with a hook?
> Can you make a pet of it like a bird
>   or put it on a leash for the young women in your house?
> Will traders barter for it?
>   Will they divide it up among the merchants?
> Can you fill its hide with harpoons
>   or its head with fishing spears?
> Any hope of subduing it is false;
>   the mere sight of it is overpowering.
>
>   (Job 40:2–9)

Yet now humans can not only catch whales, but also hunt them to near
extinction, implant radio transmitters to track them, teach them tricks in
theme parks, and catalog their DNA.

Earlier in the Bible God describes humanity's relation to a difficult,
demanding nature: "The ground is cursed on your account; you will work
hard to eat from it as long as you live. It will produce thorns and thistles
for you, and you will eat field plants. You will eat bread by the sweat of
your forehead till you return to the ground – for you were taken out of it:
you are dust, and you will return to dust" (Genesis 3:17–19). As difficult
as this promise is, there are no human-created poisons lurking in the
water. Getting food is hard, but neither the earth nor the food that comes
from it is tainted with hidden, lethal dangers.

Two thousand years later, in Renaissance England, we find an appeal –
an extremely common one in world literature – to the soothing and
morally beneficial effects of nature. How it provides a respite from and
alternative to the corruptions of society. In Shakespeare's *Twelfth Night*,
on their primitive, undeveloped island, the exiled Duke addresses his
comrades:

> Hath not old custom made this life more sweet
> Than that of painted pomp? Are not these woods
> More free from peril than the envious court?
> Here feel we not the penalty of Adam,
> The seasons' difference; as the icy fang
> And churlish chiding of the winter's wind,
> Which when it bites and blows upon my body,
> Even till I shrink with cold, I smile and say
> 'This is no flattery; these are counsellors
> That feelingly persuade me what I am.' ...
> And this our life, exempt from public haunt,
> Finds tongues in trees, books in the running brooks,
> Sermons in stones, and good in everything.

Yet once we take in the full scope of the environmental crisis, we know
every part of what would have soothed the Duke is threatened. Moun-
taintops have cell phone towers crowding each other for space; forests are
threatened by exotic species, climate change, and loggers. Each area of
wilderness must be constantly protected from encroachment, an
encroachment that need happen only once for the wilderness to be paved
over, sold at a profit, consumed.

Much more recently, hiding in a crowded attic during the Holocaust,
Anne Frank reassured herself:

The best remedy for those who are afraid, lonely, or unhappy is to go outside,
somewhere where they can be quite alone with the heavens, nature, and God.
Because only then does one feel that all is as it should be and that God wishes to
see people happy, amidst the simple beauty of nature. As long as this exists, and it
certainly always will, I know that then there will always be comfort for every
storm.[10]

Yet what would happen if Anne had gone outside, and instead of simple
beauty had seen a beach covered with plastic debris, trees dying from acid
rain, or an oil slick covering the pond?

---

[10] Anne Frank, *The Diary of a Young Girl* (Garden City, NY: Doubleday and Co., 1972),
p. 172.

3 ENVIRONMENTAL CRISIS

By "environmental crisis" I mean two things. First, the sheer scope of what we have done. Second, how the leading cultural and political institutions either directly contributed to this damage, failed to foresee it, or refused to recognize it even after it was well underway. The environmental crisis is thus not just a complex and daunting collection of problems with our bodies and the earth, it is a fundamental problem with *our* – in the broadest sense of the term – "civilization."

To make this point, consider the term *ecocide*, the essential force of which is to associate the environmental crisis with genocide in general and the Holocaust in particular.[11] There are clearly some drawbacks to this usage; genocide is typically directed at particular human communities and coordinated by a centralized authority. Generally, the environmental crisis is neither.

But "ecocide" can also help illuminate what is going on. For a start, associating environmental destruction with genocide forcefully asserts the cataclysmic nature of the threat. If the environmental crisis is like the murder of six million innocent people, it requires immediate and decisive attention. This is not a matter of some technological miscalculation that can be remedied by improving gas mileage, eating more organic vegetables, or using cloth shopping bags.

Second, like the Holocaust, the reality of ecocide calls into question the ultimate rationality of modernity. As the Germans used their technical and bureaucratic competence to create efficient forms of mass death, so today's transportation, energy, and manufacturing systems – each characterized by unprecedented sophistication – contribute to an enormously irrational and destructive overall consequence. We have the fulfillment of Hungarian Marxist Georg Lukacs's century-old warning: Modern society would combine breathtaking technological competence with a fundamental and sweeping irrationality. The machines are incredible, but the piles of garbage overflow, the seas rise, and our bloodstreams are polluted.

Third, and by implication: As any nation guilty of genocide must question its culture, politics, economics, and religion, so a modern world

---

[11] In 1988 Catholic priest Thomas Berry lamented that "After dealing with suicide, homicide, and genocide, our Western Christian moral code collapses completely: it cannot deal with biocide." *Dream of the Earth* (San Francisco: Sierra Club Books, 1988), p. 77.
  There is also Franz Broswimmer, *Ecocide: A Short History of the Mass Extinction of Species* (London: Pluto Press, 2002).

culture that is committing ecocide must do the same. How can we, collectively and as individuals, deny climate science, use thousands of toxic chemicals, and destroy the rainforest to produce cheap hamburgers for McDonald's?

Finally, some instances of environmental abuse are literally genocidal in that they have devastating effects on particular human communities. Global warming or acid rain may be somewhat widespread and random, though they certainly affect the poor more than the rich. In other cases – e.g., the consequences of uranium mining or other forms of mineral extraction on indigenous peoples – environmental damage rises to the level of physical and/or cultural destruction. The Ogoni of Nigeria have been devastated by oil drilling; the native peoples of China, Canada, and India by the Three Gorges, James Bay, and Narmada River dam complexes; racial minorities in the United States by siting of toxic facilities. For these peoples ecocide simply *is* a kind of genocide.

Indeed, in many areas of the globe economic growth has been paid for by expropriating the land, resources, and ecosystems of indigenous peoples. At the same time, indigenous peoples are disproportionately connected to settings of high biodiversity. The reduction of those settings to simplified commercial contexts – what Vandana Shiva calls "monoculture" – is simultaneously the elimination of the physical and cultural basis for indigenous cultural diversity. With the elimination of cultural diversity – the whittling away of the more than 300 million native peoples in 4,000 distinct societies – there comes a simultaneous loss of irreplaceable traditional knowledge about how human culture and nonhuman nature can mutually exist over long periods of time.[12]

Here the fate of the rivers, the land, the endangered species, and the endangered people are pretty much the same.

4 RELIGION[13] AND PHILOSOPHY

While there are exceptions, religions have generally taught us to perceive and to act on nonhuman nature in terms of human interests, beliefs, and social structures – to frame nature's significance in human terms. The

[12] For dozens of valuable accounts, see Darrell Addison Posey, ed., *Cultural and Spiritual Values of Biodiversity: A Complementary Contribution to the Global Biodiversity Assessment* (London: Intermediate Technology Publications, 1999).

[13] Unless otherwise specified, by "religion" I mean the dominant institutional or "world" religions: Judaism, Christianity, Islam, Buddhism, Hinduism, and Confucianism – which are defined by numbers of adherents and/or (in the case of Judaism) historical influence.

Judeo-Christian tradition, closely associated with a European industrial civilization that brought the environmental crisis into the modern world, was typically concerned (at best) with the "wise use" of the earth and its creatures, and not with any notion of their inherent value. If there was a moral issue in our treatment of the nonhuman, it was with the fair distribution of the fruits of human activity, combatting poverty, or anxieties that the achievements of modern science and technology would lessen the social power and prestige of religion. While nature might be a sign of God, the sign itself had little or no moral standing.

Comparable moral blindness dominated Western secular philosophy. From the Greeks to the 1970s, a series of central philosophical problems were wrestled with: what constitutes reason or knowledge, what is justice, is belief in God rational, how sensations connect to beliefs. None of these took the human relation to nature as a significant problem – either in terms of the value of nature itself or the way human actions on nature could affect other people. Virtually all of what are considered to be the major philosophers in the tradition presumed – typically without justification – that nature existed for human use. And most worked hard to establish the human difference and independence from the rest of nature. It is striking that when environmental philosophy did emerge in the 1970s, how little of the "canon" of Western philosophy could be used as a resource.[14]

Referring to both religion and philosophy, as Steven Rockefeller observed: "The social and moral traditions that have been dominant in the West ... have not involved the idea that animals, trees, or the land in their own right, as distinct from their owners or their Creator, have moral standing. Only a few saints and reformers have taught that people have direct moral responsibilities to nonhuman creatures."[15] And even the few exceptions to this general rule, who taught the aesthetic or spiritual value of nature, didn't comprehend the threat contained in the rise of capitalism and industrialization.

Since the 1980s there has been a dramatic shift. There is a vigorous, if still somewhat professionally marginalized, field of academic environmental philosophy, as well as an encompassing and dynamic discipline

---

[14] Often non-Western traditions (Taoism, Buddhism) were utilized; along with twentieth century figures Heidegger, Horkheimer, Adorno, and Marcuse. A little attention was paid to Spinoza.

[15] Steven C. Rockefeller, "Faith and Community in an Ecological Age," in Steven C. Rockefeller and John C. Elder, eds., *Spirit and Nature: Why the Environment Is a Religious Issue* (Boston: Beacon Press, 1992), p. 142.

of environmental humanities. Far more significantly, religious environmentalism is a global movement that includes theologians, institutional leadership, and lay activists. Popes, the heads of both the World and National Council of Churches, Buddhist leaders such as the Dalai Lama and Thich Nhat Hanh, and Reform and Conservative Judaism have gone on record taking environmental issues with great seriousness.

Yet we still need to reflect on how few and far between were the religious or philosophical voices in opposing the last century's juggernaut of technological development and environmental degradation. If religion and philosophy – or, to make it more immediate, leading theologians, respected philosophers, even popular moral teachers – did not see what was going on until the rivers began to catch on fire (Cayuga River, Pittsburgh), city air became increasingly unbreathable, and the cancer rates continued to rise – why? How could they have missed it? How thorough has their repentance been? When have they said: "How could we have been so blind?"

Whatever changes have been made, we may question whether they are enough. While many of their leaders and institutions have made inspiring statements, do faith communities throughout the world take climate change as seriously as they do, say, sexual relations, preserving their tax-free status, control of "holy places," or continuing doctrinal disagreements with different versions of what is essentially the same religion? Are they clear on the way their traditional concern with poverty directly connects to the devastating effects of climate change on poor people most vulnerable to drought and rising seas? Certainly, the world of philosophy, while open to environmental issues considerably more than it was, say, 30 years ago, still treats environmental issues as one of a large number of "applied philosophy" areas, in a long list that includes feminist philosophy, bioethics, professional ethics, business ethics, and the like.

Where does that leave us? Religion and philosophy are two of our critical cultural resources. If they failed so badly and for so long, how are we as isolated individuals to make sense of the kinds of facts listed earlier?

Imagine that you are on a boat, sailing far out at sea. Critical problems arise: a hole near the waterline, radio communication down. You must repair the boat, but you cannot call for help, and you are much too far from shore to get to a dock. You must repair the boat even as you are sailing on it, hoping the repairs will be adequate to keep you afloat.

The boat is our civilization. The problems are the environmental crisis. And as in the example, there is no docking and getting off, so we cannot jettison our civilization, only repair it. The failures and limitations of religion and philosophy are an impoverished tool kit, a kit itself in need of repair. How are we to repair what is so badly damaged if the resources for that repair are themselves in disarray?

5 POLITICS AND ECONOMICS

During the last century the political structure of most nations has taken one of two dominant forms. There is some variant of liberalism, marked by democratic elections, representative government, and a modicum of civil rights. And there is some variant of totalitarianism, marked by, at best, the pretense of democracy, a repressive government, and virtually no freedom to dissent.

With few exceptions these significantly different *political* forms have shared a common *economic* orientation: ever-expanding production, with that production geared (depending on the nation) to some combination of consumer goods and military power. An endless desire for cheap energy, cheap commodities, cheap food, and expensive weapons drives private corporations and state-run economic enterprises alike. There has been little concern with the enduring consequences of this pursuit. In what some thinkers have called a shared "industrial civilization," increased production and endless increases in scope and power of technology are seen as their own reward, a kind of Holy Grail of human activity, the value of which is beyond question.[16] Only when environmental problems directly threaten economic activity is the march of progress paused. Issues such as climate change, air pollution, the threat to the ozone layer from CFCs, or carcinogens in common household projects are usually raised for years, or decades, before they are taken seriously. And recommended action will typically not even be considered if it threatens economic "growth."

The result is an essential coordination of economic and political power, a coordination most often resistant to environmental sustainability or a slowdown of ecological degradation.

For example: When a die-off of bees threatens a devastating loss to their environmental service of pollination – a service that is estimated at nearly $30 billion in the United States alone – some notice is taken. We ask why this is happening and wonder what will happen if the die-off

---

[16] For an intelligent, early treatment, see Andrew McLaughlin, *Regarding Nature: Industrialism and Deep Ecology* (Albany: State University of New York Press, 1993).

continues and reaches truly epidemic proportions. But as we discover a variety of immediate answers – a fungus, a virus – we then find that there is good reason to believe that underlying causes almost always implicate some essential feature of our broader environmental practices. In the case of bees, it is weakened immune systems stemming from exposure to pesticides and biological disorientation from climate change.

And then the coordination of economic and political power returns, full-fold, to retard significant action. For pesticides are manufactured by enormously wealthy and influential chemical companies (e.g., Monsanto), whose financial contributions to politicians keeps restrictions on the use of their products to a minimum. So, action to restrain pesticide use is minimized, and whatever restrictions are put in place are subject to being revoked later when the political climate shifts and "job creation" becomes an unchallengeable priority.

The economic power of corporate giants like Monsanto, oil and gas companies, mining companies, banks, investment houses, etc., is manifest in four different ways.

First, there are a variety of media strategies. They self-consciously cultivate confusion and doubt about solid scientific findings, convincing millions that a virtual certainty or high likelihood is "really" a controversy on which authorities disagree. Even while internal memos showed an awareness of the reality of climate change, Exxon spent millions on a public relations firm tasked with cultivating the idea that climate change was simply a questionable theory rather than a reality.[17] In 2007 journalists described the "denial machine": a "well-coordinated, well-funded campaign by contrarian scientists, free-market think tanks and industry; created a paralyzing fog of doubt around climate change for nearly two decades," funded by the American Petroleum Institute, the Western Fuels Association, and ExxonMobil.[18]

[17] Geoffrey Supran and Naomi Oreskes, "Assessing ExxonMobil's climate change communications (1977–2014)," Environmental Research Letters Website. Accessed December 15, 2017, http://iopscience.iop.org/article/10.1088/1748-9326/aa815f. Studies of comparable campaigns to protect lethal substances abound. E.g., Gerald Markowitz and David Rosner, *Deceit and Denial: The Deadly Politics of Industrial Pollution* (Berkeley, CA: University of California Press, 2002); Devra Davis, *When Smoke Ran Like Water: Tales of Environmental Deception and the Battle against Pollution* (New York: Basic Books, 2004).
[18] "Global Warming Deniers Well Funded," *Newsweek* Website. Accessed February 6, 2018, www.newsweek.com/global-warming-deniers-well-funded-99775.

As well, in a process called "greenwashing," corporations represent themselves as environmentally responsible, even taking credit for changes they've made that they fiercely lobbied against.[19]

Second, corporations sway governments by direct monetary contributions. In a given year, for example, Monsanto spends 4.6 million dollars to get access and influence over members of both political parties.[20]

Third, giant corporations have a kind of ultimate or "doomsday" economic power. When threatened by troublesome environmental regulations (as with overly active unions or any other constraints), they can simply lower investment, close factories, and cut jobs. Or they can move to more business friendly – and often politically repressive – locales. The resulting economic deprivation soon obliterates concerns with global warming or cancer rates.

Fourth, through their powerful influence on popular culture in advertisements, television and movie content, and social media, they support collective values of self-concern, celebrity, consumerism, and fascination with gadgetry. You might ask yourself how many movies or TV series celebrate lives of moderation, nonviolence, austerity, contemplation, and contentment – and how many emphasize fame, sensual gratification, violence, power, and the trappings of wealth. Particular executives or corporations may be represented as evil individuals, but the system as a whole is represented as the only one possible. The bad actors are "exceptions."

This interplay of economics and politics means that over the last century or so governmental legitimacy has been tied to economic well-being, with that well-being defined in terms of continuing expansion of production and consumption. That it could be defined in other ways has been voiced by some,[21] but their voices are drowned out by a near universal clamor for jobs, development, and growth; for bigger homes, more cars, increasingly intricate phones. The extreme income inequality that haunts most of the economic behemoths – the United States and

---

[19] Jed Greer, *Greenwashing: The Reality behind Corporate Environmentalism* (Totawa, NJ: Rowman and Littlefield, 1997).

[20] Open Secretes.org Website. Accessed December 15, 2017, www.opensecrets.org/lobby/clientsum.php?id=d000000055&year=2016. For a detailed study of these processes: Dan Fagin and Marianne Lavelle, *Toxic Deception: How the Chemical Industry Manipulates Science, Bends the Law, and Endangers Your Health* (Secaucus, NJ: Birch Lane Press, 1996).

[21] An early and classic source: E. F. Schumacher, *Small Is Beautiful: Economics as If People Mattered* (New York: Harper, 2010).

China, most obviously, but also most of Latin America and Russia – drives the desire for economic growth, *not* a fundamental rethinking of the system as a whole. The recurrent inability of capitalist or state capitalist economic expansion to promote equality or a stable economic future is discounted. Rather than a rethinking of fundamental goals, we get the endless demand for more of the same.

Finally, over the last thirty years a "neoliberal" strategy of global economic treaties enshrines the freedom to pollute in international agreements. When nations sign on to these treaties, which are often necessary for their own economic development, they surrender a good deal of environmental sovereignty. The agreements enforced by international institutions such as the World Trade Organization radically diminish local environmental sovereignty.[22] For requiring warning labels on cigarettes, or forbidding polluting additives to gasoline, they can be sued by manufacturers for "restraint of trade."

As a result, only the most extreme and immediate environmental threats – e.g., the danger CFCs posed to the ozone layer – prompted coordinated action. In that case DuPont, maker of CFCs, resisted any restriction on their use, then exported them to other countries when the United States outlawed them, and in the interim managed to corner the market on their replacement.

If religion and philosophy were not adequate to the task of civilizational repair, we might have thought that the titans of industry and political leaders would save the day. With some exceptions, they have not. We are back in the boat, barely keeping ourselves afloat, even though we have a beautiful new iPhone and cars that can park themselves. At the very same time, over a billion people have little access to clean water or may have to walk four hours to get wood to cook dinner. Global warming continues, environmental toxins spread, the death of other species increases. The environmental health of the planet deteriorates.

"As human pressures on the Earth system accelerate, several critical global, regional and local thresholds are close or have been exceeded," UNEP's fifth Global Environmental Outlook says. "Once these have been passed, abrupt and

---

[22] Investor State Dispute Settlement in deals like NAFTA "give multinational corporations the power to sue the U.S. government in front of a tribunal of three corporate lawyers to demand unlimited compensation from taxpayers if they think a law or government action violates their new rights." "Investor-State Dispute Settlement (ISDS): Extraordinary Corporate Powers in 'Trade Deals'." Public Citizen Website. Accessed August 31, 2017, www.citizen.org/our-work/globalization-and-trade/investor-state-system.

possible irreversible changes to the life-support functions of the planet are likely to occur, with significant adverse implications for human well-being."[23]

And while these problems are global, they are not equally distributed. Already poorer communities and nations are suffering vastly disproportional consequences of climate change. Within nations, poor and racially oppressed groups face similar problems: African-American neighborhoods surrounded by toxic waste facilities, undocumented farmworkers poisoned by pesticides, tribal communities rendered nearly uninhabitable by the effects of oil drilling or mining. As "nature" has been treated like a casual throwaway – in the words of Pope Francis the earth now resembles an "immense pile of filth" – these human groups are treated the same way.[24]

6 RATIONALITY AND SCIENCE

How could we have let all this happen? Have we all gone nuts? What does rationality – or irrationality – mean in an age of environmental crisis?

This is an enormously complicated question, which I will examine in greater detail in Chapter 7.

However, two points stand out immediately.[25] The European Enlightenment of the (roughly) eighteenth century was based in a fundamental rejection of religious tradition and a collapse of moral meaning into an individual's self-interest. "Reason" – which had been traditionally identified with the ability to uncover essential truths about human life and the essential preconditions of human fulfillment – became reduced to the ability to find the most efficient and effective way to fulfill desires or goals that could not be rationally justified.

While such reason might take a variety of forms, the most powerful form was that of modern science – a science shaped by the commitment to understanding the natural world to control it. Scientific research took for

[23] Lauren Morello, "Is Earth Near an Environmental Tipping Point?" *Scientific American* Website. Accessed August 31, 2017, www.scientificamerican.com/article/is-earth-nearing-environmental-tipping-point/.

[24] Pope Francis, *Laudato Si*, Vatican Website. Accessed January 29, 2018, www.theguardian.com/commentisfree/2015/jun/18/pope-francis-encyclical-extract.

[25] What follows here is a summary of the Western Marxist account. See, e.g., William Leiss, *The Domination of Nature* (Toronto: McGill-Queen's University Press, 1994); and Roger S. Gottlieb, ed., *An Anthology of Western Marxism: From Lukacs and Gramsci to Socialist-Feminism* (New York: Oxford University Press, 1989).

granted (in the same way as religion, philosophy, politics, and economics) that nature existed to be dominated to meet human desires.

Of course, if human desires had actually been oriented toward long-term satisfaction, contemplative living, and equitable sharing of accomplishments in agriculture, medicine, communication, and education, the outcome might have been much more ecologically responsible. But modern science has been, with few exceptions, a creature shaped by the expectations and demands of our modern political and economic systems. The more science developed, the less it could be done without massive financial support. Such support has two sources: governments and corporations. And, as we've seen, both political and economic imperatives run counter to ecological health. The "objectivity" of science is thus shaped by the demand that it produce military power and profits. Only recently has research been directed toward stemming the tide of environmental crisis. And funding for such research is, with few exceptions, still a very small percentage of the total research budget.

With no moral grounding and rapidly developing technology, it is not surprising that since the Enlightenment there is no shortage of instances of collective madness: two catastrophic world wars within twenty-five years, mass death in concentration camps of different countries, and belief systems (Nazism, for example) whose lack of reason is palpable. It should also come as no surprise, therefore, that an environmental crisis can arise, be neglected or denied, and even when responded to get only a fraction of the attention it requires.

7 OURSELVES

Who are we if we are not an expression of our culture? Cogs in whatever economic regime is dominant? Willing, or at least not violently rebellious, subjects of our current political system? We emerge into a world of language, family structure, gender relations, technological development, scientific knowledge, and legal forms. Our vaunted individuality is typically defined by which brands we buy, which among a limited set of consumerist lifestyle options we choose, who we sleep with, or which among a series of political, religious, or spiritual viewpoints we adopt – all of which are likely to be more or less compatible with the current environmental system.

As we pay taxes, obey the law, find a place to live, and use common means of transportation (for the most part, a car), we fit into systems that are structured by social forces and traditions that existed before we did and shape our sense of the world. To understand life we will use some combination of inherited popular culture, religion, philosophy, and political ideologies.

But if religious traditions and philosophy, common sense and popular culture, economics and politics, rationality and science have all been contributors to the economic crisis and are at best being reformed into inadequate responses to it, and if these are the influences that have created us, how can we trust *ourselves* to do the right thing?

Here are five ways in which a typical person, even one concerned with environmental matters (who drives a hybrid car and always brings cloth bags to the supermarket) may find that basic features of her personality and character are complicit in the environmental crisis.

First, in a modern society[26] in which tradition, religion, family affiliation, and community ties have radically diminished, the importance of work to a person's sense of self-identity has become critically important. As we face urbanization, impersonal mass media, geographical mobility, and the spread of a frantic commodification that puts everything up for sale, it is not surprising that work takes on an exaggerated importance.

In such a society, we cannot take for granted that we belong, that we have a place. A sense of self cannot be assumed. Therefore, as adults we seek to "become" somebody – which means to have some kind of significant work identity. Meet someone new at a party, and the first identifying question to you will probably be, "What do you do?" – meaning, of course, "What *work* do you do?" You will not be asked about your parents, religion, or political beliefs. While the psychological role of work may vary across gender and class lines – with women and those from lower economic classes relying more on interpersonal, religious, or community ties – for professional and managerial groups the power of work identity is psychologically central.

This dynamic is particularly true for those who have neither immense wealth nor the closer social ties of some lower economic groups. For the broad reach of the middle class, it is (paradoxically) in the worlds of

---

[26] This is a rough way to refer to Europe, North America, Japan, the middle classes of India and China, and some other parts of Asia. It is a vast generalization to which countless counterexamples could be offered. Nevertheless, I believe that its significance in the present context is crucial.

technology, science, nationalism, the military, professionalism, and corporate power that we become who we are. Work becomes like a second home, our profession like a lover, our institutional setting like the little villages that disappeared generations ago. Of course, it is a rare work life that meets our personal needs. We may feel alienated from what we do and sense that whoever we work for cares little about us. We may be in danger of downsizing or be planning our own next career move. But even if we leave or are fired, our best hope is to go to some other place not that different from this one. We create an identity of work commitments – if not to any particular employer, then to the idea of us as "workers." Few of us want to face not having work, no matter how alienating it may be. We all need some place to go in the morning, even if it is only to log on to the network from our home computer.

Thus, many of the people responsible for the day-to-day workings of our ecologically damaging pursuit of military power, industrial expansion, ever higher consumption are often neither cold bureaucrats of growth nor immensely rich and powerful. While they may be repelled by the environmental consequences of their professional lives, their emotional dependence keeps them from responding morally to what they themselves are doing. For them, the system seems inescapable – because it is the source of their job, and thus of their sense, or a critical part of their sense, of identity and self-worth.

To maintain that connection, that work identity, what will we do? Will we, as engineers for Volkswagen did, create an automobile so sophisticated it could appear nonpolluting when tested and, when driven, emit five to ten times as much pollutant? Will we lobby for formaldehyde even as we know its destructive effects on human health? Will we persist in fossil fuel extraction, retard mass transit, export dangerous chemicals if they have been made illegal at home? Will we target African-American communities because they have less social capital with which to resist toxic waste facilities and are desperately in need of jobs?

For example: How do you get someone to design and test nuclear weapons – work that has been responsible for a significant and dangerous increase in background radiation throughout the globe? A recruiter for Livermore Laboratories, one of the two major US facilities responsible for this work during 1980s, put it simply: they sought to "get candidates' interest in the physics to outweigh their natural repugnance at the task." Often young researchers would accept a position without really knowing what they would be doing. "We would just interview people in this big room with no windows and assure them they would be working on something interesting."[27] In other words, it was the *work* that mattered: the prospect of doing something interesting, being part of a large, highly respected, and influential institution. Doing what? Perhaps for many the details didn't matter all that much: if the task matched their training, gave them a place to work, and made them somebody.

If our sense of self is dependent on public work and the dominant sources of such work have strong tendencies toward environmental destruction, for many of us there will be – or at least appear to be – no escape.

Second, we are conditioned to the ease, even in many cases the illusory ease, that the modern industrial system produces. My new car can memorize thirty-two preset radio stations and access hundreds and read a thumb drive that holds 400 hours of music. It softly beeps if I'm drifting out of the highway traffic lane and will slam on the brakes if I come too close to the car in front.

If I want to change the temperature in my home, I need only make the slightest gesture to move the thermostat. My fridge is filled with foods from thousands of miles away; my library with translations into convenient English of the world's sacred scriptures. My younger daughter, who has multiple neurological and developmental special needs, would have died without two twelve-hour operations that grafted bone chips between all her vertebrae and connected her collapsing spine to two titanium rods.

As much as it pollutes and poisons, despite the ways in which it threatens life, the modern industrial system *also* provides spectacular results, privileges, and luxuries. This is a crucial source of its power and attraction. Which of us would give up easy global transportation, antibiotics, Amazon.com, email, cheap cotton clothes, or foods (like coffee and chocolate) that come from far away?

Yet each of these attractive, enjoyable, useful things has an environmental downside. Air travel is a greenhouse gas emitter and damages the ozone layer; overuse of antibiotics continues to breed highly dangerous superbugs; cheap cotton requires enormous quantities of pesticides and damaging fertilizers; conventional coffee and chocolate cultivation injure the soil and often involve highly exploitative child labor. The multitude of casual plastics that inform everything from water bottles to ballpoint pens to throwaway razors to the rings holding six-packs of beer together have created a global tidal wave of waste. So much has accumulated in the

---

[27] Hugh Gusterson, *Nuclear Rites: A Weapons Laboratory at the End of the Cold War* (Berkeley, CA: University of California Press, 1996), p. 54.

oceans that by 2050, some estimate, there will be more plastic in the ocean than fish. If you cut open a dead albatross bird on the very remote Midway Island, 1,300 miles from the nearest city, an island without industry or commerce, you will find dozens of plastic pieces in the bird's innards: from bottle caps to cigarette lighters. The bright colors on the plastic fool the birds, who mistake them for food and offer them to their chicks.

Through the most causal actions of our daily lives, actions so casual they are barely noticeable, we have written ourselves on the body of the planet and, given the high level of toxic chemicals found in the typical bloodstream, on the inside of our bodies as well.

But such consequences are often far removed from the times of consumption. The Internet seems clean (although a *single* Google search is equivalent to turning on a 60-watt bulb for 17 seconds). Global warming seems distant from our daily commute or meat consumption. Meanwhile, we are used to the way we live – and the prospect of giving it up feels like a crazy, unnecessary, fanatical sacrifice.

There is a great deal of celebration of new technologies, some of which are truly breathtaking (operating on babies before they are born) and many flashy gimmicks (endless "improvements" on cell phones). Intellectually, there is a continual identification of humanity with reason, control, science, and perhaps someday with invulnerability and immortality. We see nature, by contrast, as the realm of mortality, fallibility, powerlessness, lack of control, and instinct. Humanity has value, and the more control it has, the more value. Nature, by contrast, has no value in itself and exists to be dominated by us. As many feminist theorists have argued, this position is compounded by projecting all "human" naturalness, vulnerability, instinct, and emotion onto women, and using their (supposed) similarity to nature as a justification for male domination over them as well.[28]

Third, widespread moral perspectives, the kind that inform "average citizens" who do not spend much time reading philosophy, lack a clear vision of moral responsibility in a world where daily actions affect people all over the world and for many years in the future. The ethical codes we follow were for the most part elaborated when the vast majority of human relations were face-to-face; or, at least, within comparatively small villages or neighborhoods. And where actions had immediate, clear

[28] The literature is quite large. For an introduction, see Irene Diamond, ed., *Reweaving the World: The Emergence of Ecofeminism* (San Francisco: Sierra Club Books, 1990).

effects. Do not murder your neighbor, or lie about him in court, or steal his horse. Care for the poor. Don't make fun of people with disabilities. Pay your laborer when he finishes his work, not the next day. These teachings make immediate, intuitive sense.

How different is the case when, in the context of the environmental crisis, I might be one of thirty engineers working on a project, the ultimate goal of which is unclear, and which will take dozens (or more) other engineers to complete and probably hundreds or even thousands more to produce and market, the effects of which are not really known and which may well be ten years or more away, and which in any case will take their place among hundreds of other new technologies, all of which affect people collectively, not individually. In my daily life, how much responsibility do I bear for a not really necessary car trip, which contributes a virtually infinitesimal but still real amount to global warming?[29] A global warming that so far hasn't bothered me too much in Boston where I live, even as it may be responsible for tens or hundreds of millions of climate refugees from an Africa stricken by drought and comparable despair and displacement from Alaska and Bangladesh to China and Nepal.[30]

Which moral teachings from the Bible, the Upanishads, Plato, Kant, John Stuart Mill, Ayn Rand, the *Declaration of Independence,* or the *Communist Manifesto* will help me think about such problems? Issues of personal and collective responsibility, guilt, sacrifice and moral resignation that arise with the environmental crisis are historically unprecedented.[31]

[29] Dale Jamieson, *Reason in a Dark Time* (New York: Oxford University Press, 2014), argues that the temporal distance and minute effects of any one person's actions mean no one is morally responsible for climate change. A similar position is held by John Broome, who suggests we do have the responsibility not to change our personal habits but to organize to change government and corporate behavior: *Climate Matters: Ethics in a Warming World* (New York: Norton, 2012). Both authors fail to note the difference between "ordinary" people who have little control over climate and those who, for example, run fossil fuel companies or lobby for them.

[30] For a visual and personal chronicle of the havoc unfolding over a decade ago: Collectif Argos, *Climate Refugees* (Cambridge, MA: MIT Press, 2007). The UN estimates 20 million refugees *per year* since 2008–2016: "Frequently Asked Questions on Climate Change Disaster and Displacement," UN Refugee Agency Website. Accessed February 26, 2018, www.unhcr.org/en-us/news/latest/2016/11/581f52dc4/frequently-asked-questions-climate-change-disaster-displacement.html.

[31] For a useful survey of many accounts of humanity's inability to deal with the moral and conceptual complexities of environmental crisis, see Willis Jenkins, "The Turn to Virtue in Climate Ethics," *Environmental Ethics* 38 (Spring 2016): 83–87.

Fourth, use of the new technologies has become so integral to daily life that many parts of a normal day involve us in practices that are dangerous or wasteful, in ways of which we almost certainly are not aware.

Consider: You have a hard day at work or in classes; you come home, make some dinner or grab a beer. Time for little rest, so you grab the remote and flick on the TV.

Except you don't. You cannot turn the TV on *because it's on already.* If it weren't on, it would not respond to the remote. It must be on, to be drawing power from the grid, to be ready for your command from the couch. Just being plugged in makes it "on."

This fact is significant because televisions, computers, rechargers plugged into sockets when they are not recharging anything, audio equipment, microwaves, DVD players, garage door openers – these and many other common home appliances draw what some call "phantom" or "standby" power. Look around your house. See how many you have. And while each particular appliance may use a vanishingly small amount, all the appliances together use an amount that is far from small. It is, in fact, between 5 and 10 percent of home energy consumption in the United States and in other developed nations.[32]

This use wastes irreplaceable fossil fuel resources and worsens global warming. Few people are aware of it, and the decision to create such appliances was not democratically discussed before they became the common currency of the modern world. There was zero informed debate or collective decision making.

Having this technology integrated into the fabric of our lives means that even if we come to see its negative effects, it is very hard to change. Individually and often collectively, we have no idea what to do about it. Compare, by contrast, the US Civil Rights movement. African-Americans forbidden from lunch counters, forced to sit in the back of the bus, punished for trying to register to vote, condemned to separate and vastly inferior public schools. Struggling to right these wrongs was difficult and dangerous. Yet what was at stake was not hard to understand. Any eight-year-old can grasp the unfairness of not letting people vote or enter a restaurant. They can see the basic injustice and comprehend the solution: open the public facilities, integrate the schools, end the voting ban.

---

[32] See Standby Power Website. Accessed August 31, 2017, http://standby.lbl.gov/summary-chart.html.

In many of the most important environmental contexts such clarity simply does not exist. Questions arise that have no simple answers and might require a high level of specialized technical knowledge even to form one of many conflicting opinions.

For example: Which of the various renewable energy options is most promising and deserves the most government support? How can transitions to a nonpolluting energy be made so that the reliability of energy for daily life is not interrupted? Does the use of natural gas produced by fracking represent a net gain in greenhouse gas reduction, and does that make it worth the water and air pollution, release of methane (fifty times more potent than CO_2) and increase in earthquakes that fracking causes? Nuclear power produces virtually no greenhouse gases, yet no safe way to store nuclear wastes (poisonous for over 100,000 years) exists. Are nuclear power plants now reliable enough to serve as a bridge technology between fossil fuels and whatever mix of solar, wind, and geothermal will replace them?

For example: Greenpeace demands that Corporation X stop using nonsustainable products (e.g., wood from old growth forests). A successful publicity campaign leads X to agree to change its ways, alter its supplier, and submit to evaluation by the Old Growth Sustainability Board or the Forest Protection Group or some such. Sounds great. And maybe it is. But how can we know that X is really doing what is claims? Or that the watchdog groups aren't fronts for corporate allies?

Even highly committed environmentalists have honest disagreements about these issues. And folks who are doing other things with their lives – teaching high school English, raising three children, taking care of aging parents, working as nurses or bus drivers or plumbers – should be forgiven for simply shrugging their shoulders.

Fifth, and perhaps most disturbingly, we are estranged from the very nature that we are assaulting. Indeed, it may be in part just because we are so estranged that we are tolerating the assault.

By analogy: If a white person hears a lot of talk about racism in American society and doesn't see what all the fuss is about, he would probably benefit from talking to some black people about their experiences and reading accounts of being black in American society. What is it like, for example, to be scared of the police, denied loans or jobs that whites get, and stereotyped negatively in popular culture? As a white person I can't know unless I talk to, or at least read accounts from, people subjected to racism. Doing so won't make me an expert on the value of affirmative action programs or racial gerrymandering in election districts, but may lead to the beginnings of understanding, sympathy, and solidarity.

What do I know of nature's beauties, capacities and interconnections? By knowledge here I do not mean the theoretical understanding one gets from science texts, microscopes, and computer models. I mean, rather, just being acquainted with nature that exists where I live. In contrast to the complicated questions about energy use posed earlier, consider these:

What are twenty plants that grow within a mile of my house?
What is the current phase of the moon?
What are five bird species that live in my neighborhood? Do they migrate?
    From where to where? What do they eat? What do they sound like?
How polluted is the nearest body of fresh water? Can it support any life?
    Could I swim in it?
What's missing that used to be here a hundred, or fifty, or five years ago?

Sadly, only a tiny percentage of us can answer these questions. Could it be that our collective lack of acquaintance with nature is one reason we can tolerate the extent to which we have degraded it? When we do pay attention to the natural world, we tend to see its surfaces and to regard it simply as a source of human pleasures: lovely scenery to amuse or calm us until the next high-tech stimulation comes around. While tens of millions of people go to America's national parks each year, most never get more than a quarter mile from a parking lot. We see the spectacular vistas, snap pictures of the wonders, and drive on, our dominant experience of the place what we see through the windshield. Backpackers get in close, but too many focus on listing conquered peaks and the latest in high-tech gear. They enjoy the great views and then return to daily lives in which the mundane trees, ponds, and insects of their neighborhood are far too ordinary to deserve attention or concern.

Graham Harvey observes that the sense of nature as kin and the widespread practice of "gifting," in which native peoples acknowledge their debt to nature by giving back, reflect more than merely a set of beliefs, but rather, a set of beliefs that compel attitudes and practices.[33] Such attitudes and practices, however, reflect indigenous peoples' very different immediate reality of dependence and reciprocity. The belief is a product of the relationship. How immediately do any of us connect to our sources of water, food, clothes, or building materials?

[33] Graham Harvey, *Animism: Respecting the Natural World* (New York: Columbia University Press, 2005).

There are, no doubt, gardeners and bird watchers among us. Tens of millions of them. And their experience has been essential in motivating some of them toward environmental concern. But even those activities can tend toward a kind of technological domination of pesticide use and genetically modified seeds by gardeners, and the aggressive "chalk up another sighting on to the next" posture of bird-watchers. And in any case, such activities unfold in a larger context of driving, computers, cell phones, appliances, lawn mowers, and expensive binoculars.

How can we save the natural world from our collective brutality if we do not love it? If we do not know it, how can we love it? And if everything else – work, ease, moral limits, the dominant institutions of our society – removes us from it?

8 HOPE?

To do the right thing morally we must be able to determine what the right thing is, and we must be capable of acting. Knowledge and agency are the preconditions of moral action. Without them, being an ethical person is not possible.

When our cultural traditions are suspect, the world too confusing to comprehend, and our own identities and daily lives compromised, how will moral action be possible?

On the one hand, the answer is simple: Despite all the factors I've described there *is* a global environmental movement. In every country activists are promoting clean energy, questioning dangerous chemicals, and trying to protect endangered species and ecosystems.

Given the dilemmas of culture and selfhood sketched earlier, what do they – do we – have as resources?

At least three things give us the capacity to resist the environmental crisis, to act morally despite these considerable obstacles.

To begin, despite everything, there is a humanly universal, deeply felt connection to the natural world. For a variety of reasons – physiological, psychological, emotional – the natural world matters to us. While our concern with other things may have obscured this connection, and we have chosen to override the depth of this tie, it still exists. Indeed, if it didn't, the environmental movement would not have the scope and power that it does.

Also, human culture is filled with varying and often contradictory perspectives. If Western religion has typically supported the human domination of nature, there are also traditional voices that celebrated nature as a gift from God, a source of spiritual insight, and a spiritual subject rather than simply a resource or a sign. If our dominant economic paradigm is ever-expanding consumption, voices early on in capitalist development challenged the idea that endless economic growth necessarily made for real human well-being.[34] Exceptions, to our human-centered, dominating, exploitative attitude toward nature can be found throughout our culture.

Finally, human culture can change, and change drastically. Ideas of human rights, democracy, gender equality, and civil disobedience did not always exist, but were brought into existence in response to developments, challenges, and threats. There has been no bigger change than the environmental crisis. And it is resulting in corresponding changes in human culture. Through a combination of reclaiming marginalized traditional voices, overcoming inconsistencies in moral teaching, and the creation of new values geared to a new technological, political, economic, and ecological reality, environmental morality has come into being.

Let's see what that morality is – and what challenges it faces.

[34] For example, Thoreau.

2

Why Does Nature Matter?

Paths to an Environmental Ethic

I WHAT'S WRONG?

In the most general terms, what is wrong with how we are treating the environment? Two answers arise immediately: First, we are mistreating, destroying, poisoning, hurting "nature." Second, in our treatment of nature, we are hurting (poisoning, injuring, lessening) human beings.

But what is "nature"? This is a question that precedes deciding whether how we treat it is wrong. On the one hand, this perfectly simple word, common in English and with comparable terms in many other languages, is not hard to understand. We have reasonably clear notions of what it means to do something naturally, to "go outside to spend some time in nature," what natural laws are, and what a nature preserve is. If I offered you a hundred dollars to go to my office and bring me all the natural stuff, you'd have no problem leaving the computer, the metal desk, and the coffee maker, and bringing the feather, the rocks, and the seashells. True, there might be some boundary cases that are difficult to determine: a leather belt, a wooden bookcase, food made with genetically modified ingredients.

But the general point is clear. In many of its everyday uses, "nature" clearly stands at odds with humanity. The nature preserve is the area without streets, stores, homes, or (if possible) cell phone towers. Laws of nature, unlike human laws, are inescapable regularities that cannot be violated by the cleverest and most hardened criminal. A natural item is one not produced or at most minimally affected by people. Natural behavior is not motivated by culture, tradition, or human reason. Bill

McKibben suggested that "wilderness" – a place where there is only nature – is a place where you can't shop.

At the same time, however, "nature" also includes people. And in some ways each person is as natural as any star or tadpole. Humans, like everything else, are composed of molecules, atoms, and subatomic particles. Throw me off the roof, and I will fall at the same rate as a boulder. Like the tadpole I am structured by my DNA, a genetic code that, like that of tadpoles, evolved over countless generations.

To complicate matters, when we say that "humans are mistreating nature," just how much of nature do we have in mind? If nature is the totality of existence, then human domination, even if morally wrong, is hardly significant: We only affect an infinitesimally small part of the universe. If nature includes natural laws – gravity, atomic structure, the laws of gases – then the idea that we can dominate it makes no sense. If nature is the earth, then clearly, we have had some real effect on species, land, waters, and air – though the vast majority of the physical earth still remains unaffected: The deepest mine is perhaps ten miles, the diameter of the earth eight thousand miles.

Some will argue that "we" can't mistreat "nature" – because, clearly, we are part of nature: It is the ground of our being, our evolutionary forbear, the source of what we need for life. But this point ignores common ways of speaking in which being part of something and mistreating it pose no contradiction. We are part of our family and can be abusive to our children or spouse. We can be part of a country that we betray for financial or ideological reasons. Cancer cells are part of our bodies and also might kill us. That people are natural in countless respects and exist within nature does not mean we cannot also be doing something immoral to the rest of nature.

In a related point, some suggest that because humans have affected so much of the earth, and we can no longer explain the behavior of "nature" without talking about human action, that "nature" as an independent realm separate from humanity no longer exists.[1] Also, there are cases where the human–nature distinction is either quite muddy or not much help. Domesticated animals are not human yet bear the stamp of their connection to us; virtually all life on the earth is now affected by human action from climate change to pollution; human bodies are both natural

---

[1] E.g., Steven Vogel, *Thinking Like a Mall: Environmental Philosophy after the End of Nature* (Cambridge, MA: MIT Press, 2015).

in the way they function and also shaped by technological aids like glasses, heart monitors, and medications.

This suggestion ignores a few relevant considerations. Nature as a realm separate from the human is not just about complete independence but about certain key differences. Among these are the overwhelming beauty it possesses and how, most decisively, the natural world functions without ego. We may plant the tree, but the tree offers shade, processes CO_2, prevents erosion, serves as home to birds and squirrels, and offers its seeds as food. It does this without arrogance, self-aggrandizement, jealousy of other trees, resentment over the trees who get more water or sunlight, anxiety about the future, or fear of death. It will give every bit of energy to growing tall and strong, and not one bit to anger over of the corporation that will clear cut it. In this way nature is profoundly different than people, even if we've altered the climate and changed the composition of the soil. And in this way, at least, nature has an independent and profoundly valuable spiritual identity.[2]

Note, as well, the unique degree to which human life is shaped by cultural norms, which we both seek to justify and can criticize and change. Unlike planets, maple trees, or sharks, part of our behavior is determined by what we believe ourselves to be – not just what we are. Or, we might say: What we believe is essential to who we are, and is not, as far as we can tell, to any other form of life. Family structure, sexual behavior, community organization, even diet are not dictated by genetic codes, but by culture. And these cultural structures are subject to justification, critique, and radical change – to a distinctly moral dimension of life.

Also, humans can drastically augment our "natural" physical powers with technology. While other animals use tools, there is virtually no comparison between the effects of their tool use and ours. Beavers build dams, crows use thorns to dig insects out of tree bark, sea gulls drop clams on rocks. Humans, by contrast, blow the tops off mountains and genetically program mice to get cancer.

Finally, humans can achieve staggering levels of immorality and irrationality, visiting untold horrors on each other, in ways far beyond the capacity of rabid dogs, aggressive ant colonies, or hungry lions. We have the capacity for gratuitous selfishness and self-destructiveness. The mass horrors of war, while perhaps benefitting each participating nations'

[2] There will be further discussion of "nature" toward the end of Chapter 3.

elites, devastate the ordinary people who fight them and the civilians who are killed. The poisoning of our own environment for military power or corporate profit has, as far as I know, not a single analog in the nonhuman realm. The pleasure people get from spectacles like bull fighting or "sports" like fox hunting suggest a kind of culturally promoted sadism. Can one even imagine any other species setting kerosene-doused rats or cats on fire (dogs die too quickly) and chasing them through slums to start fires to get residents out and make money from gentrification?[3]

Whether humans are part of or distinct from nature is really the same as any "same or different?" question, and answers to such questions always depend on context. In some ways I am no different than a star – for we both exist in the same universe. In some ways I am very different from any other person who ever lived and even from myself last year or even last week. In some contexts what is natural about people is most important, and in others what is distinctly human takes precedence.

Our context *here* is the environmental crisis. In this context the crucial difference is between those who are wreaking ecological havoc and those who are enduring it. The fact that the people doing the damage are also damaging themselves does not alter the fact that only one group on earth can ask itself: Are we doing something wrong?

So: we are part of nature, surely. And while every part of nature is distinct – tigers are distinct from ants, mushrooms, and intestinal parasites – the ways in which humans are distinct are of particular importance when we try to answer the central questions of environmental ethics.

Any traditional ethical perspective – secular or religious or spiritual – can identify in very general terms what is wrong with knowingly polluting other people's water or air. Though difficult questions about environmental racism or individual responsibility for global problems remain,[4] we can confidently assert that environmentally hurting other people is wrong.

But why is it wrong, if it is, to render species extinct? Pollute areas that people don't use? Convert wilderness to a garden – and then to more upscale condos?

---

[3] "Hot demolition" by Filipino landlords: Erhard Berner, *Defending a Place in the City: Localities and the Struggle for Local Places in Metro Manila* (Manila: Ateneo De Manila University Press, 1998), p. 144.
[4] Many of these topics will be discussed later in later chapters.

2 WHERE DOES THE VALUE OF NATURE COME FROM?

There are many ways to talk about moral relations among people. The same holds for our relationship with nature.

I will examine a number of those ways in a bit. First, though, notice that in some situations an immediate, intuitive, and often quite powerful visceral moral response may be stronger and certain than any argument. A picture of a concentration camp, a victim of a lynching, starving children, or prisoners being beheaded – such sights are revealed to us by the simple instruction: "Look at this." And having looked, we may "know" that these things are deeply wrong, and know that with greater certainty than will be revealed by any argument about general moral principles or their application.

However, history is littered with instances of moral intuitions that changed. At a given time people looked at gay marriage or women's social equality and "just knew" that they were wrong. Later, both collectively and individually, intuitions shifted. And this is because as immediate as intuitions may feel in the moment, they are the effect of a variety of complex processes of moral formation: upbringing, shared social practices, stories emphasizing certain aspects of human experience, and socially proclaimed principles. As these processes shift, new intuitions arise.

So as powerful as our intuitive moral response might be to a clear-cut forest, the Pacific garbage patch, or an average of 127 toxic chemicals in the blood of a newborn, the precise nature of these moral wrongs needs to be explored. Will this exploration – the basic task of environmental philosophy – *guarantee* the moral correctness of our conclusion? Certainly, and often unfortunately, not. The best we can do is support our moral arguments with our intuitions and test our intuitions against our arguments, our cases with our principles, and our principles with our cases, realizing that moral errors in both remain possible no matter how carefully we reason or authentically and deeply we feel.[5]

---

[5] Some will recognize here a version of John Rawls's concept of "reflective equilibrium" – the balancing of intuition and moral principles. Recent research has attempted to map intuition ("gut feelings") and reasoning onto different parts of the brain. See Jonathan Haidt, *The Righteous Mind: Why Good People Are Divided by Politics and Religion* (New York: Vintage, 2013); and Joshua Greene, *Moral Tribes: Emotion, Reason, and the Gap between Us and Them* (New York: Penguin, 2013). There is some tendency in both Greene and Haidt to confuse the immediacy of intuition (or emotion) in morality with an absence of reasoning. However, the intuitions got there through a process of learning, albeit one

3 NATURE AND MORAL SIGNIFICANCE

Aldo Leopold, American forester, naturalist, and early writer on environmental ethics, suggested that humans should change their role "from conqueror of the land community to plain member and citizen of it." This view "implies respect for his fellow-members, and also respect for the community as such."[6] To be a "plain citizen" is to have, and to recognize others as having, rights. And built into the concept of rights is that of equality. A particular right tells us what we have equality in – be it religion, speech, freedom of movement, or voting. That we have a right means we have the equal freedom to engage in those activities. Your right to freedom of speech is the way I cannot restrict you from saying what you want to say, and you cannot restrict me. Our common right to religious freedom is equality in our choice of religion (or no religion). If we violate someone else's equality without justification, our own rights, our equality, can be lessened or terminated. If we are too young or too mentally ill or otherwise impaired, we may not qualify for all the rights normal citizens have. But in all those cases specific reasons must be offered why our rights are limited. The default position is equality.

Can nature be included into this sense of equality?

Many environmental thinkers have thought so and talked about the "rights of nature" as a way to indicate a kind of fundamental moral equality with humanity. Christopher Stone argued that nature should have "standing"; i.e., to have its interests represented in a court of law by human "guardians" and be able to receive recompense of damages against it. Many other thinkers have described a comparable kind of equality in different terms. Paul Taylor argued that nature deserves "respect." Carolyn Merchant advocated "partnership." Deep ecologists like Arne Naess and ecofeminists like Karen Warren have argued for the necessity to extend moral concern far beyond the boundaries of humanity. Albert Schweitzer spoke of a "reverence for life," meaning not just human but all forms of life. Pope John Paul II instructed us to change our ways so that nature could return to its proper role as the "sister of humanity." The Qur'an warned Muslims to remember that all animals are communities,

---

that may be deeply flawed. But it is precisely because it is a process of learning that more learning, leading to change, can occur.

[6] Aldo Leopold, *A Sand County Almanac* (New York: Oxford University Press, 1949), p. 204.

just as people are. Indigenous traditions frequently speak of nature as kin. Examples could easily be extended for several pages.

Despite differences in vocabulary or cultural tradition the central thrust of these positions is similar: There is a rejection, or at least a deep questioning, of any taken-for-granted anthropocentrism – of the idea that humans are the only beings who are morally significant. And there is an advocacy of the moral significance of nature, sometimes described as a kind of moral equality with the human. In the words of thirteenth-century Jewish philosopher Maimonides: "Do not think that other beings exist just for you. They exist for themselves as well."[7]

There is, certainly, a difference between saying a tree is as morally significant as a person and saying it is morally significant at all, though perhaps in different ways and to a lesser extent. But at least the claim is widely shared that humans and nature are equal *in the sense* of being morally significant at all.

This is the fundamental point of environmental ethics – whether of a philosophical, religious, spiritual, or political orientation – and the one that gives environmental ethics its distinct and significant role in human thought.

In this chapter and the next I will explore the reasoning behind claims for nature's moral significance. In Chapter 5 we will see some of the necessary limitations that attend them. And in much of the rest of the book we will see what personal obligations and collective political change this view demands of us.

4 DOES NATURE HAVE MORAL VALUE?

Does nature have moral value of any kind? Clearly this is not a position that has a great deal of support throughout the world, though it does have some. There are limitations on our treatment of animals, though we cause untold billions of animals to suffer and die in animal agriculture and research labs. Throughout the world there are nature preserves, national parks, and the like, yet simultaneously the rainforests are being eliminated, national forests are open to gas and oil exploration, and wetlands are paved over. Our energy policies have fundamentally altered the chemistry of the oceans and decimated global coral reefs, and not nearly enough is being done to end, let alone reverse, these consequences.

---

[7] Moses Maimonides, *Guide to the Perplexed*, Part III, Chapter 13, quoted in *Judaism and Ecology, a Hadassah Study Guide* (New York: Hadassah, 1993), p. 110.

It could be replied that this situation is not that different than the way people treat each other. Millions starve while the well-off waste huge amounts of food. Many ethnic or religious communities, and often women as a group, lack equal rights and are subject to abuse. Atrocities in war or political struggle frequently kill more civilians than enemy combatants. In countless instances the fate of the aged, children, or those with disabilities is simply awful.

At the moment, we might say, moral respect is typically lacking for people as much, or nearly as much, as it is for nature.

Yet there is a crucial difference. Terrorists who bomb a café, operators of drones bombing a house, or nations who offer vastly superior rights to men, all believe (or act as if they believe) that they need reasons to do so. The terrorist or drone operator can you tell *why* killing is acceptable, perhaps even necessary: to fulfill God's will, to win the war against the West, to protect the United States, to defeat ISIS or Al-Qaeda. The denial of equality to women is justified *because* ... and then reasons are offered: tradition, the essential nature of gender, religious texts. People suffer in poverty despite "our best efforts," and the economy is really "as just as we can make it."

As morally mistaken as I (and, I imagine, some readers) think those reasons are, they are attempts at justifications.

And it is precisely the widespread belief that such reasons are not necessary when we relate to salmon, butterflies, or birch trees that signifies the different moral status of nature. Unless you have strong sociopathic tendencies, you offer reasons why you kill another person. But offer reasons why you kill a fly? When was the last time anyone offered a serious justification for eating a Thanksgiving turkey or having bacon and eggs for breakfast?[8] Squashing a beetle or pulling out a weed?

Note that the issue here is not disagreement over a particular moral practice, such as capital punishment. Both advocates and opponents of capital punishment believe that killing is a moral issue; both agree that reasons need to be given for their position. In the case of the moral status of nature something else is at stake: whether the way we treat nature is a moral issue at all. By analogy: For a traditionally oriented Muslim woman covering the hair is a religiously based moral obligation. For someone from

---

[8] When challenged, they will offer reasons, as we'll see in Chapter 4.

another culture, whether or not a woman wears a scarf may be a matter of aesthetics, comfort, or even health. There is nothing moral about it.

Why should we think that the way we treat birds, or the trees they nest in, is a moral issue? How does secular environmental ethics, or religious environmentalism, or environmental spirituality manage to include nature in the moral realm?

5 CONSEQUENCES AND TRANSFORMATION

When we consider the scope of the damage, and the terrible threats to the future, we might wonder if there is something fundamentally wrong with the way we've been acting. And because how we act is an expression of how we think, we may decide to rethink the ethical status of nature.

If *not* thinking of nature as part of our moral universe leads to climate change, an ocean with more plastic than fish, and cancer rates on Indian reservations that are eighteen times the national average, perhaps there is something moral that we have been missing.

What would it take to make this transition? Even if the failures of the current system are clear, how do we change? How do we think about nature in a new way?

Clearly at least some of the reasons we offer for *human* moral significance do not work for nature. We do not think nature deserves moral consideration because it can reason, understand ethical codes expressed in language, or make a social contract to agree to live by a political framework of rights. Nature is not moral because we can have empathetic connections *in the same way* that we can to family, close friends, or lovers. Unless we are part of a native culture, it is unlikely that nature is part of our culturally defined community to which we are joined in religious, ethnic, or political solidarity. The Golden Rule imagines symmetry between human moral actors, not a relation between, say, a man and a mosquito. Kant asks us to live under a rule that everyone else could live under – when the rest of nature lives under no rules whatsoever. John Stuart Mill wants us to be concerned with everyone's happiness – and while that might have some relevance to higher animals, it leaves out weeds, bacteria, and ants.

What follows here is less an argument about why nature deserves moral consideration, and much more a description of how we come to believe it does. While I have devoted much of my life to the study of philosophy, I'm not sure how many people are convinced by philosophical arguments. Therefore, I am offering what might a called a phenomenology of moral concern: the sensuous, cognitive, and emotional processes that lead us to see nature as something more than raw material for our needs and pleasures.

6 DEPENDENCE, CONNECTION, CARE

Despite our technological brilliance and vastly complicated culture (law, religion, art, education, and the like), it is not hard to see how we are connected to and dependent on a nature that is neither technological nor cultural. Close your mouth and pinch your nostrils shut.

Wait.

Don't change your position.

If you followed these instructions you will be reminded that each breath is our connection to nature. No breath … no connection … no life. More broadly, even a brief survey reveals the myriad ways in which nature has value for us.[9] The nonhuman world, the part we did not create or shape or design, grows our food and provides water; is the source of raw material from lumber to fossil fuels; performs ecosystem services through pollination, water purification, and protection of coastlines; serves as a spiritual model of action without ego and a source of contemplative inspiration and aesthetic beauty; in its intricacies and interdependence is endlessly fascinating; offers lessons about structure and design for human technology;[10] and directly constitutes our own bodily existence through all the unconscious processes (digestion, heartbeat, sensation, etc.) and the billions of bacteria that support us.

Insofar as it does all these things for us, we are dependent on it. And all these forms of *dependence* are also forms of *connection*. As we are connected to the people who raise our food, build our homes, or perform music we love, so we are connected to the soil in which our food grows, the trees cut down to make our dining room table, or the entrancing bird songs that brighten our hearts when we are sad.

Together dependence and connection constitute a kind of care. The natural world, while it can threaten us with lethal viruses, destructive earthquakes, ruinous tsunamis, and cancer-causing sunburn,[11] has also given us the beach at sunset, children delighting in their first snowflakes,

---

[9] For a detailed summary of these points see Stephen Kellert, *The Value of Life: Biological Diversity and Human Society* (Washington, DC: Island Press, 1995).

[10] Janine Benyus, *Biomimicry; Innovation Inspired by Nature* (New York: Harper, 2002).

[11] Note that our thinning of the ozone layer with CFCs made sunlight more dangerous.

and the experience of running across a meadow. Life may often be disappointing, painful, or tragic, but to the extent that we would rather be alive than not, nature as a totality is an enormous engine of care. It makes us possible today and created us over millions of years of evolution.

The recognition of dependence, connection, and care can lead directly to moral significance. Just because we depend on it through countless connections, and because these connections, taken as a totality, are a form of care, we begin to see that which cares for us as an object of moral concern. How, after all, do we treat the *people* upon whom we are dependent and who care for us? Certainly, in some cases we may respond with resentment at our dependence; a thoughtless taking for granted of a care that has always been present; or a hostility based in a disappointment that other people seem to be treated better than ourselves. In other cases, however, we feel deep appreciation and love. These feelings make a thoughtless mistreatment of the agent of care – a relative, friend, lover, even a stranger such as a hospital nurse – if not impossible, much less likely. We do not have to argue or reason our way to seeing the source of care as worthy of moral concern. It simply arises spontaneously.

Alternatively, we can think of nature, or the earth, as the object of *our* care. Like parents of children, whose sense of personal well-being often cannot be separated from that of their kids, we are morally and emotionally involved in the well-being of the planet, which has literally created and sustained us. Given our current technological power, the uncertainty of the future, and our need to act despite that uncertainty, we might well see ourselves caring for the planet as if we were its parents. Even though, in relation to an issue that will return, we need to remember that: "parenting the planet will require us to accept that, even if . . . we do the best we can and all goes as well as possible, we will never know the end of the story."[12]

7 IT IS US; WE ARE "IT"

In what might be called a deeper sense, we face not only a question of moral value, but also of self-identity: "*I am the rainforest protecting*

---

[12] This perspective very well presented in Sarah Krakoff, "Parenting the Planet," in Denis Arnold, ed., *The Ethics of Global Climate Change* (New York: Cambridge University Press, 2011), p. 156.

itself," said an environmental activist resisting loggers.[13] Keep in mind that we have fairly conventional ways of talking that suggest that "I" am more than just my personal body: We identify with a sports team, family, community, religious or ethnic group, or nation. In such cases a threat to the group just is a threat to the individual; the life fortunes of the groups just are essential to the life fortunes of the individual. In extreme situations the connection is so strongly felt that a particular person is willing to die for the group.

The ontological foundation for this psychological, moral, or spiritual sense of identity is asserted in a variety of ways. For example, the Buddhist concept of dependent origination, or what the contemporary Buddhist thinker Thich Nhat Hanh calls "interbeing," embodies the traditional Buddhist notion that all of existence is related. The existence, continuity, and passing away of each particular reflects the larger whole. As a concrete example, we might think of an apple. While this piece of fruit can rest in my hand, contained (as it were) in the apple are: the sun's energy, the water and minerals used by the apple tree, the tree itself, the living matter of the soil in which the tree is rooted, the insects that pollinate the tree, and people who pick, transport, store, and sell the fruit. If, in turn, we see our own identities as similarly containing or embodying air, water, pollinating insects, the health enhancing bacteria in our gut, all the species that were part of evolution's chain leading to humanity, then assaults on earth, water, air, etc. are an assault on *us*.

In Australian aboriginal tradition the primordial beings who created the decisive features of the aboriginal landscape, and the landscape, and the people who walk the land, and the ceremonies in which the history of the land is recounted, and the ritual objects and musical instruments used in the ceremonies – are all essentially connected, indeed in some sense all part of *one* being.[14] Polluting, destroying, paving over, or rendering extinct any part of this being is comparable to an attack on any particular person, perhaps comparable to chopping off a limb, blinding, or breaking a bone. The person remains but has been deeply wounded.

In environmental philosophy the perspective of "deep ecology" has argued that realizing our "ecological self" – constituted by relations to all of the biosphere rather than just the human part – can be the foundation for an environmental ethic in which all of nature has moral value. Some have asserted that "Climate change raises both the opportunity and the

[13] John Seed, *Thinking Like a Mountain* (Philadelphia: New Society Publishers, 1986), p. 6.
[14] Yimikirli, *Warlpiri Dreamings and Histories* (San Francisco: HarperCollins, 1994).

necessity of forging a planetary identity" in which I am likely to care about future generations of people, planetary health, future, and other species.[15]

It would be wonderful if the moral implications of these perspectives on identity followed directly. If the larger whole is something essential to who I am, surely, I will treat it with respect and care. Surely, I will honor its direct connection to my pleasure, contentment, physical security, health, and overall well-being. And I may. But we must remember that *self*-destructive behavior is all too common among our species. Addiction to drugs that wreck the body and mind, overeating, committed lack of exercise, violent pastimes, and wars are rampant globally. Problems of smoking and obesity have spread from the richer countries to ones that are newly able to provide what would have been out-of-reach luxuries a generation ago. As human pollute and damage themselves, there is no guarantee that even feeling part of "the land" will keep them from doing the same to everything around them.

8 THE FORM OF THE CONCERN

What does moral concern for nature look like? Many environmental thinkers talk about the "rights of nature" and indeed the country of Ecuador has enshrined that phrase in a recent change to the constitution. I suspect, however, that rights require a kind of fundamental legal equality, which, except for certain boundary cases, will not characterize humanity's relation to nature. Unless we starve ourselves, we will eat animals or plants. Unless we stop living in houses we will displace insects and earthworms to lay our foundations. Unless we completely dismantle our global economy we will continue to bring in exotic species that destabilize ecosystems or simply expand human settlements and take up space that used to be occupied by other life forms. By now 40 percent of the surface of the earth is used for agriculture; a good deal of the rest for cities, mining, roads, and recreation. All that land used to be governed by the autonomy of living beings. Now it is governed, for the most part, by humans.[16]

---

[15] Robert Socolow and Mary R. English, "Living Ethically in a Greenhouse," in Denis Arnold, ed., *The Ethics of Global Climate Change* (New York: Cambridge University Press, 2011), pp. 170–191.

[16] There are many species – rats, squirrels, monkeys, crows – that coexist in human-dominated space.

What kind of equality of rights is possible under such conditions? The answer, I suspect, is none, unless we demolish civilization and reduce human population by, say, 95 percent.[17]

We should remember that there are many moral contexts in which "rights" serve us poorly or not at all. Family conflicts are usually settled by appeals to happiness, suffering, empathy, care, and concern – not Kevin's "rights" to an expensive summer camp, Suzie's "rights" to go out with friends when it is time to visit grandma, or a spouse's "rights" to sexual pleasure when their partner isn't in the mood. While some will talk of the "rights" of refugees to be admitted to the country of their choice, it is not clear how we could prove that people have the right to live anywhere they choose. The refugees' case is made much more often, and more persuasively, by talk of compassion for their suffering, the intensity of their need, how we might feel in their place and how – in the United States at least – they are replicating the experience of our ancestors.

And this is because "rights" are designed to deal with relations of essential distance. They are, we might say, like the lines in a parking lot. You can drive whatever car, or motorcycle, or even bike, you like. Just park it within the lines so that all the other folks, who are driving whatever they like, can park as well. The lines keep us separate, allow us to coexist equally. They do not reflect or further our connections of concern for each other. They seek to promote at least modestly manageable relations among people from fundamentally different cultural, religious, and national communities; to support moral relations when care may be absent or minimal. Whatever other differences there are between us in religion, political views, or cultural style, at least we can recognize a human "right" to religious freedom, a fair trial, free speech, etc.[18] Love, mutual respect, empathic recognition – none of these need be part of rights.

But our relationship with nature cannot be one of mutual distance, at least not always and not, I suspect, essentially. Our necessary dependence and the intimacy of our connections – including the way we consume and displace it – mean that the essential distance presumed by notions of rights will not work.

[17] Some say this would be a good idea. I do not agree, but at times I have my doubts.
[18] The position developed very well by Jeffrey Stout, *Democracy and Tradition* (Princeton, NJ: Princeton University Press, 2004).

Neither, however, will the emotional interconnections that character- ize family, friendship, or romantic love. Bees, trees, and trout do not have the personalities that make for human mutuality and intimacy; and therefore, for the moral relations that depend on empathy for human others.

If nature has moral significance, but not essentially in terms of rights or specifically human intimacy, how might we think about it?

9 GRATITUDE: IMPORTANCE AND OBSTACLES

In traditional Judaism, the first thing a person does in the morning is express gratitude. "I give thanks to you, living and everlasting God, for returning my soul to my body. Great is your faithfulness." In other words: "I could have died in my sleep but here I am – alive!" What if we bracket the metaphysical aspect of this prayer – that there is a nonphysical, eternal, all-powerful, wise, and loving spirit that is the foundation of my existence – and replace that idea with one that is (by contrast) clearly and unarguably true? Nature – from the bacteria that inhabit my body and enable me to function to the air, the water, the sun, photosynthesis and all the biological processes that enable me to think, move, and see – is essential to my life and each day it is "faithful" in sustaining me.

Like the recognition of nature's care, of seeing what *it* does for *us*, we have here a foundation for a moral relation to nature in gratitude – in *our response* to that reality. Here we see that the world is a gift, something that we didn't earn and that is not cosmically guaranteed. Indeed, the chances of there being a world in which the combination of resources, temperature, atmosphere, and path of evolution would lead to humans is, to put it mildly, small.

Isn't all this something to be grateful for? Does the universe have to have a personality – beliefs, intentions, language – for us to be grateful for and to it? And if we are grateful for the universe, both as a totality and in its myriad constituent parts, how should we act toward it? If you are a musician and are given a precious violin to use, one of the centuries-old instruments valued at well over a million dollars, with what reverence will you handle it? Isn't the local park, with its pond, its old trees shading you in summer and magically changing colors in the fall, its ducks and seagulls and cormorants, where you go to refresh your spirit when you are ground down by loss or anxious about an upcoming medical appointment – isn't that park something for which you are deeply grateful? Do you litter it? Carve your initials into the trees? Toss junk into the water?

Gratitude is a central spiritual virtue; i.e., a way of thinking, feeling, and acting that, spiritual teachings assert, is an essential precondition of a contented and peaceful life; as well as something that is likely to make the person practicing the virtue kinder, more generous, and much more fun to be around.[19] And surely we know that we feel better when we are grateful than when we are envious, competitive, anxious, or disappointed.

Despite the great benefits of gratitude, most of us find it very hard to maintain. Humans, as Aldous Huxley observed, have an almost infinite capacity to take things for granted. And for that which we take for granted we tend not to feel grateful. There is a powerful and near permanent temptation to focus on what we don't have, what isn't working well, what hurts or disappoints. A miniscule splinter in a sensitive toe or a toothache in a single tooth will blot out all the parts of our body that feel just fine. A brutal cold or hot spell, freezing rain that makes driving treacherous, a thunderstorm wrecking a picnic – all these can diminish our gratitude and the moral concern that flows from it.

Similarly, in a technologized culture we may take phones, computers, cars, planes, electric stoves, automatic coffee makers and the like to be our real environment, while the trees, birds, and clouds recede into the ignored background.

As well, there may be many times when the natural world, including our own natural bodies, disappoint, frustrate, or hurt. Illness or aging, crop-damaging locusts, or crop-killing drought, even a hungry shark can make a mockery of our personal or collective goals. Nature can hurt as well as heal, destroy as well as create. An inability to accept the vulnerability that comes with the human condition can turn our thoughts to complete domination of nature, so that it never disappoints or frustrates. The consequences of the desire for total control – what Rachel Carson termed the "Neanderthal stage of science"[20] – are embedded in the environmental crisis. The endless pursuit of complete domination for complete ease and convenience has shaped the throwaway culture of plastic debris, carcinogenic pesticides, and air conditioner chemicals that nearly destroyed the protective ozone layer. It also supports the connections between the environmental crisis and patriarchy: in which men, identified with reason, knowledge, and science, are accorded superior

[19] Further discussion of virtue will arise in this chapter and especially in Chapter 5.
[20] "The 'control of nature' is a phrase conceived in arrogance, born of the Neanderthal age of biology and philosophy, when it was supposed that nature exists for the convenience of man." Rachel Carson, *Silent Spring* (New York: Fawcett Crest, 1964), p. 262.

worth and power as compared to both nature and women – who are identified with the "natural," emotions, and the body.[21] The fear of vulnerability and the necessary and natural condition of human limits drives a culture that will stop at nothing to avoid facing the realities of human weakness, fallibility, and death.

The prevalence of these obstacles means that gratitude is not just a spontaneous reaction, but also something that must be cultivated and often consciously chosen. As we wake each morning we can put our attention on what we have or what we lack; moan about an aching back or thank God/goddess/nature/our DNA that we can still walk, talk, hear, and see. We can curse the fourth large snowstorm in three weeks that will require us to shovel for hours just to get our car out of the driveway. Or we can be glad, very glad, that the snow will eventually melt, and that when it does it will nourish the trees and flowers.

On a cautionary note: We should remember that spiritual virtues exist not just in the moment but also in the larger contexts of our lives. Will we stand on the deck of our 7,000-square-foot vacation home filled with gratitude for the spectacular view – ignoring how the view is paid for by the polluting factory we own in Bangladesh? Will we cherish one particular endangered animal species that we dedicate ourselves to saving – meanwhile cheerfully eating mass-produced meat?[22] The gratitude we consciously cultivate, if it is to be more than a passing, morally insignificant emotional episode, will be reflected in action as well as experience and extend outward from our immediate setting to life as a whole.

10 SAMENESS, DIFFERENCE, AND RECOGNITION

An analogy: How did whites eventually come to see African slaves as deserving of moral consideration? For many, at least, it was a recognition of sameness, a recognition that as "I" or "we" are without question deserving of moral consideration so should any other person who is sufficiently similar. If the slave can reason, have a culture, and

---

[21] The essential point of ecofeminism. See, e.g., Susan Griffin, *Woman and Nature: The Roaring Inside Her* (New York: Counterpoint, 2013); Karen J. Warren, ed., *Women, Culture, Nature* (Bloomington: Indiana University Press, 1997).

[22] Tremendous effort has been put into saving "authentic" American buffalo by people who hold it sacred. Most of these folks are not vegetarians. See the account in Justin Farrell, *The Battle for Yellowstone: Morality and the Sacred Roots of Environmental Conflict* (Princeton, NJ: Princeton University Press, 2015), chapter 3.

possess a sense of his or her own life, the illusory superiority of whites over blacks is without foundation.

How does such a realization unfold in our relations to nature? Well, it may not. When forests are something we see through the windshield or on a calming screen saver. When water comes out of a tap. When animals are limited to domesticated pets, images on a television, or shrink-wrapped chunks of some undifferentiated mass of stuff called "meat," there is little or no reality to nature.[23] It is simply a spectacle for our amusement or a source of satisfaction.

But recognition is not impossible. In the brilliant film *The Witness*, New York contractor Eddie Lama, seeking to curry favor with a woman he wants to date, offers to care for her cat when she goes on vacation. Initially distant, the cat wins him over with purring and lap sitting. Sometime later, eating dinner, Eddie is helping himself to a chicken drumstick when he realizes that the shape of the chicken part is very similar to that of the cat, which he has explored when petting him. The cat he likes; the chicken he is about to eat. The similarity is too great. He becomes an active, proselytizing vegetarian, outfitting his work truck with video equipment, parking on the street, opening the back, and projecting images of the horrors of factory farms for passersby to see. As he loved, or at least felt affection for, the cat, he could no longer unthinkingly consume a being who had the same shape and that also stood on the earth and sought to live.

But what about the elements of nature that are considerably less "like us"? Here are two religious teachings that might offer some clues.

"When a tree is killed before its time, a moan is heard throughout the world, though not a sound is heard," says a Jewish "midrash" (an interpretive response or addition to biblical texts).

The medieval German Catholic mystic and monk Meister Eckhart suggested: "Apprehend God in all things, for God is in all things. Every single creature is full of God and is a book about God."

Many other examples could be offered, especially from native traditions.[24] But what Eckhart and the Midrash suggest is that the world is something with its own existence, destiny, and significance. The source of

---

[23] On "meat" as a mass noun without individual identity or differentiation, rather than referring to individual animals, see Carol Adams, *The Sexual Politics of Meat* (London: Bloomsbury, 2015).

[24] But because those traditions did not create the apparatus of modern environmental destruction, it seems more important to find sources of environmental ethics within the traditions of modernity.

moral concern here is not fear of the consequence for people of not seeing nature as moral, an acknowledgment of the factual reality of nature's care, or the emotional upwelling of gratitude for that care. It is, rather, a mix of admiration, wonder, and awe at what it is *in itself* – even if humanity had never come into existence. This sense may arise from nature's aesthetic beauty, complexity, interdependence, or variation in size (from the galaxy to the grain of sand to the subatomic particle). The grace of a flying bird, the persistence of a virus, the cooperation of ants, the father love of the male emperor penguin who waits for two months, warming the egg, while the mother searches for fish to bring back. Even the sheer ferocity of wasps that lay eggs in caterpillars who, upon hatching, eat their way to life through the flesh of their host.

Can we prove that because of what nature is it deserves moral consideration? Probably not, but we can't prove that people do either. Either moral concern arises out of ongoing experience and relationships, or it does not.

But we can realize that as we have our needs and goals, which we value, and cannot accomplish them without food, water, shelter, and human affection, so trees (for example) see to root in the soil, grow tall, and shed their seeds for the next generation. And to do these things they need sunlight and water, the minerals in the earth, and unpolluted air. Fish need clean, living bodies of water. No form of life needs trillions of tons of plastic garbage, radioactive waste, or genetic engineering that could unleash unexpectedly dangerous exotic organisms. As certain things are necessarily valuable to us because they are essential to our ability to fulfill our life projects, so nature has *its* values: the resources and conditions that enable each organism and ecosystem to be itself.[25] At least in these ways, all forms of life are the same. We can treat the world as material to be used or discarded at our pleasure. Or we can see that "every natural form one perceives – from the swallows swooping overhead to the fly on a blade of grass and indeed the blade of grass itself – is an experiencing form, an entity with its own predilections and sensations, albeit sensations that are very different from our own."[26]

---

[25] That nature has its own values is a view developed by Holmes Rolston, III, *Environmental Ethics: Duties to and Values in the Natural World* (Philadelphia: Temple University Press, 1988).

[26] David Abram, "The Ecology of Magic," in Peter Sauer, ed., *Finding Home: Writing on Nature and Culture from Orion Magazine* (Boston: Beacon Press, 1992), p. 183.

Such a marvelous vision does not entail rights, any more than the marvel we feel looking at a newborn baby is a support for the baby's "right" to own property. Or that the violinist with the precious instrument confers rights on the instrument. It does entail that the world is more than a background theatre for human projects. We do not treat a marvel as a background.

11 UNIVERSALITY OF NEED; CULTURES OF ADDICTION

Nature is the universal substratum of human existence. Insofar as we value our own existence, we must value it. But that returns us to the question: *How* should we value it? As something of value in its own right, or merely as a tool, a resource? A wise carpenter values his hammers and screwdrivers; a rational surgeon or a careful chef treasures her best knives. Is that all nature is to us? Yet while the vast majority of us do not depend on the surgeon's knives or the carpenter's hammers, we do all depend on air, water, sunlight, and photosynthesis. Whatever our culture teaches about nature, that it is there for the taking and use; that it is source of spiritual inspiration and moral instruction – the universality of need is present.

Does the universality of *need* create a universality of *value* that serves as a critique of any culture that fails to treat nature with moral concern? In a time when cultural relativism – the idea that moral judgement is only and always relative to the beliefs of a culture and cannot be made across different cultures – is popular, how do we criticize central tenets of a culture?

At least two kinds of argument are possible.

As we've seen, though it bears repeating, we can simply sketch the consequences of *not* taking that moral connection seriously.[27] Rather than arguing for some inherent value to nature we could simply say: "If you don't take nature seriously as a moral value, the rivers catch on fire, the climate shifts, and countless fish species are fished out."

Ironically, this form of argument might be the only way to justify the claim that *people* have moral value as well. The idea that simply by

---

[27] The idea that moral positions ultimately can be justified only by comparing the consequences of holding them was developed by Stephen Toulmin, *The Place of Reason in Ethics* (Chicago: University of Chicago Press, 1986).

rational argument we can justify some absolute, unchallengeable, universal foundation for morality has been a goal of philosophy at least since the seventeenth century. The failure of the project, I believe, is shown by the fact that attempts to complete it are repeated generation after generation. If it were possible to do, probably it would have been done by now. So, a comparable argument to the one I'm making about nature would be, for people: What happens if we don't value people morally? Look at Nazi Germany, the Jim Crow American south, modern North Korea – is that what we want?

Alternatively, we might say that a culture, such as our own, which is so attached to the endless freedom to drive fuel-inefficient cars or pollute waterways, is simply sick. By analogy: We have no trouble identifying a heavy smoker as someone who has a serious medical, including psychological, problem. They are, we say, addicted to behavior that is self-destructive. And we can say that because smoking is so antagonistic to virtually any personal goals, that it violates virtually any conception of personal health (except a concept in which smoking takes priority over every other goal). And this is true whether the person is a secular American, a fundamentalist Muslim, a Chinese communist, or a Guatemalan farmer.

Of course, different cultures or groups of people celebrate different holidays, worship (or not worship) in their own particular style and structure their families in particular ways. They will certainly have different practices around sex, death, or education. But all of them share human physiology and human dependence on nature.

Would we designate drug addiction (such as smoking, or alcoholism, or heroin use) simply as a cultural form, one group preference among others? I do not think so. Behaviors driven by addiction's relentless physiological and psychological need are not preferences. They are a kind of compulsion – and one that is destructive to virtually all other values. Any cultural relativism that tells us we cannot criticize the life of the addict leaves our medical and moral resources far too limited.

Thus, a culture that prefers to live as if there is no moral value in nature is similarly manifesting a kind of addictive compulsion to behavior that diminishes the rest of life. The "freedom to pollute" is, collectively, the same kind of freedom that the individual smoker has to smoke or the heroin addict has to reach for the needle one more time. As Stewart Ewan observed, it is not people who have power, but people's *desires*. Therefore, the ultimate power resides in those who shape desires. And a great deal of that shaping in modern society turns us away from modest, responsible, careful, reflective living.[28]

12 GIFT FROM GOD

If we take some of the teachings of the monotheistic religions seriously, the earth is a gift from God. This perspective is like our gratitude for nature being what it is, and doing what it does, but adds the dimension of attributing nature's existence to an intelligent, caring Force that brought the universe into being and has a deep love for human beings.[29]

Seeing nature as a divine gift necessarily confers value on it and a corresponding sense of horror at what has been done. The violinist described earlier would not only care for her instrument out of respect for what it is, but if it had given to her by a loving grandmother, someone who had always supported her vocation as a professional musician, she would treasure it out of respect not only for the gift, but for the giver as well.

For the serious theist *everything* on earth derives its most essential reality through its relation to God. The land, other people, education, sex, politics, or marriage – are all sanctified by being God's creation or being structured properly through God's commands. If God is kept in mind when we love our children, deal with a troublesome neighbor, conduct business affairs; or dispose of wastes, consume food, and decide on transportation, then, the theist believes, we will be acting in accord with our Creator, and with what is ultimately best for us and everyone else. In these ways, religious environmentalists are teaching that our moral recognition of nature expresses our recognition of God.[30]

The Baal Shem Tov, eighteenth-century founder of Hasidic Judaism, tells us, "The world is full of wonders and miracles, but we take our hands and cover our eyes and see nothing."[31] What is he talking about? After all, he comes from a religious tradition in which things we might all

---

[28] Quoted in David Kidner, *Nature and Experience in the Culture of Delusion* (New York: Palgrave, 2012), p. 69.

[29] There are many other religious teachings that devalue nature in comparison to the soul, heaven, angels, God, etc.

[30] See Roger S. Gottlieb, ed., *The Oxford Handbook of Religion and Ecology* (New York: Oxford University Press, 2006); and *A Greener Faith: Religious Environmentalism and our Planet's Future* (New York: Oxford University Press, 2006).

[31] I've seen this in many places, including some Jewish prayer books (e.g., *Siddur Hadash* (Bridgeport, CN: Media Judaica, n.d.), p. 80, but have yet to find the original source.

call "miracles" exist but are hardly filling up the world. The ten plagues with which God smote Egypt, the parting of the Red Sea that allowed the Israelites to escape the Egyptian chariots, Joshua making the sun stand still in the sky – these are miracles, but they do not fill up the world. They are few and far between.

It would seem the Baal Shem Tov is asking us to see the most common features of our existence, including what we would call nature, as miraculous. New leaves in spring, porpoises leaping high out of the ocean, stars dotting the night sky, our own natural ability to smell and sing. If we think of these as miracles, how are we likely to treat them? Clearly not cavalierly, sloppily, crudely, or exploitatively; but with respect and care.

"Let everything that breathes praise God," says the last line of the last biblical psalm (150). What could this possibly mean? An immaterial, infinite God is a devilishly complicated concept for humans to believe in, and clearly something far beyond a goat, a mouse, or an ant. Only humans have a language with sufficient abstractive capacity to contain the word "God"; and the idea of praising something that is not immediate to any sense is not something, as far as we can tell, of which animals are capable. While humans can tell animals to fetch, herd the sheep, and find the cocaine in the suitcase, directing them to "praise" makes no sense.

Could "Let everything that breathes praise God"? be construed to mean that people, who after all are the ones uttering the psalm, should transform themselves into beings who are capable of seeing the existence, daily life, and particular gifts of everything that breathes as praise of God? And if the very being of a horse or butterfly or salmon is praise of God, what behavior toward these beings is called for? Clearly, *not* complete disregard for their well-being, a willingness to destroy their habitat, or a license to consume them to the edge (or over the edge) of extinction.

More generally, ecotheologians have offered new models of the religious meaning of nature and of the ultimate character of the Divine. They have suggested that we might look at the earth as the body of God, see toxic chemicals as being un-kosher, treat an endangered fish as sacred, and wrap the orange sash used to identify Buddhist monks around a tree to keep it from being cut down. Simply and directly, the world leader of more than three hundred million Orthodox Christians asserted: "To pollute the world is a sin."[32]

---

[32] Gottlieb, *A Greener Faith*, p. 83.

13 VIRTUE ETHICS

It is a classic technique of moral philosophy to contrast our treatment of a rock or stick of wood with the way we (hopefully) treat people. Holding up a pencil the professor of Moral Philosophy 101 points out that "I can break this in half and if it's my pencil, there is no moral problem. But," pointing at James in the front row, "I can't do the same to him. That's the difference between having 'moral considerability' or 'rights' or being 'morally significant' and being something that has no moral standing whatsoever."

Taught this way the lesson misses a crucial point. "Why," a student trained in virtue ethics might ask, "are you breaking a perfectly good pencil in half? Isn't that a waste, and isn't waste something that goes contrary to the virtue of careful use of resources? Isn't a habit of waste something that will have bad effects on your life and that of other people?"

From the standpoint of virtue ethics, the moral standing of nature – perhaps in the very same way as the moral standing of everything else – resides in the way virtuous treatment of it is essential to human well-being. The virtues are cognitive, emotional, and practical dispositions that lead, in the long run, to individual and collective human fulfillment.[33] For example, current levels of phone use, many psychologists warn, cause social isolation, anxiety, and depression; as well as dramatic increases in nearsightedness among young people. Cell phones are destructive to the very people who think they are a good thing – or who, as described in the previous section, are psychologically addicted to the little screens. More generally, unlimited, quasi-addictive consumerism does not lead to lasting happiness, but only to a kind of endless frenzy of need, a sense that one never has enough, and an inability to enjoy what one gets for very long.

I will offer a more extended account of virtue theory in Chapter 5, but here I will simply observe how it handles a difficult problem that arises when we say that nature has rights. If it does, what are those rights, and how far do they extend? Except for the right to life, the kinds of rights attributed to citizens in the US Constitution or the UN Declaration of Human Rights are pretty much irrelevant to nature. And this is so because these statements concern freedom and equality of specifically *human*

---

[33] If, that is, they are practiced with the virtues of love, compassion, and self-awareness. Otherwise John's virtue can include a tendency to feel superior and nag Jane. For other accounts of virtue in this context see Jamieson, *Reason in a Dark Time*; and Ronald Sandler, ed., *Environmental Virtue Ethics* (Lanham, MD: Rowman and Littlefield, 2005).

activities or capacities: to practice a religion, appear before a court of law, take part in political meetings, own a weapon, or find out the news.

So, what does it mean that nature has rights, or is an object of moral concern? Seventy years ago Aldo Leopold advocated respecting nature's integrity and stability, and in 2017 an environmental philosopher claimed justice to nature requires that we allow ecosystems to maintain "their functioning, diversity, and essential identity."[34] Nature writer Edward Abbey said we should "keep it like it was"; philosopher Eric Katz argues that nature should be "preserved, set free to pursue its autonomy."[35]

But because the natural existence of all of life is one of constant use and consumption, what could this mean? That we stop eating, taking up space, building houses, walking (so that we don't step on insects or bruise plants)?

Furthermore, nothing in nature "leaves it like it was," for nature is in a constant local process of interaction and a constant global process of transformation. In the far future, astronomers tell us, our own star will explode and then contract, destroying the earth in the process, or at least leaving it so bereft of heat that no life will survive. Some seventy million years ago, we currently believe, an asteroid hit the earth, threw up massive amounts of dust, which obstructed the sunlight and dramatically lessened temperatures. The result altered the earth's climate and was instrumental in ending the age of dinosaurs and making the emergence of mammals, and eventually humans, possible. As Fred Pearce and Emma Maras have convincingly argued, the fundamental goal of "environmental restoration" or complete environmental preservation is at odds with the way evolution works. Ecosystems alter with or without human intervention; "exotic species" may often support rather than diminish their new home; biodiversity can flourish in the ruins of an industrial landscape; if we are seeking to restore, there is no way to fix what point we are trying to get back to.[36]

---

[34] Teea Kortetmäki, Applying the Capabilities Approach to Ecosystems: Resilience as Ecosystem Capability," *Environmental Ethics* 39, no. 1 (2017): 53. Other philosophers use the term "integrity."

[35] Edward Abbey, *The Long Journey Home: Some Words in Defense of the American West* (New York: Penguin, 1991), p. 145. Eric Katz, *Anne Frank's Tree: Nature's Confrontation with Technology, Domination, and the Holocaust* (Cambridge: The White Horse Press, 2015), p. 122.

[36] Emma Maris, *The Rambunctious Garden: Saving Nature in a Post-Wild World* (New York: Bloomsbury, 2013). Fred Pearce, *The New Wild: Why Invasive Species Will Be Nature's Salvation* (Boston: Beacon Press, 2016).

These theoretical problems are short-circuited by virtue theory. For virtue theory takes for granted our right to life. We will eat, at least, plant food. And in raising plant food we will displace countless organisms in the soil and try to kill as many weeds as we can. No doctrine of nature's rights, nature's equality with human beings, nature as our partner, or nature's essential value could ever make these activities, in and of themselves, morally suspect. That is, not unless we question the very existence of humans as such.[37]

What virtue ethics does is to ask, simply: What is a good life for us?

Does our refusal to accept reasonable limits to our technological powers make us satisfied? Or merely anxious when the inevitability of death, illness, and aging arise? How many times has the compulsion to "make it better" made it worse? Do we need homes this big? Do we need to eat animals raised brutally and with disastrous consequences for the rest of the ecosystem? Do we need to eat them at all? If we don't need such things, *why are we doing them*? Is it a boundless, collectively practiced greed? But greed, we know, only leads to dissatisfaction. Do we even know the consequences of what we are doing? If not, haven't we seen how often lack of awareness leads to disaster – whether in the form of addictions, the consequences of long-term, unheeded oppression, or on our own health?

Much has been written about the terrible effects of humans on the rest of life; and also on how we could know what it allowable and what isn't. The point here, however, is not just *what* has been done to nature, but *why* humans have done what they have. When people argue that the problem is the degree and the rate of change we have caused, this is certainly relevant. Since WW II the scope of environmental devastation has increased to vast and unprecedented levels. But we must ask: What has motivated us? How much has been accomplished so that human beings can live freer, more sensitive, more intelligent, more truly fulfilling lives – and how much for greed, status, military power, addictive consumption, and just plain careless stupidity? It is not just that we change the natural world because nature is in a constant state of change in any case. It is that we are changing nature in a way that leads to less life and more pain, and so often for reasons

---

[37] Some environmental thinkers have taken this route, comparing humanity to a virus or cancer. It is not, for obvious reasons, a widespread view.

that make no sense, and ultimately lead not only to the suffering of other beings, but also of ourselves.[38]

In the context of the environmental crisis virtue theory necessarily relies on particular concepts of physical and psychological well-being. These concepts reject the idea that "he who dies with the most toys wins," that shopping makes people happy, that we "need" endlessly increasing supplies of energy or an endlessly increasing Gross National Product. Rather, virtue theory claims that virtues such as awareness and gratitude, compassion and love, are much more reliable sources of human happiness. Applied to environmental practices, this means a lessening of consumption and frenetic commodity innovation, and instead a concentration on education, psychological insight, community interconnection, readily available contact with nature, and reliable ways of meeting essential physical and cultural needs.[39] As far as we can tell, these are much more trustworthy sources of human satisfaction than what we have, or at least are pursuing, now.[40]

14 NATURE AS SPIRITUAL TEACHER

I am looking out of my window in an anxious and resentful state of mind ... then ... I observe a hovering kestrel. In a moment everything is altered.[41]

I never saw a wild thing sorry for itself.[42]

Nature doesn't judge you.[43]

---

[38] This point applied well to climate change responsibility in Henry Shue, "Subsistence Emission and Luxury Emission," in Stephan Gardiner, et al., eds., *Climate Ethics: Essential Readings* (New York: Oxford University Press, 2010), pp. 101–111.

[39] Here are studies that both critique the dominant global capitalist, consumerist perspective and offer some alternatives: Vernonia Bennholdt-Thomsen, Nicholas Faraclas, and Claudia Von Werlhof, eds., *There Is an Alternative: Subsistence and Worldwide Resistance to Corporate Globalization* (London: Zed Books, 2001); William F. Fisher and Thomas Ponniah, eds., *Another World Is Possible: Popular Alternatives to Globalization at the World Social Forum* (London: Zed Books, 2003); Allan Hunt Badiner, ed., *Mindfulness in the Marketplace: Compassionate Responses to Consumerism* (Berkeley, CA: Parallax Press, 2002); Juliet Schor and Betsy Taylor, eds., *Sustainable Planet: Solutions for the Twenty-First Century* (Boston: Beacon Press, 2002).

[40] This claim is subject to the distinction between wealthy and poor nations and between those who do and those who do not already have reasonable sources of food, housing, education, and medical care and those who do not.

[41] Iris Murdoch, *The Sovereignty of the Good* (New York: Routledge, 2001), p. 84.

[42] D. H. Lawrence, "Self-pity."

[43] Malcolm Ribot, transgender man, in Jason Mark, "Outdoors for All," *Sierra Magazine* 103, no. 2 (March/April 2018): 4.

The world's religious traditions are filled with teachings instructing us that only through spiritual virtues will we have individually happy lives and collectively fulfilling societies. Alongside such teachings, and the often-inspiring lives of individuals who embody these virtues, the world of nature has been taken as a profound source of spiritual instruction.

I am not referring to the idea that one can enter an altered state and have a literal conversation with the nonhuman. Whether the hawk or spider can verbally warn us against greed or reinforce a tendency to generous compassion, I do not know. I am thinking, rather, of the way elements of the natural world function without what is commonly known in eclectic spiritual writings as "the ego"; i.e., the part of the self that is subject to anxiety, greed, competition for status, addiction, toxic relationships, self-hatred, pointless cruelty, and the like. The ego is the aspect of the human personality that is needlessly destructive, self-aggrandizing, or just plain impossible to live with. If you think of how you feel when you look at yourself, naked, in a mirror; or just before you get a grade on an important test; or when you sense yourself losing a step (or more) as you age; or find out that your childhood friend is now wonderfully successful while you are not; or if your kids are not doing well at all or your parents always make you feel small – if you can relate to any of these situations, you can get a sense of what the ego is and how it makes us suffer.

Nature lacks an ego. There is competition for food, or for a position in the pack, but not for purely symbolic status. There is fear as a predator approaches, but no anxiety over next week or next year. There is a fierce desire to live, but not to have sycophants offering coerced praise. There are instinctually governed relations between parents and offspring and between mates; but there are no divorces over jealousy, family breakups over political disagreements, or vicious arguments about money. Unlike people, nature offers without demand, lives without regret or fear of death, and cares without a contract or a request for reciprocity.

In these ways nature offers, as nineteenth-century British essayist William Hazlitt observed, a kind of constant and profound egalitarianism. Nature gives to us without "hypocrisy, caprice, nor mental reservation."[44] This generosity – the flip side of which is the way in

---

[44] William Hazlitt, "Walking," in Roger S. Gottlieb, ed., *This Sacred Earth: Religion, Nature, Environment* (New York: Routledge, 1995), p. 27.

which nature is an equal threat to all people – can provoke an awareness of that aspect of our identity that is not tied to social concerns. Wealth or social position, good grades or fame, ideology or philosophy are simply irrelevant to the feel of warm ocean waters, the smell of wild lavender, or a hungry mosquito.

To take nature as a teacher is, of course, to interpret it in this way, and to use that interpretation to help us see the possibility of our functioning in the same way, at least to some extent, as well.

Of course, as well, it is only for those of us who see the negative effects of the "normal" ego who will treasure a nature understood spiritually. And who will allow nature's model to be a model for ourselves. But this is true of spiritual life in any setting. Whether the teacher is a Buddhist saint, a Hasidic rebbe, or a medieval Christian mystic, their ideas can only be taken seriously if one is willing to deeply question the established values and goals of normality. A serious spiritual life is always at odds with a social order the foundation of which is the normal ego.

If nature's example can help us toward a spiritual rejection of that ego, or at least a management of it, then it has a deeply important value for us, and a moral concern for it may very well follow.

15 AN OBJECTION

Here is a counterargument to a good deal of what I've been saying so far, especially any suggestion that relations with nature should be characterized by emotional or moral ties such as gratitude, love, compassion, recognition, or kinship. "After all," someone might say, "you can only see nature in this warm and fuzzy light *because* of several hundred years of scientific and technological progress. Call it "domination" all you like, but try living through winter without heating or watching large numbers of babies and women die in childbirth. How many crops ruined by insects or devastating floods would it take to get you to clamor for control of nature at all costs? Nature is a heartless, unrelenting enemy of humanity. Whether it's the bacteria that make for your child's ear infection or the cancer cells in your own lungs, we must control with antibiotics and chemotherapy. After that's done, we can go for hikes in the woods and commune with the trees – no doubt wearing high-tech windbreakers and Vibram-soled boots, carrying cell phones to call for help if we get lost, and happy the car heater and sound system work when we get back to the trailhead."

There is some merit in this position, but less than meets the eye. Certainly humans, like any other species, mold their surroundings to meet their needs. Beavers build dams, birds build nests, certain ant species utilize aphids for food, and foraging mammals can graze entire ecosystems into submission. Native Americans did controlled burns in forests, hunted, fished, and planted crops. I don't mean to suggest that our necessity to manage, consume, and displace nature can ever be ended. It is precisely this permanent reality that lessens, for me at least, the idea of extending rights to nature. And there can be no doubt that struggles for food, shelter, medical care, safety, and the creation of culture have all been furthered by what environmental critics decry as the "domination of nature."

Yet three considerations are conspicuously absent from the "control is the real story" position.

The first is that feelings of gratitude and even love for nature are not dependent on achieving extensive, technologically based control. Such attitudes are richly developed in an enormous variety of indigenous cultures, in which concepts of kinship, respect, reciprocity, and appreciation are commonplace. And these concepts are not merely a convenient cover for desperate attempts to control. Rather, they serve as a limit, a boundary, a sense of proper proportion or scale in the degree of exploitation and control. Such limits have not always been observed, but they have often – and far more often than in technologically based modernity.[45] Further, awe, appreciation, and delight can also be found in Western cultures as well: from the biblical *Song of Songs* to Jesus' appreciation of the "lilies of the field." Along with the need to control and at times defend against it, appreciation for nature is a permanent feature (in wildly varying degrees) of most of human culture.

Second, "control is the answer" misses the reality of how much nature's current threat to humanity is a product of humanity's own action. Floods there have always been, but global warming makes them much worse. Cancer didn't begin in the twentieth century, but there is no doubt that the current cancer plague is to a significant degree an effect of pollution. We are growing superbugs though an overuse of bacteria; poisoning on our bodies with junk food, alcohol, and drugs; and jeopardizing our own agriculture by eliminating bats and bees. At

---

[45] There is an enormous debate on the range of native environmental practices.

this point, to use Bill McKibben's telling phrase, "more" – consumption, control, innovation, unevaluated technology – is not leading to "better."[46]

Third, so what if tree-hugging environmentalists' calls for care, kinship, gratitude, and compassion are only possible after the success of control? That does not make these ethics any less necessary – especially when we can see the practical consequences of maintaining what we've been doing already. Can't we see that something must shift?

16 WHERE ARE WE?

For each of the ways in which a moral awareness of nature might emerge, there can be a corresponding failure. We can deny the severity of the environmental crisis, discount feelings of gratitude or awe, think personal and social health depend only on continued increases in consumption and energy use, downplay our dependence on the rest of nature, treat the world as a given rather than a gift, or treasure *our* garden or pet while ignoring the effects of our actions everywhere else.

However, this is no different than how justifications for moral treatment of people are stymied by those who have beliefs that justify what others consider to be immoral. For example: a "terrorist," just about everyone agrees, is a bad person, doing bad things. However, consult the Websites of the groups "we" (the US government, NATO) label as terrorists, and you will find that these groups often use the same term to describe America in particular or the West in general.

To the person who denies the significance of acting morally at all, we can say that such an attitude would make social life impossible. They might reply that they are happy with a situation in which other people are moral and they are not. We could say they are contradicting themselves, that their assertions are inconsistent. They could reply that they didn't start the conversation, and they are happy to end it and go about their lives. They want money or power or pleasure, not to win an argument and be considered consistent. We could appeal to God's commands, and they might reply, paraphrasing Ivan in *The Brothers Karamazov*, "God is dead, so everything is permitted." We can appeal to virtue theory and ask if an immoral life makes them happy. And, they could reply, that it's good enough for them.

---

[46] Bill McKibben, *Deep Economy: The Wealth of Communities and the Durable Future* (New York: Times Books, 2007).

Yet the demand to recognize our moral connections to nature is now part of a global moral and political conversation. We have certainly not achieved any global consensus on whether nature deserves moral concern, but even people who are sure it does not know that others seriously disagree.

Those who take the moral status of nature seriously ask us to cultivate individual virtues and social practices to replace the current environmental order.

For the person, for the society, what will this transformation be like?

3

The Spirit of Ecological Democracy

Once it was the endeavor of art, literature, and philosophy to express the meaning of things and of life, to be voice of all that is dumb, to endow nature with an organ for making known her sufferings ... Today nature's tongue is taken away. Once it was thought that each utterance, word, cry, or gesture had an intrinsic meaning; today it is merely an occurrence.[1]

Animists are people who believe the world is full of persons, only some of whom are people.[2]

What we must do is incorporate the other people ... the creeping people, and the standing people, and the flying people and the swimming people ... into the councils of government.[3]

As individuals, the ways in which we take nature seriously can vary widely. We can feel a connection, respond in gratitude, appreciate with awe, see the divine, try to live virtuously, identify with other species, even perhaps believe that nature has rights. We can acknowledge that we ourselves are essentially connected to nature for daily sustenance, the overall reality of the universe, and the process of evolution that led to our emergence as a species.

And such feelings and beliefs will be reflected in how we live: recycling, veganism, limited fossil fuel consumption, reusing and wearing out rather than compulsively buying new, supporting green technology.

[1] Max Horkheimer, *The Eclipse of Reason* (New York: Continuum, 1992), p. 101.
[2] Graham Harvey, *Animism: Respecting the Living World* (New York: Columbia University Press, 2005), p. xi.
[3] Gary Snyder, *Turtle Island* (New York: New Directions, 1974), p. 108.

Yet it is clear that the decisive force for environmental destruction and environmental repair reside in collective social practices shaped by the political system. The economy is, of course, key; but in modern life, particularly in countries with highly developed governmental powers and bureaucracies, the economic system is regulated *politically*. There are environmental regulations, environmental laws, and constraints on the pursuit of profit. Indeed, a good deal of political struggle now focuses precisely on how much and what kind of environmental regulation there will be in everything from where fracking is allowed to tax benefits for electric cars.

This chapter will not propose laws or regulations; e.g., to govern chemical food additives or car emissions. My focus, rather, is on how we should conceive of the place of nature in our political system. In Chapter 5 I will investigate some of the limits to conceiving that place as equal to our own, and in Chapter 7 I will discuss methods of political transformation.

I SOMETHING ABOUT DEMOCRACY

For humanity and nature to flourish, or, at least, if we are to slow down the juggernaut of environmental devastation, the individual bonds with nature described in Chapter 2 must be manifest in our political structures. What might that might mean for one of our key political ideals: democracy?

The fundamental presumption of democracy, articulated in John Locke's *Second Treatise of Civil Government*, is both extremely simple and extremely powerful. To determine where political powers – i.e., to make laws and to punish people who violate them – comes from, let us imagine a time when such powers did not exist, and then inquire what process could bring them into existence. Locke characterizes the prepolitical time as characterized by freedom and equality. Equality arises because, having abstracted from all political relationships, no basis for specifically political inequality exists.[4] Freedom exists for the same reason, but also because free action is necessary for life. And virtually the only thing Locke presupposes is that we have a "right" to life – meaning, as I read him, that in a prepolitical condition each of us is entitled to do what we need to stay alive. To put it another way: on what basis could *you* possible argue that I shouldn't do what *I* need to do to

[4] Inequalities of strength, intelligence, health, or good looks are not at issue here.

stay alive? Or that you have a more powerful social position than I do, a more powerful right to life? Having dismantled political reality, such claims to political superiority make no sense.

How Locke gets from this nonpolitical "state of nature" to a politically organized society need not concern us. What is significant is that his two key values, freedom and equality, are essential to what that society looks like. Each of us, freely and equally, gets to shape the political system, which then will include political inequalities, but only to the extent that such inequalities further and protect our essential equality and freedom. We will designate special groups to make laws and enforce them in order that we may go about our own concerns. Political inequality may exist, then, but is acceptable only if, and to the extent that, it furthers the essential "right" to life with which we all began.

In contemporary terms this model is expressed in the right to vote, a key right that signals that each (adult, nonserious criminal, of sound mind) person has the same power to determine political structures as any other.[5] Conceived this way, democracy is an essentially *individual* process: each of us can express his or her choices in the voting booth. If the result doesn't please us, we can try again next time.

This atomistic conception of democracy has been subject to extensive criticism over the last decades. A more robust conception of democracy has emerged[6] that rejects the idea that we are essentially separate individuals and that democratic rights are aimed solely at keeping us from hurting each other. In "deliberative democracy," "communitarianism," and associated positions the goal of democracy is not equal individual freedom, but a good shared life in community. To achieve this shared life, particularly in a diverse society, democracy is partly defined by extensive dialogue so that we can hear each other's reasons, empathize with differing viewpoints, and respond to each other's real concerns.[7]

In this rich sense of democracy, political life is much more than simply adding up everyone's wants and seeing who comes out on top. Here "recognition" – being seen, heard, known – is an essential part of the democratic process. It is not just that we can worship in different

---

[5] I am ignoring the many difficulties with Locke's model: e.g., the way economic inequality makes political equality impossible and his reliance on a certain kind of labor to ground property rights – leaving out nomads and domestic workers.

[6] Or, depending on your viewpoint, been rediscovered.

[7] E.g., Jon Elster, ed., *Deliberative Democracy* (New York: Cambridge University Press, 1998); Iris Young, *Inclusion and Democracy* (Princeton, NJ: Princeton University Press, 2000).

churches, read different newspapers, or get a fair trial. It is that we can be understood – and that such understanding can be incorporated into political deliberation and social policy.

One advantage of this view over the individualistic version of democracy can be found in Locke's statement that political power exists "for the public good."[8] While this crucial point gets little further attention in Locke, it is essential to the expanded conception of democracy I am describing. How, after all, are we to know *what* the common good is if we do not communicate with the other people in our community, if we do not deliberate with them over our common situation and what each of us really needs? Without talking to each other, we will never be able to answer such questions reasonably. We will be stuck in our own beliefs and desires, and what will often be our ignorance or misunderstanding of our fellow citizens – and possibly of ourselves.

If democracy requires not just isolated decisions but knowledge of other people gathered through engaged relationships, if democracy is rooted in conversation, we can then ask: What kind of conversation is it? A culturally male model, based in the idea that interpersonal rationality rejects the distractions of emotions or purely personal preferences, would have us believe that proper democratic conversation is simply a series of assertions, justifications, and refutations: universal ethical principles and facts, connected by flawless logic, marshalled in support of competing positions.

This model is limited for many reasons, the most important of which is that when people engage in serious conversation about issues of critical importance to their community, many more forms of communication arise. Three of these are particularly important.

First, along with facts and principles there is also the depth of emotion felt by the participants, which signals the importance of the question at hand both to us and to our fellow citizens. Expressions of anger, grief, fear, confusion, joy, and gratitude are not distractions from a democratic deliberation, but an essential part. They give insight into *why* something may be crucially important to us or to our fellows. And they introduce a proper and accurate level of vulnerability into the conversation. For example, it is not just that I disagree with or don't like your position, it *frightens* me. Knowing that I am scared – or that you are – should shape

---

[8] *Second Treatise of Civil Government*, Chapter 1, Part 3.

the direction of the conversation. Leaving it out makes the conversation less real and much less likely to be productive.[9]

Rather than just the constricted "What are your reasons?" we might much more expansively inquire, "What do you have to say?" Your answer might be an expression of emotion. But it also might be our second addition to democratic conversation, someone "making a point" by telling a story. "This is what happened to me ..." may explain *why* I feel the way I do about a political issue as or more powerfully than simply claiming that my position is "rational." Your personal account of a rape can shape my perspective on sexual violence, even without a complex analysis of the politics of gender and power. A child of Holocaust survivors who tells what happened to her parents makes her anxiety over ethnic hatred or raw governmental power much clearer.

At the very least narratives, which in fact take us through the lived process of our emotional reactions to life situations, may well make us amenable to understanding or agreeing with general claims or policy recommendations. This is like the ways a good novel or a personal history can provide much more important resources for improved moral reasoning than abstract philosophical accounts of general principles. From the stories we see that other people, even people with different cultures, can suffer and triumph over adversity just as we do. Out of this sense of similarity-despite-difference, some philosophers believe, can come a moral solidarity hard to achieve in any other way. This does not mean that stories replace abstract reasoning, for stories always have to be interpreted and morals must be drawn from them. Rather, it is that stories, abstractions, and factual details exist alongside each other.

Third, as mentioned briefly in Chapter 2, sometimes we argue simply by drawing attention to a compelling reality. "Look at this," we say,

---

[9] Properly integrating emotions into democratic deliberation is not easy. There are at least two central difficulties: to act as if we don't have emotions, or to be so unaware or in thrall of emotions that we act them out without awareness, restraint, or self-understanding. The cold technocrat would have us believe he is all logic, while in fact he has simply suppressed his feelings and is acting in defense of that suppression. The person for whom their feelings are everything is unable to ask critical questions about how justified their fear or anger are; or what they believe their fear or anger entitle them to; or about the reality of *other* people's feelings.

and we all look together: at pictures of concentration camps, rape, or torture. The power of the image may be such that little conversation follows and little is needed. At any rate, it may be much more powerful than ethical generalization about violence or injustice. And at times such compelling realities will invoke powerful emotional responses and bring to mind a moving narration, a story. Who were the people in the camp? What was the awful experience of rape like? Why was this person tortured?

2 HOW FAR CAN WE GO?

Is the communication that is the heart of democratic life necessarily and only linguistic? And are the participants in democratic conversation necessarily human? Is democracy only *people* talking together? Or can we communicate in other ways than a human language, and with beings that are not human?

If our theory of democracy asserts that we can talk by telling stories, expressing emotions, and simply pointing to compelling realities, perhaps something else is possible: fundamentally different kinds of communication than that of which humans are capable. In this admittedly expanded sense of democratic conversation, we might encounter, for instance, the melting of glaciers due to global warming, the rash of pollution-caused birth abnormalities in frogs, or the emotional devastation of animals kept in zoos. We might encounter, that is, an *ecological democracy*.

3 THE VALUE OF NATURE REVISITED

In response to the environmental crisis a variety of religious environmentalists, secular environmental philosophers, spiritually oriented nature writers, and environmental organizations have asserted the moral value of nature in a variety of ways.

- Nature is a gift from God and should be treasured as such.
- Nature is permeated by a Divine Spirit.
- Because we have emerged from, depend on, and are so much like nature, we must extend our sense of moral value to it.
- Nature awes us with its scope and complexity. It is marvelous and calls forth a respect bordering on reverence.
- The interdependence and selflessness that mark the holistic character of ecosystems contain moral and spiritual lessons.

- Animals, ecosystems, or life have rights and deserve compassion.
- Environmental political action keyed to justice should recognize the "sacredness of Mother Earth."[10]

Despite their differences, all these perspectives direct us to respect the rest of life on earth. Is such an attitude compatible with our current social structures and cultures? Probably not. At least, there is little evidence that what needs to be done can be accomplished without far more change than has occurred already. As with other profound social shifts, the transformation needs to unfold simultaneously on the personal and the collective level. What would enable us to take nature seriously as part of our democratic conversation, our political community?

Let us start small. What is the personal basis for ecological democracy?

4 BECOMING CITIZENS OF A NATURAL WORLD

Significant political changes have always required deep shifts in self-identity. For example, every time a hitherto oppressed group is recognized as having been illegitimately excluded from full participation in social and political life, beliefs that justified their exclusion must be challenged and replaced with different beliefs. But, as Jean-Paul Sartre pointed out, the basis of any kind of group exclusion is not simply a matter of belief. It is, to use his term, a "passion" – i.e., a fundamental self-understanding and way of being in the world. The anti-Semite (or the racist, or sexist, or hater of any generalized social group) seeks a personal validation through *not* being a member of the despised group. He wishes to be thought "good" (strong, smart, valuable, a "real" American, or man, etc.) simply through being the opposite of some Other, a status accomplished through no effort on his part. His qualities are not earned, worked for, or maintained, they simply exist.[11]

Overcoming social oppression, then, requires that members of the dominant group come to understand their identity in a new way. Being born white or a man no longer gives you extra credit, a special place. Where something was given, it now must be earned. A kind of self-understanding must be relinquished, or even powerful legal and institutional changes (women's suffrage, affirmative action) will founder on

[10] "Principles of Environmental Justice," Greenpeace International Website. Our Core Principles. Accessed September 8, 2017, www.greenpeace.org/international/en/about/our-core-values/.
[11] Jean-Paul Sartre, *Anti-Semite and Jew* (New York: Schocken, 1995).

widespread resistance. The continued strength of racism and sexism in our society testify to this reality.

Further, a combined recognition of both difference and commonality must arise. In the case of race, for instance, a white person can come to see that love, disappointment, ambition, frustration, courage, humor, betrayal, and devotion have no color. Because people of the oppressed race possess those just as people of the dominant race do, extending both political rights and interpersonal recognition makes a fundamental sense.

At the same time, however, a fundamental *difference* persists: The oppressed group has lived a history of oppression. In the racial case it is the multiple horrors of slavery, segregation, lynching, and discrimination in virtually every public arena (housing, the army, loans, education, medical treatment, etc.) that can lead a white person to realize that because they are the heirs of a quite different history, blacks are *not* just like whites.

This analogy between overcoming social oppression among people and the foundations of ecological democracy is loose is many ways, but it does tell us something about how the way we see ourselves must shift if nature is to be included in our deliberations. We must not only pass new laws to regulate production, transform energy, and overhaul transportation. We ourselves must change. The new laws will only be passed and followed, the necessary changes in our economy arise, only if how we think of ourselves shifts as well. Neither the public, political, economic shifts, nor the subjective, personal, changes in self-understanding and experience, are possible without the other. Without the latter the former will be bitterly resisted, exist only under threat of constant revocation, and poorly (if at all) carried out. Without the former the comprehensive, global nature of the needed change will not be understood or even attempted.

To continue the analogy: the fundamental shift will require recognition of the nonhuman both for the ways it is like humanity and for the ways in which it is not: to see what we have in common and also how each bit of moss or crab has a distinct form of existence.

The change requires far more than just increased recycling, more hybrid cars, and fewer plastic bags, and it flows logically from the reality of the environmental crisis. If what is going on is *that* threatening to so much of what we hold dear, then it should not surprise us that some very significant shifts need to be made. If *this* is what our civilization has done, and if *we* necessarily are products of our civilizations, then *who we are* must change to undo or lessen the great wrongs taking place now.

5 THE ECOLOGICAL SELF

What is the ecological self, this essential building block of ecological democracy? What do we need to become that we are not, or not enough or often enough, already?

Clearly it is not the normal ego of the industrialized world that will hear trees or learn from hawks, which will, that is, recognize the nonhuman in some way as it recognizes the human. (Usually the best we can do is know when to feed the dog.) This is perhaps the fundamental difference between the modern world and that of shamans and indigenous peoples. As two Indian environmental historians put it: "Ecosystem people all over the world have viewed themselves as members of a community of beings, in coexistence with fellow creatures be they trees, birds, streams, or rocks."[12]

For a beginning, consider, in turn, a religious and a secular perspective.

What religious grounds are there for taking nature seriously in a political sense? We might believe that everything in nature is "also a community like yours" (Qur'an 6:28); or, as a Jewish Midrash teaches, be told that nature follows its Torah (its teaching, its path toward God) as we are to follow ours.[13] If the many teachings of this kind were taken to heart, we would have to allow for the depth of feeling associated with the sacred to include nature. Perhaps the experiential intensity of collective religious practice – the group recitation of sins by Jews on Yom Kippur, the solemn joy of the Eucharist, the brilliant silence of the Buddhist meditation hall – could be aroused by a glimpse of new flowers in spring, the sound of ice cracking on a bitter winter night, or the echo of howling wolves. The kind of religious concern focused on sexuality, helping the poor, and ritual correctness, would be radically expanded. Out of this expansion emerges the sense that nature is part of our community – as are the "widow, the stranger and the orphan" of the Torah, or "the poor" in Christianity and Islam.[14]

If part of our religious community, then perhaps it is worthy of political recognition and representation as well.

---

[12] Madhav Gadgil and Ramachandra Guha, *Ecology and Equity: The Use and Abuse of Nature in Contemporary India* (London: Routledge, 1995), p. 91.

[13] Shalom Rosenberg, "Concepts of Torah and Nature in Jewish Thought," in Hava Tirosh-Samuelson, ed., *Judaism and Ecology* (Cambridge, MA: Harvard University Press, 2002), pp. 189–226.

[14] Mahayana Buddhism often defines the locus of moral concern to include "all beings."

Secular moral philosophy has long talked of rights, respect, and inclusion and of the need to see other people as worthwhile because they are rational, can experience pain or pleasure, have self-awareness, or because we love them. In multiculturalism there is the assertion that different ways of being human deserve respect. The essential principle supporting all these perspectives is the idea that we can think (and, therefore, act) beyond the limitations of our individual physical body, personal self-interest, or social position. Ecological democracy invites us to extend these relational imperatives so that not only different ways of being *human* but also different ways of being *alive* or *existing* are seen as worthy of respect and care. We would see a whole range of characteristics as giving rise to ethical importance, including existing, being essential to the lives of others, responsiveness to the environment, relations to others of its species and to other species, cognition as opposed to simply responsiveness, emotional connection, radical technological innovation, complex culture, and moral responsibility. While the last three seem exclusively human, the rest clearly are not.

Alternatively, the foundations of the ecological self – and therefore of ecological democracy – can be certain primal experiences of the world. As we walk through the forest, we sense that even though no other people have come with us, we are not "alone." There is wonder as we see a colt take its first hesitant steps and mystery when we contemplate that for humans no less than herons birth and death cannot exist without each other. There are times when sunset colors light up low-lying clouds from west to east. There is the sound of wind in autumn leaves; the drenching joy of the first monsoon after months of punishing heat; the swirling, rushing flow of water over rocks in small rivers; geese coming in low and fast to land on a still lake; a flash of light as sun reflects off the wings of seagull. There is what happens when any mother – human or not – gives birth; the way plants will force themselves through the tiniest cracks in the pavement, or urban trees, despite the smog and isolation from others of their kind, give us shade and the relief of green on a city street. We can know grief as we behold a clear-cut forest or hear the news that yet another bird species has been made extinct. And we can appreciate all the things our bodies do that are not under our conscious control – from digesting food to storing memories.

As well, there are experiences that unfold over long periods of time rather than for extreme, unforgettable moments. These would include the kind of deeper acquaintance that comes with sitting with the same trees for a few minutes a day – for years; watching seasons change in an ecosystem – for decades. Knowing as intimately as we know our human partners the smells and sounds of birds, insects, flowers, and earth of a particular – *our* particular – place.

6 WHAT CAN WE BECOME?

The kinds of communication that can heal the wounds between racial groups – biographies of oppression, fiction that highlights lived experiences, political demands by the oppressed – cannot arise between people and a ravaged landscape. Dolphins do not pray in words as we do. There will be no "interfaith" services like the ones in which Jews, Christians, and Muslims celebrate their shared spiritual and political destinies. For nearly two centuries feminists have offered new political perspectives and forcefully critiqued justifications of patriarchy. But rivers cannot demand recognition.

Therefore in the case of nature the ways in which societies enlarge moral vision and therefore political democracy must take a different form. We will have to take very seriously some other parts of *ourselves* than those that we usually stress so much. If rivers and dolphins are to be part of our community without claiming their rights, then we have to see that there is part of us that has value beyond our self-representing, self-interested egos; our demands and preferences; our culturally masculine denial of vulnerability and assumed superiority over a nature *and* women thought of as fleshy, emotional, and nonrational.

You get up in the morning, see your parents or children or roommates. "How are you?" you may ask. You might notice them smiling or frowning, high energy or fighting through a hangover. If your neighbor of many years doesn't sit on her front porch anymore; if the people you regularly communicate with through tweets or Facebook posts or email or even a monthly phone call – if these people don't email, call or tweet, you sense a possible problem, you reach out, you care. If you read of communities devastated by hurricanes, you might send a contribution, or even organize supplies to be sent. You probably like it when Riff the dog or Fluffy the cat greets you with their customary tail wag or purr; and if they lie in corner, head on their paws, and barely look up when you arrive, you know that something isn't right.

This last sense of connection is not in language. And it is available to anyone – of any race or gender, nationality or religion, at virtually any historical period. Notice what it takes to connect with Riff and Fluffy: attention to the details of the body, empathy with subtle emotional cues (the drooping tail, the lack of expression in the eyes), and an imaginative extension of ourselves into their experience. But this experience, and here is perhaps the key point, resides in something within ourselves that is not tied to social identity or complicated self-descriptions. We cannot do this as lawyers or plumbers, Republicans or New Yorkers. It is not because we fervently believe in Christ or Marx, have parents who are successful brain surgeons or children who've gotten into Stanford, or prefer Apple to PC or rap to opera. Something else must come into play, for something other than all these things is at stake. And the possibility of ecological democracy, and of an adequate response to the environmental crisis at all, depends on our capacity to realize this.

The basis of our communion with nature is that we are beings that breathe and eat, sense the sun, feel the wind and rain, experience love, fear, and pleasure in our bodies, have an identity bounded by birth and death, and get to share this planet.

Take a look at the world beyond buildings, cars, cell phone screens, plate glass windows, sidewalks and televisions. In certain places it is not that hard to move away from these things and into the realm of nature. In others it is quite hard. But virtually every place has some trees, a vacant lot sprouting weeds, even small growth coming up in the cracks in the pavement. There is rain everywhere, and sky and sun and clouds.

How can we connect?

If the trees root to the earth, so do – in rather more mobile ways – our own legs. If the earth's surface is 80 percent ocean so is our own body. Human children frolicking in the grass surely can remind us of kittens playing, and ten thousand ants working together are not, seen in a certain light, all that different from workers headed for a day at the office. As the trees breathe out, we breathe in – and vice versa. We seek our own existence, our own lives, and so do the pigeons picking up crumbs in the park, the rats scurrying to the open garbage cans, seeds sprouting beneath the earth. Everything that is alive senses its surroundings, signals what it wants or is repelled by, seeks a fit for itself in where it lives. And the physical world provides for all this life: with minerals, gases, sources of energy, and food. The winds scatter seeds, the rocks are eroded into minerals, the water supports just about every life form.

What could help human beings recognize their own natural, as well as social, identity? Perhaps we might notice that when people pay detailed attention to animals with whom they are in an intimate ecological relationship that they can learn to sense the animals' reality in a way people who just see the animals as biological subjects or sources of amusement cannot. For example, Barry Lopez recounts how Eskimos knew things about wolf prints that no academic "wolf experts" could match. The natives had learned to see the game, follow tracks, and know the habits of living beings with whom they could not talk in words.[15] They could only do this because they came in touch with the "wolf" part of themselves. Buddhist deep ecologist Joanna Macy suggests that we see ourselves as beings, every atom of whose bodies were formed by the great fireball of the Big Bang fourteen billion years ago.[16] Just as Americans or Jews or Native Americans may understand themselves as having an identity constituted in part by a shared history, so all human beings can realize that the most basic building blocks of their bodies share a history with the rest of the universe.

Indigenous animist perspectives reject the essentially anthropocentric perspective in which "person" is a subcategory of "human." The Ojibwa, for instance, see "person" as encompassing the human, the animal, the wind, and the water, etc. Of course many of these persons cannot do many things humans can, but people cannot do what wind or water can either. The mountain, the fern, or the ant have a character of being, a range of qualities of existence that provoke in us qualities of experience that can be felt as real, significant, and worthy of respect as the particular qualities of the humans we encounter. We have all been taught by the modern fusion of science, technology, and capitalism to know a tree by cutting it down and seeing what it's made of and can be "good" for. This other perspective gets to know a tree by talking to it.[17]

7 THE CAPABILITIES OF ECOLOGICAL DEMOCRACY

Democracy rooted in communication requires certain abilities and virtues. Participants must be able to offer reasons in support of their position when others disagree; understand basic mathematical concepts (such as "more" and "less," "increase" or "decrease") to comprehend policy proposals; care how their actions affect others; and grasp the idea of the "public good."

An ecological democracy would require that we learn to pay attention to what nature is saying to us: both by awareness of reasonably accessible

[15] Barry Lopez, *Of Wolves and Men* (New York: Scribner's, 1979).
[16] Joanna Macy, address to American Academy of Religion, San Francisco, 2000.
[17] Nurit Bird-David, "'Animism' Revisited: Personhood, Environment, and Relational Epistemology," *Current Anthropology* 40, no. 51 (1999): S71.

scientific knowledge and by a process of attunement to plants, animals, and ecosystems. This attunement cannot be developed by talking in words with oak trees or ravens. But verbal conversation is not the only way in which humans communicate. We can connect to each other with a touch, a smile, and movements of shoulders or eyes. We relate to babies who can't talk and have relationships with people with Alzheimer's. With a variety of skills and capacities, we connect, if not beyond language, then alongside it. With intelligence, experience, and a real intention to succeed, we can come to understand what it is they are "saying" and how they are faring in life.

The goal here is to respond to the Other not by substituting your own understanding or knowledge or strength for their own, but by a quality of loving attention that allows them to continue to develop. Loving attention can change *both* sides in the relationship. It is a never-ending process of reciprocal connection that would be threatened by wanting to end it prematurely, to impose our views or needs, to control what the other says, or to retreat to a place where we only notice ourselves.[18]

Alongside nonverbal connection there is knowledge – just as caring for infants or understanding the undemocratic oppression of women requires some fact-based understanding of their situations. Ecological democracy could be supported by monitoring the health of a river or the fate of a species threatened by climate change. It could be found in the knowledge of wildlife biologists, native hunters, and experienced conservationists. It will arise in "interspecies communication": reciprocal encounters between humans and animals such as whales singing with human musicians or dolphins swimming with people (more on this in a bit).[19] In all these cases people must communicate with and respond to the particular signals that come from beings who do not live according to a human culture. But people must do so through communion, reciprocity, and understanding. Our civilization's relentless drive to control would give way to an open-minded sense of inquiry.

Intellectual knowledge can have significant effects on our sense of our relation to the nonhuman; for example, when we learn that trees communicate with each other to warn of impending threats and that healthier

---

[18] This paragraph based on the brilliant account of human relationality in Rowan Williams, *Dostoevsky – Language, Faith and Fiction* (Waco, TX: Baylor University Press, 2008).

[19] Jim Nollman, *The Man Who Talks to Whales: The Art of Interspecies Communication* (Boulder, CO: Sentient Publications, 2002); and *The Charged Border: Where Whales and Humans Meet* (New York: Henry Holt, 1999).

trees will support weaker ones to sustain the forest as a whole; that octopi, despite a radically different kind of nervous system than ours, are capable of learning complex tasks; that impalas groom each other, mongooses share babysitting, and elephants weep for their dead mates. We can realize that our own acts of intelligence, love, and compassion do not separate us, but rather connect us to the realm of nature from which we emerged.[20] And that this shared reality makes possible a shared political life.

As well, we may attune to nature by becoming aware of the consequences of our collective *lack* of attunement. If we look long and hard at the way frogs are "succumbing to parasites, to pesticides, to increases in ultraviolet radiation [from the hole in Ozone layer], to global warming," then we will see that "frogs are telling us a lot."[21] We can "read" the growth rings of trees and see how their health has been diminished by changes in the soil caused by acid rain.[22] We can hear the silence of the extinguished species, how the mechanical throb of a dam replaces the whoosh of a running river, or the enormous thud of a chunk of Arctic ice breaking off from global warming. We can listen to our own grief when we find out that the placental blood of newborn babies carries 127 toxic chemicals. We can see the groups victimized by environmental racism, who are as natural as tigers or dolphins, succumbing to environmentally caused asthma, cancer, lead poisoning, and stress. We can observe the dying off of coral, bats, and bees – knowing the tragic loss of biodiversity, beauty, and ecosystem services this will cause. These phenomena tell us that our society is not functioning as a democracy should. This is similar to the way we know a purely human democracy is not working if large numbers of people are outside the educational or economic systems, if

---

[20] When certain trees (willows and maples were tested) are subject to extreme defoliation, neighboring trees will increase production of the defensive chemicals in their leaves, as if having been "warned" by the defoliated ones. Jack C. Shultz, "Tree Tactics," *Natural History* 92 (May 1983). On the rat adopting the rabbits, see Jeffrey Moussaieff Masson, *When Elephants Weep: The Emotional Lives of Animals* (New York: Delacorte, 1995). Another astounding example concerns a species of small river fish in Latin America: pairs of the fish will swim to a new area to see if it is safe for feeding. If one holds back, thereby lessening danger to itself, its partner will shun contact with it when they return to the group. This and the other examples of animal reciprocity are in Lee Dugatkin, *Cheating Monkeys and Citizen Bees: The Nature of Cooperation in Animals and Humans* (New York: Free Press, 1999).

[21] William Souder, *A Plague of Frogs: Unraveling an Environmental Mystery* (Minneapolis: University of Minnesota Press, 2000), p. 287.

[22] Christopher Uhl, *Developing Ecological Consciousness: Path to a Sustainable World* (Lanham, MD: Rowman and Littlefield, 2004), pp. 127–131.

leaders don't care for the common good, or if people by and large do not trust the government.

The vision of an ecological democracy both furthers and transcends the broadest conceptions of progressive democracy, setting it off from modern liberalism, most of modern secular radicalism, and virtually all politically conservative thought. For this is, again, not about nature's "rights." We will continue to eat, use, and compete with nature, trampling on insects or uprooting plants in ways that would not be morally acceptable if done to people. But we can honor the reciprocity of our relationship with the Earth, and out of that honor limit our use to that which makes moral and spiritual sense. If we respect what we use, we are not so likely to use it all up or waste so much of it; if we attune ourselves to other life forms we may look – hard – for ways to coexist rather than to obliterate.[23] If listening to nature is recognized as an essential civic obligation, then a radically different awareness can be the foundation of radically different environmental practices.

If we redefine the "we" of the democratic community to include the natural as well as the social, we will no longer, in Charles Taylor's definition, be "modern." Taylor argues that the hallmark of modern politics is seeing the social order as founded purely on human action, rather than on some event and force that is out of time, some transcendent Power or Personality. In the modern mind, he says, political legitimacy rests only on ourselves.[24] With this definition Taylor wants to distinguish between religious and secular society, as well he might. But what he ignores is the reality that human society is founded in, on, and within nature and that some kind of compatibility with nature is a condition for its flourishing. If this is not literally a "transcendental condition" in Taylor's' sense, it is not a purely human one either. Taylor's humanism, like most forms, is an unreflective anthropocentrism that denies our obvious dependence on and connection to that which is not human.

Similarly, when Alasdair MacIntyre proclaims "I can only answer the question 'What am I to do?' if I can answer the prior question 'Of what story or stories do I find myself a part?'"[25] He seems to presuppose that

---

[23] Residents in Maine resisted the use of polluting pesticides to kill the highly annoying black flies. If you can't deal with the flies for a few weeks, they suggested, don't come to Maine. Sue Hubbell, *Broadsides from the Other Orders: A Book of Bugs* (New York: Random House, 1993), pp. 74–89.

[24] Charles Taylor, *Modern Social Imaginaries* (Durham, NC: Duke University Press, 2004).

[25] Alasdair MacIntyre, *After Virtue* (Notre Dame, IN: University of Notre Dame Press, 1981), p. 216.

meaning in our lives can *only* come from essentially human cultural structures. Our existence as natural, living beings, in a community of other living beings, would not, I suspect, be nearly enough for MacIntyre. Nor should it be enough for us as the *only* structure of self-understanding. But that does not mean it cannot be one of our "stories" – a narrative centered by bodily life, sensory experience, and living connection that we share with the nonhuman.[26] Because of the environmental crisis this story is of critical importance now. But the context that makes this recovery of natural identity so important is not the same as the recovery itself. To the extent that it is possible, we must abstract from the context to undertake the recovery. Our very social identity makes a turning away from that identity necessary.

Finally, there is Hannah Arendt's definition of "the political" as requiring some form of individual or group self-representation. For Arendt politics is a kind of public performance – action geared to understanding and evaluation by another.[27] Yet Arendt takes for granted that such self-representation can only take symbolic, linguistic form. By contrast I believe that all forms of life present themselves to us – as we do to them. True, they do not do so in a human language. But as living beings they are present in and respond to the world. Even nonliving structures – rivers, mountains, oceans – can be altered, polluted, or protected. The comportment and responsiveness of nature is not aimed at people the way a human political statement is. And so the task of ecological democracy is to make ourselves the kind of beings who can orient ourselves to nature so that we experience its presentation *as* aimed at us. If we can respond politically to babies crying from hunger, so we can respond to poisoned fish and coral bleached white.

8 EXAMPLES

Here are some examples to help us think what ecological democracy *means*, rather than why it is (or is not) *justified*. This is a description of what, in some very small ways, it feels like – as in Chapter 2, a "phenomenology."

Empathy. Richard Rorty claims that any search for a "universal human essence" as the foundation for moral treatment of other people

---

[26] Such a sense of shared narrative is essential to a good deal of native tradition. For a modern attempt, see the award-winning film, *The Universe Story*.

[27] Hannah Arendt, *The Human Condition* (Chicago: University of Chicago Press, 1958).

is fruitless. There are far too many moral perspectives and codes and far too little chance to come to agreement across moral differences. Rather, we can enlarge our moral community by learning to see others as "like us" in contingent ways. Most important, we learn to understand the content of others' suffering and victimization. My moral respect for someone very different than myself does not arise because I can argue him into agreement, or because he can do that to me, or because of our shared universal human essence, but because I recognize his pain, disappointment, frustration, and fear as like my own.

Similarly, Kwame Anthony Appiah suggests that a true "cosmopolitan" does not necessarily expect to reach agreement with people of different cultures but does believe that virtually everyone can be talked to. And that conversation across differences promotes a kind of acquaintance that may be the best available support of peaceful coexistence. This acquaintance can generate a kind of thinking of oneself into the life situation of the other person.[28]

Can Rorty's and Appiah's approaches be extended to the nonhuman, who are "like us" in many important ways, even though they are clearly not universally or even locally "human" – and therefore most emphatically also very different?

In the case of animals in factory farms or laboratories empathic understanding of another's suffering is not that hard to come by. Their misery is obvious and palpable – which is the reason that food industry and pharmaceutical companies have been criminalizing unauthorized sharing of information (especially videos) of such places. As Jane Goodall, Mark Bekoff, and many others have argued, and what animal researchers have denied for years – animals have emotions – is both elementary and necessary knowledge for anyone who works closely *with* animals, as opposed to working *on* them. And it is why there is an animal rights movement that argues for representing the experience and interests of animals alongside the experiences and interests of people.

Can a modern city dweller find a similar empathic connection not only to the nonhuman but also the nonanimal? Does it even make sense to talk of extending empathy to ecosystems destroyed or species eliminated? When a particular type of tree can no longer survive because of acid rain, is that species' death a communication to which, if we were to "listen,"

---

[28] Richard Rorty, *Contingency, Irony, Solidarity* (New York: Cambridge University Press, 1989); Kwame Anthony Appiah, *Ethics in a World of Strangers* (New York: W. W. Norton, 2007).

we could make some kind of first personal and then political connection? Even if the *tree* does not intend to communicate in the sense of possessing a consciousness that includes a representation of us, can *we* not imagine what it would be like to live in a world in which the necessary conditions of our own existence gradually disappeared? It might be a planet without a protective ozone layer, or in which the loss of phytoplankton destroyed the oceanic food chain, or in which genetic engineering or pesticides bred killer organisms. If we can imagine such a world (sadly, not altogether different from the one we are in) and what it would be like to live in it, is it that much of leap to respond to the plight of the tree species in a comparable situation? If we can relate to the sufferings of an oppressed group, even one culturally different and geographically separate from ourselves, can we do the same for other species? Is it too much of a stretch to speak, as some are now doing, of "plant liberation" and plants as morally significant?[29] When I saw a grove of the last remaining redwood trees in California, was it only personal eccentricity that led me to think of nothing so much as survivors of the Holocaust?

Religious Tradition. Despite the anthropocentrism that permeates Western culture, countless cultural statements also suggest that nature, both collectively and as individuals, has a kind of spiritual subjectivity.[30] These directives are relevant for the still very large number of people from modernized societies who receive moral instruction from religious sources. Many passages in the Bible, for example, take nature seriously as an aid to understanding and worshipping God. Here nature is clearly not depicted as an inert collection of objects designed only to help humans achieve whatever they want. Rather, the physical universe gleams with a kind of ecstatic light that invites us to see the rest of Creation as joined with humans in the divine drama of existence. In the Psalms we hear that "The heavens declare the glory of God . . . and their voice goes out into all the earth"; and that the "sea and everything in it" can sing God's praises.[31] A traditional prayer integral to the Jewish daily service begins,

---

[29] Matthew Hall, *Plants as Persons: A Philosophical Botany* (Albany: State University of New York Press, 2011).
[30] There are sources in non-Western tradition as well. For example: Buddhism contains a large collection of Jataka tales – stories of Buddha's earlier incarnations as either an animal or a person who devoted himself to the care and protection of animals. Again: while shamanism typically reflects a sense of direct connection to the nonhuman, modern technological mass society is unlikely to turn to shamanism to any significant degree. To our loss, no doubt.
[31] Psalm 19:1, 4; Psalm 96:11.

"The soul of every living thing shall praise you, O God." There were periods in European history when animals were brought into Catholic cathedrals to be blessed by priests. These texts and practices do not assert that nature is a "sign" of God's greatness, power, or generosity, though clearly that idea is present in other places. Nor do they limit themselves to saying that "we" (humans) should praise God *because* of what God has created. Rather, they clearly state that creation *itself* does the praising. And that nonhuman beings are considered worthy of some sacramental connection.

Yet if nature is, in some sense, not only a product of the divine but also a response to it, surely it might be worthwhile to investigate how it is faring under the current environmental regime, to pay close attention to how it responds to current conditions, and to advocate for it not just in Sunday sermons but in political contexts where policies are formed. As many Christian leaders have advocated for political acceptance of undocumented immigrants, particularly those brought to the United States as children, so a rather smaller number have advocated for the representation of the interests of nature. This is a nature that, if recognized, could return to being, in Pope John Paul's words, the "sister of humanity." But if in reality our sister, should not "she" be taken seriously as part of our democracy?

A religious understanding of the life of other beings can be extended from theology to science. This is admittedly a stretch, but actually not foreign to the significant number of scientists who are also religious. Here is an illuminating example: famed animal researcher – "ethologist" – Mark Bekoff describes some marvelous instances of animal cognition and emotional bonds. What is he doing when he tries to understand animals in these terms?[32] Based in his faith that God permeates the cosmos, Protestant process ecotheologian Jay McDaniel asks, in response to Bekoff's research: is not our knowledge of the cosmos a kind of knowledge of God?

If all things live and move and have their being in God, then when we try to imagine what it is like to be inside a coyote or penguin, a bluejay or a small child we are, in our way, exploring the very mind of God. And when scientists try – as for instance serious students of animal consciousness do – to comprehend what it is like to be inside the skin of other living beings, they too are praying. Of course they would not call it prayer. They would call it understanding. But in their way they are reaching out to ask: "What is it like to be you, who are different from me?

---

[32] Marc Bekoff, *Minding Animals* (New York: Oxford University Press, 2002).

And how are things for you?" When we find ourselves entering into imaginative empathy, we are simultaneously entering a space where science and religion meet. We are reaching out to something beyond ourselves, trustful that there is a greater whole in which all living beings are small but included.[33]

McDaniel's *theological* version of the point can be translated into *political* terms in this way: If we can reach beyond ourselves to people of different cultures, beliefs, and desires, believing that to have a peaceful and fulfilling social order we must learn to listen to them, perhaps we can also reach beyond ourselves to different *species*, and learn how to listen to them as well. If we can conceive of justice between industrial society and indigenous tribes, before we outfit them with literacy and Nike windbreakers, can we not conceive of justice between people and eagles, whales, or mountainous bioregions?

Interspecies communication provides an experience of relational reciprocity that does not depend on the Other having a human ego or speaking a human language. A fascinating example: Musician Jim Nollman outfitted a boat so that he could amplify the sound of his guitar underwater. From time to time whales would gather round, and he and they would exchange riffs. In Nollman's view "interspecies communication" cannot mean putting apes in cages and teaching them sign language, for such a context is not *communication*, but a *training* in which only one side shapes the encounter. "If it is truly to be considered communication, then it should also be based upon mutual respect. It must develop as an open-ended dialogue where both participants have the equal power to direct the course and subject matter of the learning experience."[34]

Communication requires that both sides are free to approach or retreat, and that the terms of the interaction are decided mutually, according to a slow and delicate evolving process of interspecies protocol. It is striking that one time, when Nollman was attempting to play music with whales near Hawaii, he was forbidden to do so because the whales were an endangered species, and people were not allowed to interact with them. *Unless*, of course the person had scientific credentials and was "studying" them (e.g., attaching radio transmitters to track their movements) for the sake of "knowledge." An interaction of equality was prohibited but one of human-centered control was not!

---

[33] Jay McDaniel, Panel on the work of Mark Bekoff, American Academy of Religion, November 20, 2004.
[34] Nollman, *The Man Who Talks to Whales*, p. 11.

Whales could be "subjects" (really, "objects") but not, in Nollman's telling phrase, "neighbors."

Interspecies communication may also simply involve a recognition of the fundamental otherness of a nonhuman being. In Annie Dillard's classic essay "Living Like Weasels," the author has a brief, revelatory meeting with an animal who is dissimilar to her in countless ways, yet has its own very real experience of the world – and in just that sense is exactly the same.[35] Like Dillard, the weasel too is the center of a very particular life. This revelation is a dramatic extension, but not necessarily totally different, than the recognition that a human being of vastly different values, tastes, sexuality, education, and age is – just as we are – a person alive in the world. Ultimately this realization can extend far beyond the human. That is why there can be ethical perspectives based in "reverence for life," such as that articulated by Albert Schweitzer: "To affirm life is to deepen, to make more inward, and to exalt the will to live. At the same time the man [sic] who has become a thinking being feels a compulsion to give to every will to live the same reverence for life that he gives to his own."[36]

Agriculture. Biodynamic farming aims to make soil richer and healthier after growing food than before. In this form of agriculture the complex community – water, minerals, trillions of trillions of insects, worms, bacteria, and fungi – that makes up the soil is considered a partner rather than a "raw material," and humans need to be sensitive to the signs of illness and distress caused by chemically oriented pesticides, fertilizers, and genetically modified seeds. Essential to the process is the belief that: "Everything in nature reveals something of its essential character in its form and gesture. Careful observations of nature – in shade and full sun, in wet and dry areas, on different soils – will yield a more fluid grasp of the elements. So eventually one learns to *read* the language of nature."[37]

It could be argued that the biodynamic farmer is not "reading" nature, but simply using a metaphorical flourish to paper over the same old detached, objective measuring of fertility, temperature, number of worms,

[35] Annie Dillard, "Living Like Weasels," in *Teaching a Stone to Talk* (New York: Harper 2013).

[36] Albert Schweitzer, *Out of My Life and Thought* (Baltimore: Johns Hopkins University Press 1998), p. 157.

[37] Biodynamic Farming and Gardening Association Website. Accessed June 24, 2013, www.biodynamics.com/biodynamics.html.

etc. To some extent, this is true. Yet metaphors are not external to the ways in which we interact with each other, but essential to them. For human behavior, even human speech, can *also* be objectified as measurable responses of a process or being that (not "whom") we understand only to control and make use of. Subjects in social science experiments, targets of political propaganda or advertising, potential customers for shady salesmen – all these may be thought of and treated like objects. We can recognize – or fail to recognize – the internal, subjective, "for itself" reality of people, dogs, hawks, minnows, palm trees, even bacteria. To the extent that we have ever managed such a recognition for other humans, democracy is possible. If it can be extended, if only partially and briefly, beyond the human, ecological democracy is possible as well.

Forest Care: While indigenous traditions have long talked of nature as kin, ancestors of present tribes, or part of their community, I am not sure to what degree contemporary, dominant, nonindigenous cultures are capable of learning directly from native peoples. Given the critical differences in our immediate experience of and (seeming!) independence from forests, rivers, and animals, imitating native intelligence in these matters might be impossible.

Or it might not. Here is an example: the Menominee Tribe has been in control of its forest resources since 1854, when the Wolf River treaty created their reservation. In appearance its 220,000-acre forest in Northeast Wisconsin looks wild and untouched. Yet in truth it has been highly managed – in a sustainable way – by the tribe. Over two *billion* board feet of lumber have been removed, yet the total mass of wood in the forest is greater than it was a century and a half ago. Towering white pines fill the forests, along with ruffed grouse, eagles, ospreys, woodcocks, bobcats, coyotes, otter, marten, fox, white-tailed deer, and bears. With many of its members still living close to the land, the forest provides meat and furs, maple syrup and ginseng. Continual monitoring ensures the Menominee that their forest will continue for generations – serving human needs while maintaining its own exosystemic integrity. As one elder said, "Everything we have comes from Mother Earth – from the air we breathe to the food we eat – and we need to honor her for that. In treating the forest well, we honor Mother Earth."[38] If an

---

[38] Paula Rogers Huff and Marshall Pecore, "Case Study: Menominee Tribal Enterprises," Menominee Website. www.menominee.edu/sdi/csstdy.htm#A.

orthodox vegetarian would strongly object to the hunting element here, at least the bears and deer have some place to live.

9 OBJECTIONS TO ECOLOGICAL DEMOCRACY

What is the "real," sober, hard-assed way to deal with environmental problems – in particular, with global warming? An influential environmental economist tells us that "no realistic progress on climate change will be achieved by hope, trust, responsible citizenship, environmental ethics, or guilt."[39] Instead, we need a careful cost-benefit analysis and the imposition of economic policies (e.g., carbon tax) that can be shown to make economic sense.

Yet the view that economic benefit is the only real driver for political life leaves us mired in the same cultural perspective that got us here. If economics is what really matters, then short-term economic gain will lead polluting companies to do everything they can to keep things as they are for as long as they are able. As well, the notion that people will act on a rational, calm, cool-headed appraisal of their long-term economic interests seems blind to the actual course of human history. If people are not motivated by "hope, trust, responsible citizenship, and ethics," if our motivations do not change – we get consumerism, addictions, and ignoring the necessity to repair roads and bridges. People are not particularly rational, even when their economic interests are involved, if by rational we mean carefully pursuing long-term interests. If they were, how many would ever fight in wars? It's also best to keep in mind that there are no economic motivations without "ethics" – because economic motivations depend on what people value, and value is an ethical category, not (at least not solely) an economic one.

More broadly, someone might say that the whole enterprise of ecological democracy rests on a category mistake. Empathy, compassion, "attunement" (to other species or even to people) are moral responses appropriate to personal life or spirituality, but have no place in a political context aimed at a collective, rational concept of justice. Impersonal justice, it might be argued, is the only practical and reasonable foundation for a mass society of enormously varying strangers: people whom we don't know, might not particularly like, and whose fates matter little to

[39] William Nordhaus, *A Question of Balance: Weighing the Options on Global Warming Policies* (New Haven, CT: Yale University Press, 2008), p. 20.

us. Our emotions, our attachment to our particular creeds or "mysticisms,"[40] might motivate us, but have to place in public exchange.

For example, highly influential liberal philosopher John Rawls asserts that what we need for justice are basic assumptions: that free and equal people have interests, that we can recognize other people's interests and the value of living together, and that this living together continues over generations. "Comprehensive doctrines" of morality, religion, spirituality, the meaning of life, and so forth are external to the fundamental political constitution – and fundamental deliberation – of a liberal, democratic, secular society based on these assumptions. Because in our pluralistic, heterogeneous society comprehensive doctrines may be enormously different and often opposed, we can only enter reasonable political conversation with each other if we appeal to reasons that all of us can recognize.[41] By clear implication, the moral value of nature, and even more the idea that nature should be consulted and represented in political life, is not one of those.

In its most general terms, this objection raises a crucial question: What does specifically modern political life require? I believe something very different than what it needed during the Enlightenment, whose vision of democracy stressed individualism, a rejection of traditional social ties, and a response to centuries of bloody and pointless religious conflict. Isolation from each other and an attempt to evade alternative religious frameworks fits a time when reigning social structures of inherited power, social hierarchy, and religious dogma are the rule. In a world of nuclear threat, modern states need something like the UN. Facing the environmental crisis may require that democracy be redefined to include attunement and communication with other species and life as a whole.

The fate of a nature unprotected by intellectual and emotional connection is clear to see in any photo of the human and natural aftermath of hurricanes worsened by global warming. And so is the fate of racial minorities or the poor in terms of an environment permeated by pollution and disproportionately vulnerable to climate change. If the scope of the problem poses an overwhelming problem to existing perspectives, what philosopher Mary Midgely calls a "conceptual emergency," that doesn't

---

[40] Walter F. Barber and Robert V. Bartlett repeatedly use this term to marginalize such beliefs. *Deliberative Environmental Politics: Democracy and Ecological Rationality* (Cambridge, MA: MIT Press, 2005).

[41] E.g., John Rawls, *Political Liberalism* (New York: Columbia University Press, 1993).

mean a new framework cannot be devised.[42] And just like, for example "*gay* marriage," we should expect the new framework to break some of our taken for granted conceptual boundaries. And while many philosophers have lamented that the ethical (hence political) dimensions of this crisis are just too complicated and unprecedented for people to understand,[43] somehow tens of millions of people globally are taking the crisis seriously and are acting. There is thus a vast difference between "impossible" and "very, very hard."

In regards to Rawls's claim that the foundation of our political system should be principles derived from the "original position" – an imagined situation in which we do not know our own race, gender, economic position, religion, or even present or future generation – perhaps what is needed is to add in: and we *don't know what species we will be either.* Rawls wants equal access to well-being, with inequalities benefitting everyone. But who is everyone? Does it include trout? Crows? Squids? Worms? Clearly this is a radical idea. But wasn't the notion that society is "for everyone," – meaning all people – a radical break with the entrenched belief that some people just are worth more than others? If we move beyond the speciesism that privileges those who can verbally demand justice in a human language, which seems to the be the dividing line for most leading political theorists, then perhaps we could conceive of another radical, to many incomprehensible, notion – that "everyone" includes all of life. Why is seeing universal value in all of life more "mystical" than seeing it in all people? I suggest that it is not. And that political deliberation, therefore, no matter how "basic" or "essential," cannot do without comprehensive doctrines, or "mysticism," or some kind of fundamental orientation toward human existence that is ultimately chosen, rather than resting on some impersonal rationality. The support for such an orientation is, again, simply and only what happens when we do – or do not (as in the present) – chose it.

Here is a related criticism. Steven Vogel, responding to the idea that nature could be included as fellow participants in political dialogue,

---

[42] Mary Midgley, "Individualism and the Concept of Gaia," in Ken Booth, et al., eds., *How Might We Live? Global Ethics in a New Century* (Cambridge: Cambridge University Press, 2001), p. 40.

[43] E.g.: "People are not equipped with the mental and emotional repertoire to deal with such a vast scale of events ..." Bruno Latour, "Agency at the Time of the Anthropocene," *New Literary History* 45 (2014): 1.

makes what he takes to be a crucial distinction.[44] Animals may communicate, but they do not make "validity claims"; i.e., they do not assert or contest issues of truth, legitimacy, fairness, or rationality. Captive monkeys may respond to unequal distributions of food with anger, but they cannot *say* what is *wrong* with giving some more and some less. Similarly, while *we* can reflect on what we are doing, nature itself cannot deliberate with us. It cannot demand justice, list grievances, or argue about why it is wrong to so pollute rivers that they cannot support life. Nature just suffers in silence. Democracy, the argument concludes, might well be concerned about the fate of nature, but nature itself cannot be part of democracy.

This point has some merit. But it is not clear where that merit leads. Is argumentation the only form of democratic interaction? Is articulating a point of view the only way a person can express themselves in democratic interactions? When we consider the welfare of children, those with Alzheimer's, or those with very limited intelligence or who are illiterate, are we not obliged to listen, observe, and take note of what it is like to be them? And to do so for political reasons leading to political outcomes? True, they cannot argue with us, but in *our* communications with other people, is that the only way we engage? If my wife is sitting crying, is that not something that deserves my attention as much as if she upbraids me for being insensitive? If a person, red faced and trembling, shakes her fist at us in rage, do we not need to open ourselves to what might be going on? If the poor sharecropper simply points to his starving children, is that not a communication that is essential to our deliberations? If we define deliberation as argument, then yes, only humans can do it. But if we expand deliberation to include all interpretable manifestations of the body, then nature joins in. Can it do all that humans can do? No. But humans don't seem to be able to function without committing monstrous injustice and globally destructive irrationalities, whereas nature does neither. That difference alone might be reason enough to expand our sense of deliberation.

In an ecological democracy only humans would argue about policies, property rights, taxation, and regulation of chemicals. But *how* they would argue would be rooted in a sense of felt connection based on direct experience, imagination, and knowledge. How we argue and what we

[44] Steven Vogel, "Habermas and the Ethics of Nature," in Roger S. Gottlieb, ed., *The Ecological Community* (New York: Routledge, 1997); *Thinking Like a Mall* (Cambridge, MA: MIT Press, 2012), pp. 175–192.

believe would be shaped by our experience of life outside of the purely human realm. *Communion* would be a condition for *deliberation*. We have learned, I suspect, that without some empathic connection to persecuted groups progress in social justice will be very limited. The same is true for our understanding of the nonhuman realm.

Finally, it has been argued both by both Marxists and some thinkers oriented to varieties of postmodernism, that my whole construction of "nature" as an Other to be communicated with, attuned to, and empathized with is mistaken because "nature" is "always already" a human construct. William Cronon made this point in a controversial article about the concept of wilderness, challenging deep ecologists and other crunchy types with the fact that what people termed and how they valued a "wilderness" depended on their own cultural and historical situation.[45] Similarly, many have argued that what we consider "natural" changes with the amount of technology at our disposal, our economy, and our social position. Nature, supposedly defined by an absence of the human, is always perceived through human interests and beliefs. There is no getting beyond the human, the social, and language.

If we consider the wide variety of ways in which we represent, for example, polar bears, we will see that they have been seen as ferocious killers, enemies to be eliminated, heroic survivors, victims of human aggression, and a species whose fate signals climate change. What are they really? Nothing in particular, the critic charges, but just a reality completely dependent on our shifting, socially based, perceptions.[46]

This perspective often also raises the issue of the countless borderline or "hybrid" entities that refute the idea of an absolute "nature–human" duality. Genetic engineering creates glow in the dark tomatoes and pigs with vastly more "meat"; people's bodies and minds are shaped by pacemakers and psychotropic chemicals; endangered species are nursed in captivity and then released to the "wild"; every "wilderness" area is dependent on legal protections; the entire earth (or at least its waters and surface) is altered by greenhouse gases; tens of thousands of human-made chemicals permeate the flesh of animals and plants alike. If "nature" is the realm without the human, it is long gone.

---

[45] William Cronon, "The Trouble with Wilderness," in J. Baird Calicott, ed., *The Great New Wilderness Debate* (Athens: University of Georgia Press, 1998), pp. 471–500.

[46] On the fate of the bears, as well as the history of human concern, see Jon Mooallem, *Wild Ones: A Sometimes Dismaying, Weirdly Reassuring Story about Looking at People Looking at Animals in America* (New York: Penguin, 2013).

Therefore, the argument goes, we need not be thinking about including "nature" in democracy, nor reflect on our moral connections to nature, because nature is just whatever people think "nature" is at any given time anyway and because of human action the human–nature distinction has lost any value.[47]

I have a great deal of trouble with this position. To begin, notice that the fact that I see my wife through the eyes of my experience, hopes, social position, and personal history surely does not mean that she is not a being in her own right; or that I can, unless I am psychotic, see her any way I (or my social position, historical setting, etc.) please; or that I do not have to communicate with her as a separate, independent being. Of course, who we are colors our relationship with nature, just as it does with everything else. That coloring is just part of what makes the relationship possible, not something that means the relationship is "really" just another aspect of *our* selves. No knower can have knowledge except from the standpoint of his/her species, history, and culture. In this dialectical relationship between knower and known we see the condition of knowledge as such, and not anything particularly applicable to nature. As humans we are always representing the Other – whether that other is dad, someone who prays differently, or a polar bear.

So, if relationship and representation just are the conditions of living together with other beings on this planet, then, it should be clear, relationship and representation don't refute the reality of these other beings. We can always ask if our representations are accurate, fair, or useful. If they are products of our social situation, we can ask what that tells us about how we are living and how both might be improved.

As well, as soon as we try to give an account of who we are and what this history or culture or social position is that determines our perception of nature, it will turn out that we must in part appeal to what nature is to explain the history and culture and social position that are determining what we believe. Our human condition grows out of earth, air, water, DNA, gravity, and the microbes that make our digestion possible. We could not know what humans are without reference to our physiology, the biological conditions of the planet, or the history of evolution.

Because humans interact with trees, gibbons, or the ocean does not mean there is no significant difference between them all. If a seagull drops a mussel onto a road to crack it open, does that mean there is no

---

[47] E.g., Timothy Morton, *Ecology without Nature* (Cambridge MA: Harvard University Press, 2009); Steven Vogel, *Thinking Like a Mall* (Cambridge, MA: MIT Press, 2014).

significant differences between the birds, shellfish, and roads? Of course humans have affected life on earth. That does not mean there is no difference between humans and the rest of life. At the least, as I've observed earlier: nature is that realm in which beings function without egos and from whom we cannot demand explanations of or justifications for behavior. It is only humans of whom we can ask: "Can't you see that what you are doing is wrong?" The connection between these two points is simple: It is because only humans act out of egos that only humans need to be morally reflective and, at times, morally criticized. Even whales who might have radio transmitters inserted into their bodies and be physiologically depressed because of all the undersea noise humans make, raise their young, act in solidarity with their pods, and sing their magnificent songs without arrogance, insecurity over their worth compared to other whales, or a desire to dominate the entire ocean. Trees sustain each other in forests and are now shaped by climate change, but they do not plot to cover the entire world and wipe out all other forms of vegetation. No matter how much humans affect whales and trees, such beings will never have our gifts or our tragic, world-altering weaknesses.

10 PRACTICING DEMOCRACY

Here is another way to think of what an ecological democracy could mean – and what it would take.

Ever since Christopher Stone raised the question of whether or not trees have "standing,"[48] – i.e., whether they could be represented as having interests in a law court or legislatures – environmental philosophers have discussed the possibility that nonhuman natural beings, whether individuals, species, entire ecosystems, or nonsentient features of landscape such as mountains or rivers, could be part of our moral or political system.

In a recent effort, John Hadley argues for Animal Property Rights.[49] His argument is significant but simple. There already exist some restrictions on human treatment of animals; e.g., there is the Endangered Species Act, some states have limited exploitation in farms, people can be punished for "animal cruelty." Thus, as a society we have decided that

---

[48] Christopher Stone, *Should Trees Have Standing: Law, Morality, and the Environment*, 3rd ed. (New York: Oxford University Press, 2010).

[49] John Hadley, *Animal Property Rights: A Theory of Habitat Rights for Wild Animals* (Lanham, MD: Lexington Books, 2015).

animals have some moral value. To have moral value is, among other things, to have a life worth living and to be deserving of some protection. Therefore, the conditions of animals' lives are also worth protecting and reserving for their use. Animals have a right to use territory in which their species-specific needs can be met. Aware of the inevitability of competing claims to property, Hadley matches animals' needs for survival not against comparable human needs, but against nonessential human wants. In a choice between survival for people or animals, he will choose people; but in a choice between things people want but don't need and the life of animals, he will support the latter.

Hadley and other environmental thinkers have argued that we already have moral and legal structures in place for representatives of those who cannot advocate for themselves. People with intellectual disabilities, infants, and dementia sufferers may have "guardians" to protect legally guaranteed interests.[50] Through familiar democratic institutions (courts, legislatures, etc.) Hadley would extend such protection to wild animals. And there would be, as there is now in other contexts, reasoned debate over who gets what, the distinction between needs and luxuries, and how conflicts got resolved.

I am sympathetic to Hadley's general intent, though I have, as I've said already, questions about the centrality of rights in the conversation. We can, and often do, assert the moral value of a being *without* asserting that it has rights.[51] We love our pets and our children and seek their well-being. But not, I don't think, because we are concerned with their rights. We would be furious if someone denied our kids' legal equality or free speech. But *we* would not be *motivated* by concern for their rights, but by concern with their happiness, welfare, personal fulfillment, and the like. The same might be said of our gardens and our rivers. Doubtless it may be difficult to determine what is essential to the well-being of animals, forests, or humans who cannot speak. But is this fundamentally different

---

[50] Such advocacy depends on the way claims for those represented for are rooted in detailed acquaintance and also contestable. Michael Saward, "The Representative Claim," *Contemporary Political Theory* 5, no. 3 (2006). For an account of what representation for wild animals, as opposed to domestic ones, might look like, see Erica von Essen and Michael P. Allen, "The Republican Zoopolis: Towards a New Legitimate Framework for Relational Animal Ethics," *Ethics and the Environment* 21, no. 1 (Spring 2016). Accessed May 7, 2017, http://search.proquest.com.ezproxy.wpi.edu/docview/1799542737?pq-origsite=summon&accountid=29120.

[51] This approach is sometimes called "relational animal rights theory," in which a relation, rather than simply a negative duty not to harm, forms the basis for norms of human–animal connection.

than deciding what, beyond a minimal amount of food, oxygen, and water, is essential for those of us who can speak as well? The line between need and want will always be subject to enormous disagreement.

Imagine, then, that just as humans who cannot verbally communicate are represented, so can animals. And extend this to the nonanimal world as well. Of course, many problems remain. Do we represent species, subspecies, and groups of animals in particular areas, and/or individual animals? Each abandoned human infant typically gets his/her own guardian; will each wolf or whale? How do we handle exotic or invasive species? How much do we intervene to protect and when do we "let nature take its course"?

These details, as difficult and important as they are, are not my immediate concern. I am wondering, rather: what do *we* have to do to become the kind of people who could be guardians, or at least evaluate the claims of guardians, for other species. For example: when would we qualify to serve on the jury of cases where demands are made in the name of a species or a swamp; or what would we need to know to intelligently decide which environmental policies to support?

And here we find a real and significant objection to ecological democracy: Knowledgeable evaluation of policy alternatives is far too much to ask of any but the most committed, and typically professionally trained, observer. For example; should we dam the local river for flood control and hydroelectric power? What would that do to the fish, insects, and birds who depend on free-flowing water? Or to people for whom the river is a source of physical beauty, spiritual peace, recreation, and income? How much water should we take for local agriculture without damaging the ecological balance? If we are submerging buildings, how many toxins will be released into the water? Would the increased renewable energy and lessened need for fossil fuels compensate for the negative ecological effects? Who would get the benefit of the cheap power produced? And what would we be doing with that energy?

That very few people possess intelligent views on these matters suggests that policy questions cannot be left to nonexperts: people whose lives are focused on earning a living, graduating from college, raising children, or caring for aging parents. Technical environmental issues – like designing seaports or evaluating pesticides – are the business of those in the know: biologists, engineers, and economists. Certainly recent elections (in both the last few years, and the last several decades) leave many of us despairing over electorates that are easily manipulated, horribly uninformed, and unfailingly attracted to oversimplified "solutions." How could ordinary voters offer informed views on environmental issues?

As real as they might be, none of these dispiriting facts leave us with a better alternative than democracy – for the simple reason that no plausible candidate for something better exists. In the contemporary United States we can see how rule by the rich is working out. Past experiments with unlimited power in a dictatorial elite (the Soviet Union comes to mind) have been practical and moral disasters. Unchecked by some input from the mass of ordinary people, ruling elites have virtually always developed interests that separate them from those they dominate.[52] And we have seen the consequences of undemocratic rule by "experts." Far too often money, power, and ego shape the application of expertise. Technical knowledge, while quite real, is clearly no guarantee of moral behavior or successful policies. Thus, the people, as limited as we are, are the best we've got. And it is the people, already, who serve on juries and vote on representatives who make laws about contexts where humans have guardians.

Ultimately, the very idea of democracy proposes, *all* government power derives from the consent of the governed. Laws are made, policies formulated and carried out, judicial decisions made – all by people chosen through electoral processes or chosen by such people. If ordinary people are too ignorant, stupid, self-centered, or intellectually limited to understand the needs of a river's ecosystem, or what will happen to the mountain if all the wolves are shot and the deer left to multiply unchecked, then how does it make sense that they choose – or choose those who will choose – people responsible for deciding when to go to war, how to structure a national health care system, or how to set interest rates? As well, we should remember that many times "ordinary" people have identified significant environmental problems before "experts" did. Typically, they lacked technical knowledge, but deep acquaintance with the context prompted them to acquire it.[53]

In short: ecological democracy cannot be rejected simply because ordinary people aren't "good" (smart, caring, informed) enough to do it.

---

[52] This is the "iron law of oligarchy" described a century ago in Robert Michels, *Political Parties: A Sociological Study of the Oligarchical Tendencies of Modern Democracy* (Los Angeles: HardPress Publishing, 2013).

[53] The toxics movement in the United States is a prime example. See further discussion in Chapter 8.

11 MAKE IT BETTER

Here are two examples how ordinary people could become significantly more able to make an ecological democracy work. What I am suggesting is a vast distance from what is fully necessary. The results would only be, at best, an improvement.

We can return to analogies from more familiar contexts.

How is a citizen to respond to issues of racial justice? Can proposals like affirmative action, financial reparations for past injustice, or redress for environmental racism be understood without a modicum of understanding of the history of race relations in the United States? When white people feel that blacks are demanding too much, making too much of a fuss, acting entitled when they should improve themselves like immigrant groups, would it make a difference if, besides some awareness of the horrors of slavery, they knew about the systemic, "legal" segregation and subjugation of blacks that followed the end of slavery? That for decades any advocacy of racial equality in Mississippi could be punished by a fine or imprisonment? That in Nebraska a white person could not marry someone of one-eighth nonwhite blood? That even phone booths had to be segregated in Oklahoma?[54] That the GI Bill, responsible for the advancement of so many WWII veterans, was segregated? The concentrated force of such laws and policies, and their effects over time, shape the present condition of race relations, which cannot be understood without knowledge of them.

What do we need to know about our collective environmental past? We could be educated about what where we live was like 30, 100, or 500 years ago; about the source and severity of pollution; about cleanup efforts. We could be told about the animals that used to live here that no longer do; about interconnections among species and between species and climate. We could get a painful sense of what would be lost – in health, personal experience, ecosystem services, and cultural meaning – if our neighborhood were polluted or paved over. We could learn our *natural* history just as we do our national, ethnic, or religious history.

Of course, such highly detailed knowledge of a natural setting is liable to be hard to come by and to exclude other natural settings. We can only know so much. If we are not environmental professionals, we'll be lucky to get detailed knowledge of one place if that. But there is no reason we

[54] Smithsonian Website. Accessed May 7, 2017, http://americanhistory.si.edu/brown/history/ 1-segregated/detail/jim-crow-laws.html.

cannot come to understand that any given area has a deep and complex natural structure; that this structure is being affected now by human action; and that choices we make today will become central to any future history.

Having learned all that about one small piece of the earth's surface, a person may by imaginative extension know at least some of the crucial questions to ask about any other part. And can perhaps overcome, however slightly, the limitation that every generation knows only the changes in its surroundings it has witnessed firsthand. Born into a time of melting icecaps and huge storms, experiencing "unhealthy" air twenty-three days each summer – such things become normal. But there are ways of overcoming, at least to some extent, such natural limitations on both knowledge and imagination. People in Appalachia can study the destroyed mountains and see what they used to look like. People who eat fruit (that's almost all of us) can get a thorough acquaintance of the role of bats and bees in pollination and then witness their recent precipitous decline. Students could take a "field trip" to live in a polluted neighborhood subject to environmental racism.

Yet intellectual knowledge of environmental history, even of a comparatively small area, may still be too, and I use the term "advisedly," *impersonal* to provide the crucial sense of personal connection. The extension of our political system to an ecological democracy may also require a level of intimate personal contact.

This claim may seem strange. We know what intimacy is between people – close friends, family, lovers. What could "intimacy" be between, say, a person and a tree? Here is an example of what I have in mind.

Students in my Philosophy and the Environment course are required to find a nearby tree of their choice and quite simply hang out with it for fifteen to twenty minutes three or four times a week for the term. They must keep a written record of the experience, a kind of journal in which they record what occurs. I assure them that if it is legible, they can write what they like, including "What a stupid waste of time, Gottlieb is an idiot" or "I'm bored out of my mind." While a few go that route and are clearly untouched by the assignment, most do not. They reflect on other trees they have known, use the occasion to recall past contacts with the nonhuman realm, give their trees a name, wonder if their own driving habits have contributed to tree-damaging acid rain, write "So long" to the tree at the term's end and vow, many of them, to return for visits next fall.

Given my university's seven-week terms, the process is necessarily short. Still, it is a more directly connected, a more *intimate* connection than many people have with nature. For this is emphatically *not* a "wilderness experience" of tramping through distant forests and conquering mountains. Our vaguely suburban campus is near a small, urban park, never out of range of traffic noises or the built environment. The connection that develops between student and tree is not dependent solely on the spectacular, though most students learn to find beauty in the single tree; nor on the excitement of adventure in the wilds or the awe-inspiring effects of Great Places. The student's experience is limited, ordinary, and above all *particular*.

In the affection, respect, and intimacy of witnessing one tree at different times of the day or night, in cold or warm weather, sometimes in rain or snow, a relationship sometimes emerges that alters the student's understanding of nature as a whole. From a resource, a background, a source of fun and aesthetic beauty, it becomes as well a source of solace and mutuality. And thus, I am suggesting, it becomes a being that is capable of being responded to in the realm not just of personal affection but of political recognition.

12   GETTING TO GO

Many factors can lead a marginalized, oppressed group forward politically. Sometimes, as with slavery, the root economic structure of the domination is incompatible with other social forces. Sometimes an activist movement undermines the weight of tradition with detailed critique and an alternative vision of human relations, as in modern feminism.

Sometimes, along with such structural and collective political challenges, there is a personal, relational basis for the change. In the history of gay rights we can find the Stonewall rebellion, campaigns for political office, and explicit demands for legal changes, including the right to gay marriage. But as a comparatively small minority raising demands that run contrary to a seemingly unshakable weight of long-standing beliefs, the gay movement had another resource: personal connections among gay and straight people. As gay people, emboldened by collective struggle and the history of other movements, came out of the closet to their friends, family, and coworkers, the single best predictor of whether or not a straight person would support gay rights was whether or not they had a close relationship with a gay person. If they knew a sibling, uncle, or woman they sang with in the church choir, they were more likely to see them as individuals whose happiness or suffering mattered and as worthy of political recognition.

Repeated experience of the same tree, or pond, or bird over an extensive period of time – hopefully far longer than the seven weeks of my class – can provide a reason to value, and to seek political representation for, nature. Such experience is precisely the kind of connection that an expanded sense of communicative democracy requires. Of course, trees do not defend their identity or proclaim their rights or argue for specific policies. But they do flourish or sicken, stand tall or droop, connect in a fulfilling way with the rest of the ecosystem or not. And as they do all those things, they are telling us who they are and what they need.

The appeal I've been making to education and personal experience is a familiar one in strategies for social change. And it is not insignificant. People *can* be educated to eat healthier foods and place fewer demands on the health care system; to use stress reduction techniques to lessen uncontrolled aggression; to learn about, and thereby increase respect for, other cultural traditions. In the case of our acquaintance with and relation to the natural world, similar possibilities exist.

However, there are significant differences. For one thing, technological overload creates us as people for whom nature is often too distant or dull to arouse our interest and attention. If we are conditioned to the nonstop stimulus of cell phones, Internet, and television, sitting with a tree or watching birds might be far too slow for our hyped-up minds. Further, the predictable consequence of a deep acquaintance and respectful relation to nature would run counter to dominant social forces advocating endlessly increasing consumption and a self-monitoring focused almost exclusively on our "needs." As movies criticizing religion or depicting interracial relationships were prohibited by the stringent Hays rules in mid-twentieth-century America, so education aimed at cultivating a sensibility in which respect for nature is essential, and worth challenging prevailing norms of consumption, would likely be quickly identified as dangerously subversive. We can look for an instructive example to the government of Thailand, eager to pursue conventional forms of capitalist economic development, which forbade the traditional Buddhist teaching of restraint in consumption.[55] While there is a simplicity movement in the United States, it surely is not something that was taught in the public schools. And the same is true for deep knowledge of nature.

[55] David Cockrell and EcoSpirit New England, "Appendix B," in The Seventh Principle Project, *Green Sanctuary: Eco-Spirituality for Liberal Religious Congregations*. Available from The Seventh Principle Project Website: www.uuaspp.org.

Yet the difficulty, even the impossibility, of achieving a fundamental social transformation is *not* a reason to fail to argue for it. While history frequently tells us that things will be worse than we ever thought, from time to time they get better than we ever imagined. Surely that latter outcome is at least slightly more likely if we can share the idea that we can and should cultivate our acquaintance with the natural world; and that such acquaintance could, bit by bit, play a role in the creation of an ecological democracy.

4

Can We Talk?

Understanding the "Other Side" in the Animal Rights Debates

I WHAT IS IT ABOUT ANIMALS?[1]

Why a special chapter on animals? I have not, after all, included separate accounts of our relations with trees or bacteria. The reason is that there are a number of ways in which animals stand out from other nonhuman life forms.

To begin, in many species of animals, particularly the "higher" mammals, we can recognize ourselves. We see family groupings, mothers giving birth, children moving from helplessness to adult autonomy through growth and education, the expression of recognizable emotions, comprehensible bodily responses to attraction or threat, bonds of friendship and play, careful thinking, learning, and intelligence. Even an animal whose neurological structure is as different from ours as an octopus can be observed carefully responding to a problem situation and devising a reasonable solution; e.g., learning how to get food himself by observing another octopus opening a trick box. However much we may hug trees or find God in the mountains, however thrilled we are by sunset colors or the sound of a stream, we rarely feel a comparable recognition of immediate, living similarity.

Given the typical self-absorption of the normal human ego, it is perhaps more important how animals respond to us with a precision that makes us feel seen and understood. The pigeons come when we spread out the breadcrumbs, Fluffy the cat cuddles into the exact space by our

---

[1] This chapter benefitted greatly from comments by John Sanbonmatsu.

hip to enjoy a nap when we do. Deer flee our approach in hunting season, sheepdogs control the sheep. I heard birds in my childhood neighborhood come to the open window and respond to music created by my extraordinarily gifted flutist brother. Dogs can learn as many as 150 (and in a documented case, over 1,000[2]) words and warn people who are about to faint from low blood pressure. Dolphins allow us to swim with them, often distinguishing the degree of physical intensity their human play dates can handle.

Further, just because of the emotional bonds between humans and animals, there is a distinct tendency to analyze our relations to them in human terms. A gorilla locked behind bars in a zoo, his face pressed to the bars, his eyes deadened with hopelessness, closely and painfully resembles a person in a prison; and it is not much of a stretch to argue that, because the gorilla is innocent of any crime, he is being held unjustly. And indeed in 2015 animal rights activists demanded that two chimpanzees be granted the writ of *habeas corpus*: to be either put on trial or freed.[3] Similarly, theorists Sue Donaldson and Will Kymlicka have offered a "political theory of animal rights" in which they divided up animals into the wild, who deserve sovereignty comparable to foreign nations; the liminal (e.g., squirrels, birds in cities) who may be thought of us noncitizen aliens; and the domestic, who deserve rights comparable to people. In each case Donaldson and Kymlicka apply to animals the fruits of long-standing traditions of political theory designed for people.[4]

While there are attempts (such as I have offered in the previous chapter) to expand the circle much further to include ecosystems or rivers or forests, applying human concepts to animals is much easier. A general right to life we might share with trees, but animals can be confined, be subject to cruelty, suffer loneliness because they are deprived of needed social contact, become recognizably depressed, mourn for dead mates, miss their familiar human companions or take joy in their return. Their

[2] "Dog Understands 1022 Words | Super Smart Animals | BBC Earth," YouTube video. Accessed February 27, 2018, www.youtube.com/watch?v=Ip_uVTWfXyI.

[3] Initially, the suit was granted. "Judge Recognizes Two Chimpanzees as Legal Persons, Grants them Writ of Habeas Corpus," Nonhuman rights blog Website. Accessed January 8, 2018, www.nonhumanrights.org/blog/judge-recognizes-two-chimpanzees-as-legal-persons-grants-them-writ-of-habeas-corpus/.

[4] Sue Donaldson and Will Kymlicka, *Zoopolis: A Political Theory of Animal Rights* (New York: Oxford University Press, 2011).

right to speak can be overridden by having, as is customarily done to dogs in labs, their vocal chords removed. As individuals they can be given cancer, castrated, kept lactating their entire lives, forced to breed, and have parts of their anatomies (e.g., chickens' sensitive beaks) routinely removed. When we think of happiness or misery, freedom or slavery, humans and animals seem to be in the same boat.

Therefore, our relations to animals must occupy a special place in a discussion of environmental ethics.

Given how similar animals are to humans, and the ease with which we can sense their pains and pleasures, happiness or misery, the question of their moral standing is much more accessible than that of rivers or flowers. One need only point to the brief, typically poorly shot videos of animals in industrial farms or foxes gnawing off their own limbs in traps, or rabbits with chemicals dripped into their eyes to test cosmetics, and the only reasonable, sane, humane response seems to be: "For God's sake, stop it."

Alongside this visceral response ethicists and animal activists have articulated numerous reasons why we should stop it: because animals feel pleasure and pain, have emotions with which we can empathize, possess a subjective experience of relationships, desires and projects (e.g., to protect their young, to build a next, to migrate). And because so many of the ways in which we justify our treatment of animals make no sense. There can now be little doubt that they are intelligent like us, have emotions like us, have relationships like us, communicate like us, and use tools like us. For some it is even clear that they are beloved of God as we are. Therefore it is only the rankest prejudice – a "speciesism" akin to racism or anti-Semitism or sexism – that would allow us to continue doing what we have been doing.

Yet we do not stop it. Despite the good political work of animal rights organizations and the compelling arguments of animal rights theorists the clear majority of our uses of animals continues. There are exceptions, but the sheer number of animals consumed and used remains unbearably high: about one hundred and fifty billion per year eaten; in experiments, over one hundred million used.

Stop? No. For those of us who believe that it's an open-and-shut case, that virtually nothing can be said in defense of the other side, this leads to a kind of moral confusion. How can we be so right – and yet our arguments and insights have so little effect? And how can people who might in other ways be kind, generous, and morally reflective on a host of ethical issues so casually buy the burger and grill the chicken, and not wonder what is being done to animals in the name of progress and convenience?[5]

That is why rather than rehearsing the arguments for moral treatment of animals once again in this chapter, I will offer something a little different. How, I am asking, can we talk to the "other side"? Is there any way to reach through the pervasive atmosphere of self-righteousness, distrust, and invective to talk, and, perhaps above all, to listen?

2 POWERFUL FEELINGS

Animals can be such a vital, powerful presence that we often have vital and powerful responses to them. These responses, we may think, lead to obvious truths and easily agreed on, shared values.

Alas, just the opposite is true. Our encounters with animals can result in complicated, divisive, and downright hostile encounters with our fellow humans. Folks who just want to show off a little wealth and wear a warm coat are accused by People for the Ethical Treatment of Animals of wearing "The look that kills!" and might end up with ruinous red dye tossed on their $8,000 mink. Your mother serves a beautifully done up turkey, and you dismiss it as a needlessly slaughtered fellow creature rather than an act of love. The research scientist thinks he's trying to cure cancer and is accused of careerist opportunism on the flesh of the 100 million animal bodies per year. A farmer whose family has raised chickens for generations, or a global corporation providing beef at a tiny fraction of what meat used to cost, are told that they are causing global warming by all the oil they use and the rainforests destroyed to plant soybeans to feed cows, and they are accused of causing mass starvation because what they feed the animals could feed the world's poor. Somebody is just trying to put food on his family's table, and a referendum in Massachusetts takes his job away by making greyhound racing illegal. A father wants to bond with his son in the Great Outdoors – and hears that sport hunting is cruel, patriarchal.

Should we just forget about all this conflict? Leave the whole subject to someone else? For the most part that is what we do. We can think and feel what we think and feel and leave the ravings of the animal fanatics, the inventory in the labs, the blood on the slaughterhouse floor to others.

[5] Carol J. Adams laments how frequently meat is served at feminist conferences: "The Feminist Traffic in Animals," in Greta Gaard, ed., *Ecofeminism: Women, Animals, Nature* (Philadelphia: Temple University Press, 2010), pp. 195–218.

Yet if you have opened the pages of this book you probably have some interest in the hard work of thinking about morality – and, as I'm presenting it here, thinking about morality is not something we can do alone or just with people who think like us. Rather, it requires that we take seriously people who think very differently. So, let us look at some reasons why it can be so hard to come to agreement on how humans treat animals.

As I have seen from my students, talk shows, intellectuals writing on both sides, and public statements of animal rights groups and the meat industry, these feelings can translate into moral intuitions so immediate and forceful that we feel they could not be wrong. When other people have *opposing* powerful feelings and intuitions, it is easy to be dismissive. How can "they" be so naive? Unthinking? Pretentious? Who are *they* to guilt trip me and tell the whole world it is wrong? And who are *they* to live without a heart?

These powerful, opposing intuitions can be summarized this way:

The Animal Rights activist intuitions. *Animals love their mates and their children, they romp on the grass and tussle with each other. They delight in soaring across a dawn sky, running through the forest, chewing their cud. And despite the very rare time when they hurt people, they are pretty much defenseless against us. And think of how much suffering we cause them. If you really, really look at them, listen to their screams, take in their wounds, how can you continue to do this to them?*

People First intuitions. *People are more important than animals. They just are. And anyway life is hard enough already – if I want a steak or fried chicken, I'll just have it. They taste good. And the idea that some rat or pigeon has rights is just, well, ridiculous. People need food. Science needs lab animals. People all over the world are starving and sick or oppressed in countless ways, and you want me to worry about a cow or a mouse? Get real. If you want to go gaga over your labradoodle, that's fine. But leave the rest of us alone.*

Things would ease off a bit if we could say at this point, "Why don't we all just agree to disagree? If you don't want to eat meat or wear fur, no one is making you. People have different beliefs about God, vote for different political parties, and like different music and food, so why can't each of us get along with people who have differences about eating meat, using animals in experiments, or the amount of space a veal calf should have in his cage before he's slaughtered?"

This would be a welcome, calming response. With people so attached to their opinions, we're not going to convince anyone. We should just leave well enough alone and keep to ourselves.

Yet it will not work.

And it will not work because whether a particular "difference" is allowable is part of the problem itself. As individuals, as a society, we must draw lines: between differences that are a matter of taste (like a really bad wardrobe) and differences that will put you in jail (like abusing your kids). We (some of us, anyway) have learned to accept people who have different names for God than we do. But we *cannot* let people routinely whip their five-year-olds. Or have sex with them. If you think that's okay, too bad. For a whole bunch of reasons, such differences are just, well, *too* different – so morally wrong that they must be outlawed.

So, while when we think about animals the option of tolerance for differences might be an option, but for many people it clearly is not.

At the same time, even if we think our views are so morally right that people on the other side are not just different but wrong, and *so* wrong that what they do should be illegal and considered an ethical outrage, whichever side *we* are on, there still are an awful lot of people on the *other* side. If we are going to get along with these people morally – thinking of them as moral agents who deserve respect for their choices just as we do – at the very least, we had better try to understand them. As well, such understanding might lead us to a bit of common ground in which both sides could get something they want.

For this to work, our powerful intuitions must coexist with the faith that people who feel and think differently should not be swept aside as simply cruel or naïve. We cannot talk reasonably to these people, or even think intelligently about them, unless we entertain life from *their* point of view. When views have a long-standing, broad acceptance – as human superiority, meat eating, and the scientific exploitation of animals do – we must take them seriously on their own terms. Similarly, when so many people are moral vegetarians, or oppose using animals in science, as do now, it will not work to write them off as mush-brained, sentimental hippies. Especially because many of those opposed to animal exploitation are among the most universally respected people in history: Einstein, Gandhi, Steve Jobs, Thomas Edison, Leo Tolstoy, Rosa Parks, Benjamin Franklin, etc.

If either side is dismissed at the beginning, attempts to communicate with – or even to comprehend – these different people will be doomed from the outset. And where would that leave us? Well, perhaps exactly where we are right now. But is that where we want to be?

Another strategy to end the conversation quickly would arise if the People First types observed that even though there are legal limits on what you can do to your pets, and some slowly adopted and very minimal standards dictating the treatment of animals in labs, animal rights supporters are still a tiny minority. "You can feel what you want," a People First person might mutter, "and yell about animal cruelty as loud as you please, but you haven't got a real chance, and you are just too outnumbered."

For two reasons this quick dismissal does not really work. First, the vast majority has been wrong before. Very, very wrong. One need only think of slavery, or of societies in which women have no political rights, or times when we were ruled by hereditary aristocracies. All these were the accepted norms of their day. All were opposed at first only by tiny minorities. Do any of us want to be like people who thought it was perfectly fine to keep slaves? Or exploit peasants? Or beat their wives? If we claim to be moral – and don't we all want to think we are basically decent? – shouldn't we take a few minutes and really listen to the other side?

Second, the animal rights position, small minority though it is, is making something of an inroad in social life. Vegetarians[6] may be a small number, but they are a steadily growing number. In terms of wild animals, the United States has – however inconsistently applied – an Endangered Species Act, which says that normal property rights can be suspended if activity on privately owned land threatens to erase a species. There are sizable movements to outlaw bullfighting in Spain and Mexico. An NFL quarterback went to jail for training dogs to fight each other and killing them when they didn't. Information about the disastrous effects of factory farms continues to spread and have a minimal but real effect. So, while a People First type might have the law and culture on his or her side *now*, the balance could be slowly shifting.

Despite the power of our intuitions, then, and the certainty of the moral ideas to which they give rise, a truly moral conversation – in which

---

[6] I will use "vegetarians" as a stand-in vegans as well, realizing that there are significant differences between them. A recent study suggested that there are over seven million vegetarians in the United States, approximately 15 percent of them vegans. *Vegetarian Times* Website. Accessed May 9, 2010, www.vegetariantimes.com/article/vegetarianism-in-america.

we open ourselves to what the other person is saying and find as much truth in it as possible – seems to be called for.

3 VEAL PARMESAN

Just as our relations with strangers and with family, as employees and as citizens, as professionals or as soldiers, involve different moral values and imperatives, so might our different kinds of relations with animals. Do the principles or values that we use in one context make sense for others?

Consider: we use animals for food, for work, for scientific experiments. There are pets and wild animals and zoo animals. Animals are prey for hunters, sacrifices for some religions, companions to the blind, and somewhere in Asia (I forget where exactly) monkeys serve food in a restaurant.

How are we to make sense of all these different contexts? I will not offer a simple, universal rule, because I think that if I did it would be so abstract that we would not really know what it meant until I described how it operated in each context. (After all, we talk about the "rights" of workers and hospital patients, to healthcare and free speech, of religion and carrying weapons. Does using the one term ("rights") really tell us how we are supposed to act in all these differing settings?) Because this is not a book just on animals, there is no space to examine all these contexts. But we can compare two very different contexts and see how the differences affect our responses.

Here is one: When you order a delicious veal parmesan at a fancy Italian restaurant you are consuming the flesh of a living being who had been confined in a cage so small that he could barely move, always in the dark so that his flesh would be pale, without any company (which he needs, being a social animal), and to preserve the delicacy of his taste never fed the solid food he requires.

Clearly there are all sorts of *cultural* reasons to keep eating that veal parmesan. It has been a delicacy for a very long time. It tastes great. People earn a living raising, cooking, and serving it. Yet if you lean in the animal rights direction, as I do, it might seem pretty easy to dismiss all such defenses of veal by pointing out that slavery was culturally supported, and that people made money off of Jewish slave labor in concentration camps. But this quick dismissal does not work when you are talking to someone who remembers how his family really enjoyed his grandmother's cooking; whose heart opens in the memory of everyone sighing with pleasure around the dining room table; or who is paying for his son's alternative medical treatments for debilitating asthma by working at Ricci's Italian Paradise. The painful truth is that the vast majority of people simply do not, and never will, equate cages for veal calves with concentration camps. So, comparing the treatment of animals to the horrors humans have inflicted on each other might be morally valid, but it may not reach many of the people you need to convince.[7]

Yet it *is* very hard to defend the way veal calves are raised without saying flat out that the pain of animals is morally meaningless: that we can cut down trees, mine the earth, hammer brass – and in the same way do what we want to any animal that is not human. This is a kind of orthodox anthropocentrism – people are the center of all things and the beings out on the periphery do not count. Yet, interestingly, even people who believe this sort of thing typically do not believe it *completely*; and it is that lack of completeness that leaves an opening for the other side.

For example: a good number of the veal parmesan eaters (or servers) doubtless have their own special, favorite pets that they would not dream of treating the way veal calves are treated – whose welfare, happiness, and pleasure count for something. They have their "favorite animals" who stand out from the rest, and this both in terms of their own particular companion, but also in terms of favorite species: we love our dogs, but pigs – intelligent and graceful animals – are consigned to the slaughter.[8] The fundamental inconsistency here – that the pain of our pets matters but that of our dinner does not – creates a deep logical hole that is very hard to climb out of. And you cannot climb out of it by arguing that we are usually a lot nicer to our family than to strangers. You might not be obligated to help people in faraway places who are starving, but you cannot enslave or eat them.

So when we look at veal – and indeed meat eating generally – what we have is a deeply entrenched social practice that is, when examined, pretty much without any moral justification. Whether or not this moral indefensibility extends to hunting buffalo thousands of years ago by stampeding them over a cliff,[9] or to the Inuit peoples in the Arctic

[7] A critique of meat eating by Charles Patterson was titled, in a nod of one of the Holocaust's largest concentration camps, *Eternal Treblinka: Our Treatment of Animals and the Holocaust* (New York: Lantern Books, 2002).
[8] Heinrich Himmler, an essential architect of the Holocaust, once commented that his fellow SS members no doubt all had their "favorite Jew," whom, he was delighted to say, they killed anyway. Lucy Davidowicz, *The War against the Jews* (New York: Bantam, 1975), p. 200.
[9] Head-Smashed-In Buffalo Jump World Heritage Site in Alberta, Canada, commemorates this practice.

Circle who pursue seals now, is really beside the point. Right now, we are talking about mass-produced animals who end up in shrink-wrapped packages at the local supermarket and "local" free-range animals who would, let's face it, rather not offer their flesh for our dinner tables. We can add, just to make the issues even clearer: the mass production of meat in factory farms creates concentrated waste, pollutes surrounding areas, uses land and plant food that could feed hungry people, leads to deforestation, and contributes quite significantly to global warming. In anything like the quantity it is being currently consumed in many countries, it is also very unhealthy for people.

What can the veal eater say in response? Not much, which is why his or her response is generally laughter, contempt, not looking at films of factory farms and slaughterhouses, saying, "That's just the way we do things around here," and repeating, "It tastes good," as if that were sufficient *justification* to keep eating it. One usually gets a lot of attitude, but very little reasoned argument.

So if the cheerful meat eater does not want to engage seriously with an animal rights advocate's claims that July 4th barbecues are like Nazi death camps, what are we to do?

Well, and initially this might seem to be beside the point, we can start by recognizing that the moral failure of modern meat eating is not the end of the story. For if the modern meat eater is doing something morally wrong every time she whips out her Visa card to pay for prime rib, she is surely not the only one who commits moral wrongs. I remember a telling conversation I once had with a highly intelligent and passionate animal rights advocate. We had just been part of a panel discussion at a national meeting in San Francisco. And while the panel was all pretty much pro-animal rights some of the questions from the large audience had been quite hostile to our position. "Ahh, Roger," she complained, real pain in her eyes, "they don't get it. After all that's been written, they just don't get it." "You're right," I commiserated. "But of course, all of us have our moral limitations. You've come to this conference from Texas, I from Boston. Think of how jet travel damages the ozone layer and how the money we spent on this not really necessary trip could have been spent on other things." She stared at me for a second. This wasn't the moral solidarity and self-righteous mutual appreciation she had expected. The pain in her eyes blinked out, and a kind of vagueness replaced it as she backed out of the room, barely murmuring her goodbyes.

In other words, *yes* eating meat, at least the way we do it here and now, is wrong.[10] But *yes* as well there are *many* other things we do that do not add up morally. Like everyone else I know, I am morally flawed, at times deeply. And indeed, every animal rights activist, including the ones who believe that our mass consumption of animals is a kind of Holocaust, lives in a way that harms animals. Such activists drive their cars and plug into the power grid, thus contributing to the global warming that is eradicating countless species. Even their fully vegan diet involves large-scale agriculture that displaces animals. And when their children are sick, they do not reject "out of principle" medicines that have been developed though testing on animals.

The bind we are all in, and one of the things that distinguishes ethics in an age of environmental crisis, is that short of dropping out completely, we cannot help but be part of the problem. Certainly, we will be less of a part if we stop eating animal products and refuse to buy consumer products tested on animals. But so long as we are functioning members of this society, we will be a part nevertheless.

As well, the sad truth is that a lot of people who love animals can at the same time be uncaring about other people. They might give large donations for animal shelters but nothing for world hunger, peace activism, or to stop abuse against women. They might cherish animals deeply but think of and speak to animal-eating humans with hatred and verbal violence. They might take refuge in a comforting sense of superiority, endlessly taking the moral inventory of everyone else's moral failings while never seriously examining their own. In other words, they might be great about animals and only mediocre on most other moral concerns.

This line of thought does not eradicate the tensions between People First and Animal Rights. It does, however, enable the morally critical Animal Rights activist to approach his or her adversary with a less arrogant and more modest posture.

At this point there may be some comfort for both sides to be found in what is probably for most readers an unexpected source: the vegetarian perspective of Rabbi Abraham Isaac Kook, who at his death in 1935 was the chief rabbi of prestate Israel.[11] As an esteemed leader of Orthodox

---

[10] I am leaving aside practices from the distant past, as well as those of indigenous peoples. I am not leaving aside "humane" or "locavore" practices – unless those animals sign statements willing their bodies to our dinner table.

[11] "Rav Kook on Vegetarianism," Orot.com Website. Accessed January 8, 2018, http://orot .com/rav-kook-on-vegetarianism/.

Jewry, Kook functioned in a community in which meat eating – and lots of it – was the accepted rule. There was no way he could simply demand vegetarianism from his followers: The ruling would not have been understood, and certainly not followed. But Kook was not about to issue such a simple, absolute rule. In fact, he argued that biblical history showed that humans, though ultimately headed for a nonmeat diet, simply were not capable of it yet. In Genesis God initially gives Adam and Eve only vegetable food to eat. After the "sinful generation" of Noah, however, God told people they could eat flesh. At the same time, Kook pointed out, there are many biblical restrictions on what and how we eat: We are not allowed to boil the kid in its mother's milk, or take the mother bird along with the eggs, or eat blood. There are foods that are forbidden.

Thus, the way we eat is a matter in which God's commands operate. It is morally significant. These rules, said Kook, indicate not just what God wants, but also that humans have a long way to go before they will be able to live truly moral lives. This process starts with some restrictions on what we can do to animals. It will end up in an ideal of respect and care, including a refusal to use animals for food. We are not capable of the end point yet, but our observance of rules that limit our behavior will help us move toward that point.

One does not have to be an Orthodox Jew, or a religious believer of any kind, to appreciate the force of this position. One need only see that a partial improvement is better than no improvement at all, even in the realm of morality. And that the practical truth or at least the practical relevance, of any moral claim – animal rights, women's rights, gay marriage, what we owe to people starving faraway – is only as powerful as the level of moral development of the people to whom we are talking. No matter how right a moral claim is, if humanity is not ready to take in its truth, it will have no social consequence. Like so much else in life, the effectiveness of a moral truth depends on where we are historically and socially.

So, if the vast majority of people on this earth are not yet morally capable of being vegetarians, and if all the anti–meat eaters are themselves morally flawed, what can the moral vegetarian say to the lover of veal parmesan? Perhaps something like this:

First: *would you treat your pet this way?*[12] *If not, what's the difference?* Second, *I'm hardly morally perfect myself, and there are indeed a*

---

[12] Of course, huge numbers of pets are treated dreadfully.

lot of other moral issues besides the abuse of animals. So when I talk to you now I know I'm not coming from any position of moral superiority. I'll see if I can help you on this issue, and God knows you can probably help me on another one. So I'm asking you as a fellow struggler in the long effort of moral betterment to consider that veal calf. And third: *what can we agree on that would make all this at least a little better?*

This last question has some resonance in the real world. For in some countries there has been agreement on legal restrictions on how you can raise veal, and in other matters relating to animals as well. If these new laws are not nearly enough for the moral vegetarian, I completely understand. If the endless murder of animals just is different than not buying fair trade coffee or driving too much, we still live in a society in which the clear majority simply do not agree with a strong animal rights position. As in other areas moral life it is often, perhaps typically, not a case of "enough." It usually is, at best, a case of getting a "little bit better."

4 ANIMALS IN THE LAB

Here's another context. Your child has been born with cystic fibrosis (CF), a generally fatal genetic condition in which a missing enzyme leads to lung and digestive problems. While CF used to spell a quite early death for everyone, recent research has now enabled many to live into their thirties and forties.

If it is your child, doomed to a life of frequent lung infections, rounds of seemingly endless coughing, near constant chest physical therapy to clear the distinctly thick and immovable CF mucous, do you care how many lab animals must die to find something that will enable your child to have a somewhat longer, somewhat more tolerable, life? In forty years the median survival age for CF has gone from 10 to 37. *That's* what you're counting, not the number of mice that were used up to develop treatments, and potentially a cure, for your child.

If meat eating, in particular veal, is an immoral self-indulgence (no matter how culturally supported, tasty, and emotionally resonant), the use of animals for research to cure deadly diseases is something else. Here we have what at least looks like a clear choice: allow a child to suffer and die young or do what needs to be done for people at the expense of animals.

The Animal Rights defender can say that there is no reason to prefer the human to the animal. And we should be aware that whatever a given, deeply affected individual may feel, certain choices should not, by collective social decision, be available. Perhaps we are no more justified in experimenting on animals to save human lives than we are in experimenting on humans. Could we choose a thousand random children and use them for experiments to save other children? If we couldn't with humans, why with rats? Even if we don't accept the human–animal equivalence, we can also raise questions of degree and scope. How many animals would you sacrifice for a cure for a single human health problem? A million? A hundred million? A hundred billion? And for what disease? – for one that afflicts some 300,000 in the United States like CF? For one that afflicts 300? Or 3? How many animals would you kill to help with diseases that are bothersome but not life-threatening? E.g., allergies or acne? What about diseases that are often the result of lifestyle problems? Should we kill millions of mice to help people with their alcoholism or heroin, obesity or video game addiction? Or to develop prosthetic limbs for people maimed in accidents they caused while drunk? Is there no limit on how other species are supposed to compensate for our suffering?

Perhaps if it were myself or my child, I would vote for no limit whatsoever. Such is the moral relation of parent to child, or the impulse for personal survival; and also the degree to which I privilege humans over animals. Yet even though I might respond in such a way, that does not necessarily mean that I should be the one who determines moral and legal norms. It is not necessarily that the most personally affected should have the final say. For in such a situation I might also demand no limit to other people's sacrifices for my or my child's health and survival as well. I might demand a twentyfold increase in research funding through the imposition of a tax on everyone who doesn't have CF; I might argue that CF get funding from less lethal health problems. I might want experiments done on poor children from poor countries. There might be no end to what I would demand. That doesn't mean such demands carry moral weight, or enough moral weight to override other people's problems, or other people's acceptance of my or my child's imminent death.

There is a further consideration, one that changes the choice we are facing from simply either "animals in labs" or "no animals in labs."

Using animals for research costs money; money for health care is limited; and there are a lot of other things that we can do with that money that are good for people's health and do *not* involve animal cruelty. We can clean up the environment so fewer people get cancer from pollution; we can teach people to have better health habits, so lifestyle diseases diminish; we can encourage people not to eat animal foods because they are a big contributor to ill health. These measures will not hurt animals at all; in fact, they will help animals *and* people

Of course, such activities are not likely to generate medicines that can be sold, and thus make considerable amounts of money for drug companies. Nor are they likely to lead to high-profile careers for medical researchers. These are often low-tech, comparatively low-status activities that, nevertheless, can have potentially enormous health benefits. Suppose, to take one example, we changed the current ratio of money-for-cure to money-for-prevention in cancer – now at about 98 percent to 2 percent – to something closer to, just for argument's sake, fifty–fifty. How many animals would be saved? And how many humans as well – especially considering that by some estimates environmental causes are implicated in millions of cancer cases?[13]

Yet even the best environmental regimens and an entire population doing yoga, meditating, and eating nothing but salads, brown rice, and lentil stew will not end genetic health problems like CF. We will still have the desperate parent and the sick child, the people with a terrible illness and the animals whose lives we will want to sacrifice to find better treatments.

Perhaps once again the only approach with a reasonable chance of success is to try to make things a little better. First, stop all the stupid, wasteful, even insane animal experiments: the ones that drip cosmetics into rabbits' eyes until they go blind; or that smash monkey's heads into walls to see if having heads smashed into a wall will injure the brain; or that test how long it takes to make animals crazy by randomly subjecting them to electric shocks.[14]

As for the CF experiments? Well, even if they are wrong, perhaps we could agree to talk about them later. Just as it would be an improvement, even if not necessarily good enough, to better the living conditions of veal calves, so there is a lot that can be done to limit animal experiments *before* we get around to stopping the research aimed at curing lethal inherited illnesses.

In a moral life we are often faced with difficult choices. Sometimes these are really false choices, and we should make sure we know why we must "choose between A and B." Maybe there is a C that would work out for us all – like the holistic and preventative health measures described

---

[13] "Cancer Prevention," World Health Organization Website. Accessed January 5, 2017, www.who.int/cancer/prevention/en/.
[14] All actual experiments and practices.

earlier. But at times, and sadly, there is no way out of the painful alternatives is possible. "People are born to trouble," said Job, "as the sparks fly upwards." "Life," said the Buddha, "is suffering." We will have pain in this life, and so will everyone else, and no amount of moral goodness will ever take that away.

5 ANIMALS KILL AND EAT OTHER ANIMALS, WHY SHOULDN'T WE? AND THE JOY OF HUNTING

To be honest, these are positions that it is often hard for me to take seriously. Yet I have heard them so many times from students and from people at my public lectures that my inability to see their force is clearly my problem.

The first is often articulated as the desire to live more "naturally," to "learn from nature." The lions eat the gazelles, the hawks eat the rabbits, and those o-so-cute dolphins at Sea World do not live on bean sprouts, but on lots and lots of fish. Why should people alone be restricted from this vast banquet? If we are tougher, or at least smarter, than all the other animals, that's just their blues. If the lion is truly the "king of the forest" no one will be telling *him* to lay off. People should have the same privilege. Vegans live in a fantasy world in which killing and being eaten don't exist. Meat eaters are realists who celebrate real life. And in their meat eating they will be reminded of the cycle of birth and death that defines human and animal existence.[15]

This argument gets even more emphatic in the context of hunting. We are, say some hunters, getting back into nature, experiencing the wilderness as our forebears did, tracking and killing in a primordial struggle that bonds us with the circle of life the way humans used to before we were made weak and decadent by civilization. There is a mystic connection between hunter and animal that all those who buy packaged hot dogs can never understand. And those of you who criticize hunting as a brutal celebration of death do not comprehend the respect, the love even, that passes between hunter and prey. Hunting, says philosopher Lawrence Cahoone, displays an "anachronistic self-sufficiency" and responsibility, "local ecological expertise" and most reliably, a "kind of

---

[15] A pointed critique of this last point is Saryta Rodriguez, "Sierra Club's Bogus Argument for Eating Animals," Free From Harm Website. Accessed February 2, 2018, https://freefromharm.org/common-justifications-for-eating-animals/sierra-clubs-bogus-argument-eating-animals/.

animal honesty."[16] A hunting Website affirms: "Hunters ARE animal lovers; sounds surprising to some, but we hunt where they live, appreciate their family units, cunning hunting methods, and intimately observe them in their true environment. Hunters respect and appreciate wildlife in an entirely different way... in the wild!"[17]

What bothers me so much about these arguments? Two things, at least.

First, we do not want to live "the way the animals do" because we want to live like people, not any other kind of animal. And that means we want to live in a society guided by moral norms. We do not just accept "what is," but frequently talk about "what ought to be." Do you want to live "naturally" and have a stronger male take your wife or girlfriend away, as is done in some animal communities? Or have to be the mate of the guy in the pack with the biggest muscles? Do you want to be eaten for food yourself? Or, like some male spiders, to have sex and then get your head bitten off?

I think not.

In terms of hunting: if people want to experience the primordial struggle between hunter and prey, let them have that experience. They will walk to wherever they are going to hunt, using weapons and wearing clothes they have made themselves. Their total consumption of meat will depend on the hunt and the hunt alone. No more $200 boots and toasty down parkas. No going out for steak afterwards or driving to the national forest for deer season. When today's hunters want to try it this way, they will at least be more honest. I still wonder why they cannot commune with a living being without killing it. Perhaps they could connect to animals by tracking them, taking pictures, or writing poems. But until they make the real sacrifices needed to "get back to the primordial," their stated desire seems a little insincere.

The point to all of this is that as attractive as a moral position seems initially, if you cannot live by it, it does not amount to much. By that I do not mean perfection. I am not suggesting that if we cannot love our neighbors exactly as ourselves we should totally abandon the religions that tell us to; or that if do not always take other people's rights seriously we should abolish the *Declaration of Independence*. I do mean that if we

[16] Lawrence Cahoone, "Hunting as a Moral Good," *Environmental Values* 18 (2009): 82–83. See also Jose Ortega y Gasset, *Meditations on Hunting* (New York: Charles Scribner and Sons, 1972).

[17] Eye of the Hunter Website. Accessed January 28, 2018, www.eyeofthehunter.com/hunters-animal-lovers/.

put forward a moral position that seems to require a certain amount of responsibility, and we are not willing to try to live up to that responsibility, we should not pretend it is really something we believe in. It is pretty clear that our hunters will not live like Native Americans of a thousand years ago; and that the person who wants to live "like nature" will also want his or her own life and property protected by a moral code and a good police force.

Thus, my arguments, I am convinced, win. But so what? Is that the best we can hope for in a moral conversation? Could it be that something more important is going on than my own knee-jerk rejection of moral stands I do not like?

I think there is. And here is part of it. Any widely held belief – even one that is inconsistent, poorly informed, or just dead wrong – almost always has some connection of vital importance to the people who hold it. If we truly are to understand one another, to develop our moral life through connected conversation with other viewpoints, and to create a moral community *together*, we must try to find out what it is that binds people to positions we completely reject.

At this point some people will point to revolutions or activist social protest movements and say *that* is how we should respond to moral evil, not by trying to find out what is vital and authentic in it. We do not need to "understand" Nazis, wife beaters, racists, or homophobes – we just need to confront and defeat them. Indeed, that may be the case in some situations, though it might certainly be argued that often a lot of unnecessary antagonism, self-righteous condemnation of other people, and outright violence slows things down or leads to a continuation of violence in the end. Maybe feminism in the United States would be further advanced now if the movement in the 1970s and 1980s had showed more compassion or at least understanding for men; or at least consciously sought men as allies. Perhaps violent anticolonial revolutions tend to create violent postcolonial governments. Maybe nonviolence – political and emotional – is a more effective, long-term answer to the problems of profound injustice. And maybe it is not. Maybe entrenched power and privilege are simply impervious, no matter what the strategy of those seeking fundamental change.

In any case, here I am concerned with sustaining a moral community, which includes trying to hear and be heard by people who think very differently than I do. Here the goal is understanding and connection, not victory and correctness. Political power, including possibly forcing other people to change how they act whatever they think, will be discussed in Chapter 7.

The hunters, and those who would think nature teaches us to act without moral limits, are expressing, however indirectly, a yearning to find some source of value, meaning, and connection that is beyond the human. They seek to learn from nature, probably in the hope that what is so often missing in their own lives can be gotten from some source outside the weaknesses and disappointments of society. In nature there is vitality, honesty, strength, and acceptance of fate. In nature the only masks are part of an evolutionary strategy, like the butterflies whose markings make them look poisonous when they are not. In nature there is no waste, and everything fits, and everybody's death is someone else's life – or at least so it may seem to those of us trapped by television, roads, bureaucratic regulations, the tax code, and email.

If the way hunters root authenticity and love of life in violent power repels me, and if a good deal of hunting really is a celebration of power and death, it may also be the case that at least some hunters are authentically seeking a spiritual struggle without the ambiguities and irrelevance of so much of conventional existence. Life or death, clear success or empty-handed failure, you hit the death point on the moose or you don't. In every wild animal there is a worthy opponent – because they will never lie or cheat in the struggle, never hire a shady lawyer to help them prevail, never call you names or guilt trip you. They will simply fight to the death with a clarity and a love of life that inspires our own.

If any of these speculations about the deeper motivations of people whose attitudes toward animals I reject are true, then there is a basis for communication between us. Even, perhaps, for some solidarity. For I too seek some wisdom and inspiration in the realm of nature, and I too admire the clarity and integrity of animals. If I can see what is beautiful in what other people think and want, as well as what is wrong, I will have upped my chances at finding allies, and at least will have learned to be a little less angry, superior, and self-righteous. I can diminish my own ethical smugness, which only hides my insecurity, and probably all the pain I feel as well. And maybe I and the people whom I am so sure are wrong can join on things we both support, like protecting wilderness. Better they should hunt and join Sierra Club to help protect the forest and the animals in it, than be so alienated from all the soft-hearted and morally superior environmentalists like me that they ignore everything but the next kill.

6 ANIMALS CAN WREAK HAVOC ON OTHER SPECIES AND ON ECOSYSTEMS

In the industrialized world it is very rare for animals to be a threat to people. The occasional snarling German shepherd, the deer that eats the lettuce from your carefully tended garden, pests in the grain supply – these can be unpleasant but are very small exceptions to a general rule in which domination runs from people to animals, not the other way. People, after all, kill about fifty million sharks a year; sharks kill a few dozen people at most.

But there are ecological contexts in which animals are very significant threats and have done irreparable damage to other animal species and indeed to ecosystems as a whole. Consider, for example, the case of feral cats in the United States. Lost or escaped or simply abandoned when no longer wanted, these cats have multiplied to a population in the tens of millions. They, in turn, kill billions of small rodents and millions of birds a year. Some of those birds are members of endangered species, and feral cats, many believe, are a big factor in making those birds endangered.

Do we have the right to kill the cats to save the birds?

Then there are rabbits in Australia, whose effects make America's feral cats look like child's play. Introduced for food in the late eighteenth century, some rabbits escaped or were let loose, exploded as a population, and have since been responsible for widespread ecological damage including erosion, plant species loss, and alteration of rainforest ecosystems. They have also threatened the Australian food supply by eating what sheep farmers wanted their sheep to graze on.

Should we kill the rabbits to save the trees whose bark the rabbits eat and the birds who live in the rainforests the rabbits destabilize? Should we kill the rabbits to make it easier for Australian farmers and keep the price of mutton low?

Often the most difficult aspect of living a moral life is not figuring out what is right, or even the decision to be moral rather than a scoundrel. It is what to do when faced by competing obligations, by conflicts not between right and wrong but between right and right. The tension between the rights of individual animals to be free from human violence and the survival of species and indeed whole ecosystems is real and painful. In academia a little growth industry for philosophers has involved writers on both sides of the issue – some for animal rights, some for a more "holistic," ecological approach – accusing the other side of just not understanding why their chosen policy of protecting the ecosystem or leaving the animals alone is dead wrong. Practically, there has been real live conflict between those who would control the feral cats by trapping and killing them, and the cat defenders who destroy the traps.[18]

While I tend toward the holistic, control the feral populations, protect a threatened species against an overpopulated one direction, I know there are arguments on the other side. Some might ask to know why we cannot simply catch the feral cats and sterilize them (as is sometimes done). Others wonder if posing a casual question "Should we kill the cats?" really takes in that each of these animals is a unique center of intelligence and experience. More challengingly, some might demand that I consider "culling" the human herd to save all the species *it* is threatening instead. And if I will not even consider that possibility, and am so quick to ask about killing the cats, why is that?[19]

But which side is "right" is not my concern right now. Instead, I will just point out some things about moral life that this conflict reveals.

Once certain kinds of actions are taken, it is too late to avoid painful conflict. "We" decide to colonize Australia, eat meat, bring in rabbits. "We" decide that anyone who wants a pet cat can have one, that sterilizing cats is optional, and that if they get to be too much of a bother you can just get rid of them. We also take animals to ecosystems where they have no natural enemies, try to create new businesses (tent caterpillars, which destroy trees in the northeastern United States, came from the attempt to create a domestic silk industry), or get careless. If we get caught up in the immediate problem (cats vs. birds) we might not pay enough moral attention to the processes that led to these consequences, to the decisions and values which make them inevitable.

Therefore, the question that intrigues me about animals that threaten species loss is not "What should we do about the animals?" but "What should we do about ourselves?" In an age of global warming many problems that seem to be about other things will come back to this one.

---

[18] Novelist T. C. Boyle explored in fictional terms the conflict between an ecosystem manager concerned with the overall health of an offshore California island and a fierce defender of the domestic-turned-wild pigs that were being poisoned and shot to "protect" the rest of the species. *When the Killing's Done* (New York: Viking, 2011).

[19] John Sanbonmatsu, author of many excellent pieces on animal–human relations, in private conversation.

Feral cats *are* a problem, no doubt. Just ask the birds they kill. But along with our conservationist concern over the birds, maybe we should worry about what *we* eat – and everything else we do. Perhaps we should control ourselves first, and deal with the animals later.

How much of what threatens animals comes from animals? And how much from us? Feral cats are bad for birds and rabbits in Australia are terrible for the Australian rainforest. But so are habitat loss from endless housing developments and large-scale agriculture, industrial meat pro-duction, pesticides in the food chain, and global warming. Should we kill the feral cats and the rabbits? Maybe we should. But maybe we should do so only *after* we develop a comprehensive plan for human land use that leaves some room for the rest of the animals, have learned how to farm without poisonous chemicals, and have drastically scaled back on energy use. Maybe the focus on those "damn cats" is a way of taking the focus off ourselves. In any case, if we concentrate on ourselves first, and try to institute some changes in the way *we* live, we might be so busy we wouldn't have the time and energy to worry about the cats.

Of course, in the short run it is easier just to poison some cats or shoot some rabbits (though the rabbit problem hasn't gone away, rabbits being a remarkably resilient species). And the conservationists have a point when they warn that if we wait for large-scale social changes it will be too late for many bird species. But if all our attention goes to the short-term, if we give ourselves tacit permission to continue with the same old policies for population, housing, energy use, agricul-ture, and transportation, then these policies will continue to decimate the environment and eliminate species far more than anything cats and rabbits could ever do.

7 WHAT THEN MUST WE DO?

Animals suffer for lots of reasons: They freeze to death in bad winters, get torn to shreds by predators, and grow old and starve because they can no longer hunt. If you put enough sad music on the screen as we witness such moments, doubtless many an eye will fill with tears. But such tears are easily remedied by a moment's reflection on the cycle of birth and death. If people are born, we will die. And the same goes for animals.

But there are other forms of suffering that do not go down so easy. The sea birds covered in oil, the fox gnawing off its leg in a fur hunter's trap, the long lines of cows waiting to be bludgeoned and then have their throats slit, the millions of mice to be used for God knows what, including the ones who have been genetically engineered to get cancer ("onco-mice," they are called).[20] Not to mention whole species, thousands of them, dying off because humans have taken their habitat, or brought in exotic species against which they have no evolved defenses, or just eaten too many.

What happens when we look at their pain? Quite often not a whole lot, for most of us do not bother to look. Or if we do what we see is an abstraction: *x* million killed in experiments, *x* thousands of species lost. But what if we do look, willing to accept whatever feelings arise, at – say – polar bears, who must cannibalize each other because global warming has melted so much ice that their ability to hunt is drastically curtailed. Magnificent creatures clad in thick white fur, superbly adapted to the frigid ice and snow, at home even in the sea. Mothers that protect their young, playful cubs, hunters of seals. They are dying – not from old age or struggles with predators or competition within the herd – but because we are killing them. Through global warming. Reckless sport hunting. Human-made toxins that build up in their flesh.

Ultimately, however, it is not just the suffering of the individual polar bears that gets to us, or even the potential loss of this majestic species, it is how hard it is to *look at ourselves*. To save the polar bear and all the rest how much would *we* have to change? How much of our economy, culture, and family life? How many laws would we have to pass? How many Thanksgiving get-togethers would feel (and taste) differently? Would we have to give up our dream of endless economic expansion so that we left some room for other species? Would we have to convince all the folks who believe that charbroiled steak equals a good time that tofu is just as good? Would we have to say that the whole human enterprise of the last 10,000 years – seeking more and more power, wealth, control, technical expertise, and shopping – should be (deeply, seriously, essentially) restrained?

Between the intensity of the pain we feel, the guilt over our own complicity, and the seeming impossibility of what *all* of us would have to transform, we are left in a difficult and contorted moral position. Guilt for ourselves and rage against "the others" who "just don't get it." The need to do something to "make it all stop" and the certain realization that

---

[20] Approximately 100 million mice per year. PETA Website. Accessed January 3, 2018, www.peta.org/issues/animals-used-for-experimentation/animals-laboratories/mice-rats-laboratories/.

we can't. A life that seems hard enough already, in which these animal rights types want to add in *more* things to feel upset about.

It is all too much.

There is no way out of this conflict and confusion. That is, no way that will lead to a simple fix of the problems, or a universally accepted way for people on different sides to come together and create a calm, reasoned, agreeable moral conversation. Like calling for women's equality in the seventeenth century (as a very few did), or demands to end slavery in 1800, according full respect for animals is just something that is not psychologically, and hence morally, possible now. Every minute of every day our civilization may indeed be committing monstrous crimes, and perhaps the anguished, "extremist" cries of animal rights activists are just what we need to wake us up. I suspect, however, that in this case whatever changes we make will necessarily be gradual, more based in quiet understanding and slow, moderate improvements than wholesale moral condemnations.

Probably some animal rights activists, and perhaps even the animals themselves, would think this is a cowardly cop-out in the face of mass slaughter. Perhaps it is. But we should remember that the long struggle for women's social and legal equality is far from over; and that while the slaves were freed in 1865, over a century later African Americans were still fighting for basic civil rights. In all the changes that have taken place, who knows how much was accomplished by anger, verbal violence, and coercive laws, and how much by the slow, patient work of moral conversation – by doing our best to connect despite bitter disagreement? Maybe reflecting on this history will tell us that even now we could be a little satisfied with limited gains that make life a little better, rather than clinging with rage and despair to an impossible ideal.

In the meantime, those of us who pay attention can at least acknowledge how upset this makes us. We can commiserate with other people's moral limits, knowing we have plenty ourselves. We can ask ourselves what the difference is between the golden retriever who sleeps on our bed at night and the bacon we eat for breakfast. And if we are really willing to feel the full range and intensity of our emotions about our animal cousins, to take in their pain and our responsibility for it, and to have compassion for them and for our fellow humans at the same time, who knows what might result?

5

Where Do We Draw the Line?

Limits and Virtues

I DISABILITY AND DEMOCRACY

Through relations of knowledge, trust, and intimate experience, people with severe intellectual disabilities (SID) can have representatives or guardians who speak for them. In this way SID folks can be part of the democratic conversation, at least in the sense that their needs and preferences can be made known to the larger community. In my own experience as coparent and colegal guardian of my thirty-two-year-old daughter, this process requires that I have extensive communicative experience of my daughter's life, that I am able to present social or even political issues to her in ways she can understand, that I can abstract from issues far too complex for her (the details of a new health care bill, which side to support in the Syrian Civil War) and present that which is essential in her mind: did, for instance, candidate Donald Trump mock a reporter who has (Esther's favored term) "special needs." Will some policy help the environment or hurt it? Who is, and who is not, in favor of her most precious political value – peace?

As our daughter, Esther receives all the care, protection, and love that my wife and I can provide. As a citizen of the United States and, more important, of Massachusetts, she is supported in a group home, has a day program in which she volunteers (with one-on-one support) at an old age/nursing home, and receives excellent health care. With our help she advocates for herself: complains if a staff person is disrespectful or negligent and asks for the kind of day program (volunteering with seniors) that she seeks.

Through a remarkable amount of courage and effort on her part, enormous financial support from the government, and tens of thousands of hours of labor on the part of her parents, she has a life in our society. She votes; gives talks in local elementary schools about having special needs; offers her thoughts, sometimes quite insightful and sometimes not, at our synagogue's Torah study; plays adapted basketball; and is part of a special needs singing group. In all this she has been helped by legal changes guaranteeing access, care, and education for persons with disabilities. But in truth few of those legal changes would have been of much help without the tireless advocacy of parents, teachers, friends, and medical specialists, who went far beyond the usual to help us, and, since turning twenty-two and leaving school, the social service agency that oversees both her residence and her day program.

Disability theorists have argued that democracy is not a universal and equal set of rights for individual, emotionally isolated, autonomous, self-sufficient, healthy adults. Rather, democracy depends on ongoing relations of trust, personal connections based in extensive personal knowledge, and help being present when needed. This is because as young children, diminished elders, people who go through difficult periods of ill health or emotional strain; as people who may be talented in some areas but quite "slow" in others; as modern people dependent on countless other people to produce our food, build our homes, and manage the technologies that transport us, keep us warm and amused, and support the economic structures – our entire lives are based in relationships.

And yet there is something quite particular about Esther. For a start, if Esther's enormously complex medical needs were broadly generalized, society would, if not cease to function, have to function very differently. The Esthers of the world, to the extent that they receive what they need, can only do so because they are a small fraction of the population.[1] This level of care is not universalizable.[2] As well my wife, a psychotherapist, and myself, a college teacher, have quantities of free time that are unheard of for the vast majority of workers.

How is this relevant to environmental ethics? Because I have argued that our ethical connections with nature are not rights, but bonds such as compassion, love, appreciation, gratitude, empathy, awe, and recognition. And that these connections, unlike the traditional conception of rights-based, autonomous, individualistic democracy, can be the basis

---

[1] For a variety of reasons, including pollution, the percentage is growing.

[2] Unless we abolished military expenditures and money wasted on junk consumerism.

for an ecological democracy – for a new conception of democracy that reaches beyond the purely human to the more than human.

What Esther shows us, however, is that whatever else this new model offers, it does *not* offer equality.

2 PROBLEMS WITH EQUALITY

Most of moral and political theory concentrates on equality and its surrogates: fairness, justice, overcoming prejudice, ending oppression, delegitimizing ideologies of domination. While virtue theory and feminist care ethic may be exceptions, they also spend a good deal of energy confronting the question of how not to be prejudiced or unfair. Yet moral life is filled with *inequality* – with unequal distributions of money, time, energy, empathy, understanding, desire, approval, and resources. We may aspire to a society in which every being receives the love and care they need. We may remember Marx' promise of communism: "From each according to his ability to each according to his needs." We may, like the Bodhisattva of Mahayana Buddhism, feel the sufferings and the joys of others as if they were our own. But in reality, I give far more to Esther than to anyone else I know, and the government does as well.

Let us turn to the broader framework of the human relation with nature.

In a hurry to make an important job interview you back out of your driveway much too fast. There is a sudden and frightening thud as your car hits something.

What is it?

At that moment, I suspect, all talk of nature's equality with the human, all critiques of anthropocentrism, all affinity with the biosphere might shrink to the wish that it be, if possible, a casually placed bicycle or a potted plant. But if not, that it be a squirrel or even a neighbor's dog rather than a child.

Does this reveal an unjustified moral hierarchy in which people always come out on top? If so, it is a moral pattern to be found virtually everywhere – even among the vast majority of environmentalists. And this is true not just for isolated accidents, but for our entire way of life. Each person lives in a place where there used to be plants, insects, birds, and small mammals. Almost all the food we eat comes from an agriculture that displaces native species. The mechanisms of modernization, wealth accumulation, and just getting by routinely require that we privilege people over the rest of life. And with the possible exception of indigenous peoples, this is as true of poorer countries as wealthy ones – especially given how much such countries are subject to polluting and destructive resource extraction and export-oriented monoculture.

Is the primacy of the human a bad thing? In *some* ways, perhaps not – and I say that despite my long-standing commitment to the environmentalist cause. (Notice the emphasis on "some" – a point to which I will return.)

For the moment, though, we can just observe that there are some exceptions to this "people first" rule. There is a religious tradition (the Jains) in which the pinnacle of spiritual development is self-annihilation as an alternative to the destruction (eating, displacing, using) of any other life form. Some people might prefer the death of a stranger's child to their own dog and might not care very much for other people's dogs. Or if they are orthodox dog lovers, might well be unconcerned with the cows they barbecue on July 4 or the turkeys they roast on Thanksgiving. And even the rare case of the extreme nature lover who loves all of nature and can barely spare a thought to humans, has another hierarchy, like the anthropocentric one, only reversed.

Preferences and inconsistencies abound. People will mobilize to push stranded whales off the beach while opiate addicts, stranded in their own way, lack for treatment. Bird lovers put out bird food while homeless people are starving nearby. Dog owners, I'm one, feed their tens of millions of pet dogs on the flesh of millions of dead animals of other species. And note that even the people who feed birds, keep dogs, or try to save the whales, will be living in many ways that privilege humans over the rest of nature.

This inconsistency applies within our relations to nature as well. In Louisiana a small but devoted activist group labors to preserve bird species from habitat loss and pollution. But they also seek to use the resorted habitat and cleaned waters to fish. They love the birds, but don't extend that love to the myriad fish they seek to catch and eat.[3] At a small college in California a researcher devotes her life to trying to save an obscure butterfly from extinction – while the college itself specializes in training students to exploit animals in zoos and movies.[4] Even in the

---

[3] Justin Nobel, "Louisiana Is Restoring Its Barrier Islands to Defend Against Hurricanes and Rising Seas," *Audubon* (Fall 2017).

[4] Jon Mooallem, *Wild Ones: A Sometimes Dismaying, Weirdly Reassuring Story about Looking at People Looking at Animals in America* (New York: Penguin, 2013), pp. 154–160.

deepest arenas of domination, there is inconsistency. The Humane Slaughter Act, which limits how animals are to be treated in slaughter-houses, does not cover chickens. Mice, rats, and birds are exempt from the Animal Welfare Act.[5]

There are cases of a kind of in-your-face rhetoric in which radical environmentalists claim to side with animals over people.[6] How much of this is sincere and how much simply a conscious overstatement is another question. None of these folks, as far as I am aware, starved themselves, stopped driving or heating their homes, or did without any basic creature comforts for themselves or their families to make more room for other species.

For the most part, these decidedly unequal ways of relating to other beings need not be justified or even articulated. They are taken for granted, embedded in a thousand cultural traditions, legal codes, and personal habits. Animals will starve during the winter, and we will save the people. "Weeds" are pulled so we can widen the driveway or spruce up the baseball field. Countless square miles of forest or marsh are leveled so that we can build new roads, malls, housing, and places for recreation.

So current moral practice is generally and for the most part, people first. For the rare exceptions, there is generally some other kind of deep inconsistency – some individual animals or species or particular locations (a pond, a woods) before people, people before the rest.

But the fundamental inequalities that necessarily arise do not mean that our relations with nature – or indeed with other people – lack essential elements of ethical connection. I will try to show how this is so by focusing on inequalities of love and knowledge in the context of the sacred and by employing virtues ethics as a source of human guidance and restraint.

[5] Kim Starwood, "Animal Rights: Moral Crusade or Social Movement?" in John Sorenson, ed., *Critical Animal Studies: Thinking the Unthinkable* (Toronto: Canadian Scholars Press, 2014), p. 302.

[6] In a provocative short story collection, Mark Martin, ed., several authors proclaim that in a conflict between people and bears *I'm With the Bears* (London: Verso, 2011). Poet Robinson Jeffers suggested that "I'd rather – except the penalties – kill a man than a hawk." "Hurt Hawks," Tim Hunt, ed., *The Collected Poetry of Robinson Jeffers*, Vol. 1 (Palo Alto, CA: Stanford University Press, 1988), p. 377.

3 THE INCONSISTENT SACRED; LIMITATIONS OF LOVE AND KNOWLEDGE

The sacred, we may remember, is that which is precious beyond measure, experienced as a gift, an object of most profound and sincere gratitude – that is the sacred. Thus defined the concept, while originating in religious contexts, need not be limited to them. How can our sense of the sacred shape our relation to nature – and how is it necessarily inconsistent? Here is an example from my life.

Although I live within the city of Boston, I am fortunate to be just a few blocks from a lovely pond. A mile and a half around, surrounded by trees, graced by turtles, seagulls, geese, cormorants, the occasional heron, and a few magnificent white swans, the pond reflects the changing sky of moon, sun, snow, and rain and offers a space for joggers, lovers, pensive dog walkers, and frisky dogs. It serves as a source of natural beauty for harried, overworked, chronically anxious city dwellers and as a kind of emotional transfer station. People go to the pond feeling depressed, at a loss, hemmed in by life – and come back feeling a bit more hopeful, a bit lighter in spirit and mind, a bit more – strange to say – alive.

I have been fortunate to have seen a fair amount of this planet: trekking in the Himalayas, Colorado, Montana, and Idaho; enjoying beaches on Cape Cod, southern India, the Mediterranean's Formentera, Mexico, and northern California. I've see deer and yak, hawks and eagles, coyotes and dolphins and whales. All these are magnificent, all worthy of life.

But Jamaica Pond is *my* sacred space above all others. I've lived near it virtually all of my adult life and turned to it countless times for recreation, pleasure, and emotional and spiritual sustenance. I know each curve of the path that surrounds it; the order of the trees flowering in spring; the colors that will emerge in the fall; what it looks like by moonlight when it's frozen in February; and how the far side, a wooded hillside, glows with sunset colors. I've taken countless "nature" photographs of it; jogged (increasingly slowly over the years) around it thousands of times, and shared excited moments with strangers by pointing out turtles sunning themselves on a fallen branch or a blue heron standing in the shallows.

As much as I've enjoyed the other places I've been, nothing has touched my heart as much as these comparatively undramatic few hundred acres.

As with the sacred, so with knowledge.

I grieve for the destruction of the rainforest and the beaches covered with plastic refuse in the isolated islands of the Pacific. But these I know only from secondhand sources: pictures on my computer screen, articles from journalists. But if something goes wrong in the pond, I know it. When a beloved tree falls from age or illness, I run my hands over the trunk and whisper a blessing. When pollution was washed in from unusually high rainfall, I could smell it. I cannot love, or care, or know any other spot on this earth as I do this one. As I must love and care for my own children in a way I cannot with anyone else's, and as I will walk my dog, and take her to the vet if she is ill, and perhaps one day rest my hand on her head as she dies, so my love for the pond area is central in a way that no other place can be.

It has often been said that we must know nature to love it and do both in order to protect it. But that necessarily means that we will know and love some parts far more than others.

For I am limited: in length of years, in attention, in capacity for both knowledge and love. And I believe that almost everyone else is too.

And so *of course* we are inconsistent, play favorites, give more to some people than others, more to our own species than others, or more to our chosen pets or species or spots than others. More to our families than our neighbors. More to our country than other countries. There is nothing unethical about this inequality, unless we think that we should love without exception, equally to all. That is the life of a saint, or an abstraction of ethical theory. It is not the lives of the rest of us.

And this inequality does not just arise in our personal lives, but in the larger settings of social policy as well. For practical reasons, not every person or every group can get equal consideration or support. Without a transformation of our society so dramatic that it is beyond the reach of anything but political or spiritual fantasy (an appealing one, but a fantasy nevertheless), some will make out better than others.

We may offer government-sponsored healthcare, but the rich will still have far better resources than the poor. When we try to redress past injustices with programs such as affirmative action that will privilege some groups over others, and perhaps disadvantage many who had little or no role in the initial injustice. Noisy highways will afflict some neighborhoods rather than others; groups with social capital will be able to resist pollution far better than those who lack it. Some religious holidays will be days off for everyone and receive recognition in the broader culture; others will not. We can make sure everyone gets an attorney if they can't afford one, but does anyone believe that an overworked public defender handling multiple cases at the same time is as effective a high-priced specialist handling just one case?

We can do our best to make sure that all receive jury trials and get the right to vote, and that even celebrity sexual predators are punished. We can outlaw slavery and discrimination in education or housing. But ingrained social structures will limit all of these: juries will reflect social prejudices; gerrymandering and voter suppression laws will limit the electoral power of racial minorities. It is still often a struggle to get sexual violence taken seriously.

In the realm of environmental concern, comparable inequalities arise. The cuddly or awesome animals – pandas, elephants – get groups dedicated to their well-being (or at least survival); and the rats in labs, the mice bred to get cancer, or the pigs genetically engineered to carry far too much weight on their arthritis-laden joints get virtually no concern – at least no effective concern – whatsoever. Focusing on one issue leaves out all the others. Or else the concern expressed is so broad and vague – partnership with nature, reverence for life – that no particular concern is addressed at all.

4 A LIFE WORTH LIVING

We would like to guarantee my neighbor's right not to be killed and eaten; but I, and everyone else including the most principled vegan, will kill plants, insects, and animals through participating in the modern world. We can, as Donaldson and Kymlicka[7] do, list a whole series of duties that we owe animals; e.g., extensive and equal medical care, the right to be fully present in public spaces, a complete end to virtually all forms of animal exploitation, not inflicting noise in the ocean and thereby disturbing sea mammals. Fulfilling these duties would require far more resources than we have, and certainly more than we would be willing to expend. The same is true if we include plants, natural features such as rivers or mountains, ecosystems, or the entire earth. Some ecosystems and individuals will suffer so that we can do what is important to us – in the same way some people receive less care, consideration, comfort, and protection than the rest of us.

Is there nevertheless a way to ask at what point human suffering may be preferable to nonhuman suffering? To say: "We privilege people over

---

[7] Sue Donaldson and Will Kymlicka, *Zoopolis: A Political Theory of Animal Rights* (New York: Oxford University Press, 2011).

nature and over most animals; we privilege our family, friends, little town, or cultural group over others. The rich and powerful, no matter what any of us claim, will continue to have it better than the rest of us. That is regrettable but inevitable. But, in this policy, with these actions, you have gone too far."

How would we begin to draw the line regarding our treatment of nature? Leaving aside the question of social inequality, I will take it for granted that it is good that humans, like sparrows or dolphins, are alive. And in the case of the kind of species we are, this means not only food, shelter, and (within limits) reproduction, but also a culture: science, spirituality, art, creativity, and political life.

But does the goodness of life we share with all other species include an acceptance of a form of life that is destructive to ourselves as well as to countless individuals, species, and ecosystems? Is there a source of restraint, of reasonable limits to human action, that does not depend on the absolute equivalence of all forms of life – an equivalence that cannot be observed in any case because the consumption and displacement of other forms of life is essential to ours? Is it possible to find a basis for restraint not in some competing rights, or in ranking living beings so that we think it important to love golden retrievers and protect gorillas and simultaneously trample on trout? Perhaps the answer could be found not in more detailed descriptions of fish and pine trees to see if they "really" deserve moral consideration, but in individual and collective self-examination.[8]

Let us begin with suffering. Entire moral systems have been built on the assumption that suffering is bad and should be avoided and happiness (defined in various ways) should be promoted. But this framework is always, and necessarily, conditioned by our assessment of what is causing the suffering. A person's suffering must meet certain basic conditions for us to see it as a reason to condemn or change the acts that lead to the suffering. When slavery was abolished, slaveholders suffered greatly: what a loss of money, of status, of mint julips on the porch while the darkies worked in the fields. But slavery was abolished nevertheless, and I doubt if any abolitionists gave the slave-owners' very

---

[8] For an argument that moral concern should be extended beyond people and animals to plants, see Andrew F. Smith, *A Critique of the Moral Defense of Vegetarianism* (New York: Palgrave Macmillan, 2016). It is, of course, commonplace of many native world views.

real suffering a second thought – because justice takes priority over attachment to an unjust way of life.

Consider another example. Addicts always want more – and suffer greatly from not getting it. Yet while we might offer heroin addicts medical treatment, counseling, or a word of reassurance, we are not motivated to meet what they think are their needs by getting them more dope. Instead, we make a judgment that meeting their desires is not rational, will not help them, and will simply be part of an endlessly increasing cycle.

Suppose we came to believe that current forms of life in the developed nations (and some "developing" ones such as India and China) are not only immoral but, necessarily, unavoidably destructive. We would have to make this case in detail, specifying the harmful effects of such things as what is being produced and how it is being distributed; the dominant social values being communicated; what types of people receive public respect and political power; how resources are used; how people work and what they are working for; the overall health of human relationships of family, romantic love, and friendship; and the creation of an ever-growing surplus population of unemployed and refugees from climate change.

Thus rather than arguing that a particular action or policy is bad because it violates the rights of trees or hawks, I am offering another criteria: the action and policy must not stem from a form of life that produces misery for the very people who are practicing it. When we want to do something, and the motivations for that action are unsustainable, addictive, or consumerist, then the mere fact that we "want to" is not a sufficient motivation. When the action or policy has to do with exploiting animals, or clearing a forest, or using five hundred billion plastic bags and thirty-five billion plastic water bottles a year,[9] we can ask: Is this a desire that will support a reasonable, fulfilling, self-respecting life? And if it does not, isn't that reason to reflect and change the way in which we have been living?

Consider the nearby wetland, 37 acres of marsh, home to an endangered species of butterfly, offering the usual ecosystem services of water purification and containment of excess water from storms. There is also

---

[9] EcoWatch Website. Accessed May 21, 2017. www.ecowatch.com/22-facts-about-plastic-pollution-and-10-things-we-can-do-about-it-1881885971.html.

a raised platform from which water birds can be seen and a well-used path that allows walkers to skirt the outside of the area, occasionally experiencing the rabbits, muskrats, turtles, and snakes; the changing foliage of the seasons; and the sounds of birds, insects, and leaves tossed by wind.

Now consider Mr. Big, the local real estate developer, who wants to turn the area into an upscale condo development. If we say that all the beings that live in the marsh have a right to continue, Mr. Big can easily reply: "Don't you realize that everywhere you live, eat out, and shop used to be something like this marsh? Want to give back the land you've taken? Didn't think so. And think of the jobs the work will provide and how the increased real estate taxes will help the local school system. You really think some acres of mud and some snakes are worth more than educating our children and giving their parents work?"

Mr. Big has a point. Anyone reading this book benefits in some way from what we have done to the rest of the earth. But just because something has gone on in the past does not mean we can't resist it being repeated. Here are some questions that can be part of that resistance, questions designed to illuminate the human consequences of living without ecological limits or care.

Why do we need more condos? Is there no rundown housing stock that could be renovated? Does the constantly expanding size of the typical US home reflect real human needs or a compulsive attraction to conspicuous consumption? Are we rewarding wealthy people whose jobs are environmentally destructive in other ways? How will the people who buy the expensive condos pay for them? Will their jobs be fulfilling in any way? Will the economic pressure of the mortgage lead them to other forms of damaging consumption or to stress self-medicated with alcohol, drugs, compulsive gambling, and sexual infidelity? What will the condos be made of? Is the manufacturing process toxic or benign? Can the materials be recycled? Will public transportation to the area be an option – or will it require more driving, greenhouse gases, and traffic noise, yet fewer places for people to walk? What will the loss of the marsh do to local water control from the ever-larger storms? What will it do to the psychology of people who now go there for peace and quiet and the by now well-established psychological healing powers of a natural setting? When we look at what the marsh contains, do we not feel that something of value would be lost if it were obliterated? How happy, satisfied, or content can we be if we do not recognize this? Doesn't virtue of any kind require that we recognize

things of significant value – and in the case of environmental virtue that
we see the value in nature?[10]

5 SPIRITUAL VIRTUE

These questions rest in the belief that there are better or worse ways to
live, that by now we should have seen enough of our current social form
to know that it is deeply unsatisfying in countless ways. There is no dearth
of social psychological research to support this claim.[11]

In answer to the question of what uses of nature are permitted and
which are not, I suggest this standard: the ones that reflect spiritual virtues
of self-awareness, acceptance, gratitude, compassion, and love. *Self-awareness* would require that we ask: *Why* are we doing what we are
doing? What needs, values, and hidden psychological wounds prompt our
individual action? What social forces – in our educational system, the
mass media, and our religious institutions – are encouraging us to think
and feel as we do? What illusions are bred in us? For instance, that success
measured in possessions, fame, or power will lead to happiness. This type
of illusion fuels relentless economic expansion and technological and
substance abuse forms of escape. An alternative can be found in *gratitude*
for what we have rather than an endless, addictive drive for more. And in
a *compassionate* connection to other people and other life forms, rather
than a personal identity that can disregard the consequences of our form
of life on others. A *loving* connection is the surest path to human satisfaction – to other people and to the world around us. When we consider how
much time and money is expended on domestic animals, and the rise of
the use of therapy animals in different contexts, is it not obvious that as a
culture modernity is suffering from a lack of love? Finally, without a basic
acceptance of certain realities – that we are all subject to aging, illness and
death, that satisfying every whim is a distraction from the essential tasks

---

[10] Holmes Rolston, III, "Environmental Virtue Ethics: Half the Truth but Dangerous as the
Whole," in Ronald Sandler and Philip Cafaro, eds., *Environmental Virtue Ethics*
(Totawa, NJ: Rowman and Littlefield, 2005), pp. 61–78.

[11] Anxiety or depressive disorders together afflict nearly one-quarter of the United States.
Forty-five million Americans suffer from some sort of mental illness. "Data on Behavioral
Health," American Psychological Association Website. Accessed January 16, 2018,
www.apa.org/helpcenter/data-behavioral-health.aspx. Despite the remarkable collective
wealth of our society, only a third of Americans report being happy. Alexander Sifferlan,
"Here's How Happy Americans Are Right Now," *Time Magazine* Website. Accessed
January 15, 2018, http://time.com/4871720/how-happy-are-americans/.

of life, that kindness and generosity make us feel better than gated communities or a gated heart – will we not continue to build a society based in meaningless violence, addiction, fear, and depression? Alongside nature, the poor, victims of military aggression and racial, ethnic, and gender hatred suffer in the service of a society geared to drastic inequality, consumerist distractions, and unaccountable political power.

Many environmental thinkers or activists might question my approach. "Once again," they might say, "you are making human fulfillment the measure. This stress on human virtue is just a thinly disguised anthropocentrism. What if human fulfillment required the continued annihilation of marshlands and all their inhabitants? Or mass 'produced' chicken? You would have to endorse it. Ecosystems and individual animals, life outside of human happiness, they all have *inherent value*, whether we like it or not, whether recognizing it makes us happy or miserable. It's not all about *us*!"

Given the position I tried to develop in this book already, how could I disagree? I cannot. Yet there are at least two things that can be said in defense of the virtue approach as a way of limiting human actions and redirecting our environmentally destructive civilization.

First, notice that because humans are part of the environment, our integral connections to nature as obvious as each breath, any environmental destroying civilization is one that is destroying people as well. Not all at once, and not equally, but surely. If "over 1 million seabirds and 100,000 sea mammals are killed by pollution every year," it should come as no surprise that estimates of people dying from the same cause range from three to nine million.[12] There cannot be a society that meets our authentic, long-term physical and psychological needs and continues to extinguish other forms of life and torture, enslave, and consume animals. It may be theoretically, abstractly possible that humans could live fulfilled lives while wreaking devastation on the rest of the natural world, but it is not actually, empirically possible. And this is true because, despite the ways in which we are culturally and technologically distinct from the rest of the planet, we are also part of it. And thus, as Horkheimer and Adorno observed, if nature is considered as an inherently valueless collection of

---

[12] Birds and Animals: "Eleven Facts about Pollution," Do Something Website. Accessed January 3, 2018, www.dosomething.org/us/facts/11-facts-about-pollution. Pamela Das and Richard Horton, "Pollution, Health, and the Planet: Time for Decisive Action," *The Lancet* Website. Accessed January 3, 2018, www.thelancet.com/journals/lancet/article/PIIS0140-6736(17)32588-6/fulltext.

resources to be dominated, humans too will be considered in just that way. Recognition of the value of life either extends from people to nature, or it will be withdrawn from people as well.[13]

Second, the development of virtue is not a distinct issue from that of recognizing and implementing the demands of justice, recognizing rights, or extending care, but an integral part. Justice, rights, and care without spiritual virtue are impossible or, at least, very partial. Recognizing the inherent value of the Other – whether that Other is defined in terms of gender, race, nationality, ethnicity, or species – requires the ability and willingness to see the value in other people or other species and to sacrifice short-term pleasures for long term, stable, flourishing. But without self-awareness we are unlikely to recognize consumerist desires for what they are: insatiable patterns of lack that motivate relentless assaults on natural resources while keeping us permanently anxious and ill at ease. Without informed gratitude for what we have, we will miss the ways in which trees, birds, clean water, and a relatively stable climate are essential to our economic and emotional well-being. Without compassion for others, we will never understand them well enough to see when they are being oppressed, nor recognize how much we have in common with beings whose interests and experiences we have dismissed as both essentially different and essentially inferior.

I call compassion, awareness, and the rest spiritual virtues, while others might call them simply "moral" or "psychological." For me "spiritual" implies a serious challenge to the conventional ego, the "normal" well-adjusted person of society, and offers instead a radically different understanding of human identity and fulfillment.

Here is one small example: "Who is rich," asks the Talmud. And answers: "The person who is satisfied with what they have."[14] If this classically spiritual teaching were assimilated to popular consciousness, a host of personal and collective forms of behavior would shift. Far less energy would pour into the endless drive to economic expansion, the lure of shiny new toys, or expensive consumerist experiences. We would not measure social well-being by gross national product rather than any reasonable index of satisfaction. As well, the individual pursuit of wealth

---

[13] Max Horkheimer and Theodor Adorno, *The Dialectic of Enlightenment* (New York: Seabury, 1974). This is just as true as the fact that turning some people into slaves would not, in the long run, produce happiness for the rest.

[14] Avot 4:1. A common theme in world religions. One Christian version is Jesus' admonition (Matthew 10:21) that before a rich person could follow him, the person's wealth would have to be given to the poor.

and the collective drive toward economic expansion creates a psychological compulsion that makes awareness of the immediate *and* long-term consequences of one's actions hard to impossible. Never mind what we are doing to the air or the climate, we must build new factories, create gigantic, energy consuming servers for Google, and get new phones every year. In China they eat far more meat and drive far more cars than they used to, but it is common for young people to grow up never, ever, seeing a star.[15]

The virtue of compassion is frequently praised as a source of holiness in religious terms and deep satisfaction by secular psychology.[16] As a response to the world, compassion is easiest when it doesn't cost us much and when the object of compassion is someone we care about. It gets progressively harder when the object of compassion feels increasingly different, alien, or even antagonistic, and when our own reserves of responsiveness are diminished. It is easy to feel compassion for the victims of a terrorist attack, nearly impossible to feel it for the alienated, rageful, deluded attackers. The suffering of dogs – especially the ones with beautiful long hair and deep soulful eyes – calls forth a widespread, immediate response. Dirty, mangy, flea-bitten mutts do less for us; coyotes, which threaten our pets, typically not at all.

What does it mean to feel compassion for nature? In the case of the "higher" mammals this is not too hard to understand. Like us, they have a nervous system capable of experiencing excruciating pain, are social and often family oriented, are capable of emotional bonds. What about snakes or lizards, frogs or bumblebees? What about trees, fleas, or jellyfish? As far as we can tell none of these have emotional lives, and in the case of trees it is doubtful whether they have, in any reasonable sense of the term, desires that can be frustrated or painful sensations. What does compassion mean for beings so different from ourselves?

Perhaps only a realization of the shared realities of life. The energies of the tree reach up toward the sun and root down into the earth for nourishment and physical support. The tree, just like ourselves, expresses an energy that seeks to engage with its surroundings and continue on doing the things that it needs to do. It seeks to live. And in a variety of

---

[15] I have had students from China report this to me.
[16] For one of many summaries of psychological benefits, Emma Seppala, "The Compassionate Mind," Association for Psychological Science Website. Accessed January 12, 2018, www.psychologicalscience.org/observer/the-compassionate-mind.

ways, though probably not any of them that we would call "emotional," it is connected to other trees in solidarity and support.

Is that fundamental reality enough for us to recognize a commonality despite all the ways in which it is different from people? Is it enough that we are fellow voyagers on what seems to be an extremely rare voyage of life? And is it enough to know that just like ourselves, its time on the voyage is limited – that there will come a time when its roots will no longer be able to hold, its ability to make leaves will dwindle, its trunk will splinter? Is that commonality enough for us to care whether it lives or dies – and whether what we do or fail to do contributes to its health or ensures its death?

The psychological value of compassion is the way it takes us out of our ego – out of the part of ourselves that is engaged in the never-ending pursuit of pleasure, power, profit, excitement, reassurance, recognition, and status and that is too often prey to anxiety, depression, endless grief, rage, self-hatred, and addiction. By thinking out of ourselves, and into the reality of another, our own compulsions may be lessened.[17] Compassion is thus a possible source of the well-being of the person manifesting it, and certainly, a virtue the practice of which is likely to make the practitioner much better company – not only for people, but for trees as well.

We can ask: How much does any action or any given social policy manifest compassion? When we buy the shrink-wrapped hamburger "meat" in the supermarket are we aware that this is actually the flesh of a dead animal murdered for our pleasure and the owner's profit? And that the industrial farms where the cow was bred has effects on global warming and local water quality that hurts other living beings? When ground is broken for a new parking lot or condo development, can we think of all the life cut down and scraped away even as we think of the jobs, tax revenues, and recreation that may result? When racially oppressed groups find their neighborhoods vastly overburdened with pollution, what kind of community – or lack of community – does our unthinking acceptance of environmental racism create?

While compassion can be a challenge, what is the alternative? Without compassion how can we connect to others except as objects of use, enemies to be conquered, or fellow bargainers we hope to better in deal? Without compassion we are walled off from the experience of other people, and walled into our own limited, often unpleasant minds. Is such

---

[17] Out-of-control compassion, of course, can turn into a lack of boundaries, codependence, and authoritarian paternalism.

an isolation a source of security or, really, of loneliness and anxiety so deep we must flee into distractions to escape?

Perhaps if we recognized that compassion is a partial antidote to the psychological afflictions of modernity, we could exercise it in a sufficiently expansive way to include the more than human.

Three limiting conditions to this line of thought need to be acknowledged.

I am clearly relying on a certain image of what human psychological health and fulfillment look like.[18] Other images might stress personal accomplishment, thrilling adventures, religious orthodoxy, or the accumulation of fame, power, and pleasure. Among these, only religious orthodoxy has any kind of overlap with the stress on spiritual virtue I've offered. In response, we might simply accept that people get to choose what "health" or "fulfillment" are for them, and let them see, over time, whether they are right. On the other hand, there seems to be an enormous amount of evidence that people are happier, all things being equal,[19] when they are grateful, compassionate, loving, and so forth. If we are to consult evidence, it would seem the evidence is more on my side than that of Ayn Rand, Hugh Hefner, Donald Trump, or the surfers globe-trotting in search of the next perfect wave.

Next, compassion must in many cases, and particularly in ecological ones, be joined with knowledge. Buddhist tradition speaks of "upaya" – loosely translated as "skill in means." We cannot act to lessen the suffering of another unless we have some idea of why the being suffers and what would reduce the suffering. What is killing the trees? Poisoning the villagers? Making so many in the United States depressed and anxious? Just seeing the pain, and wanting to help, is not enough. And this leads us back to the way love and knowledge go together in our relation to the ecological crisis.

Further, and often revealed through upaya itself, we often find ourselves torn by the reality of countless objects of compassion. Children starving, young girls kidnapped by terrorists, civilians killed by drones, island nations threatened by rising seas caused by climate change, an aging parent needing help, children with Down syndrome or cerebral

---

[18] In a groundbreaking article G. E. M. Anscombe stressed the necessary relationship between ethical theory and what she called "moral psychology" – beliefs about the social and psychological conditions of human fulfillment "Modern Moral Philosophy," *Philosophy* 33, no. 124 (January 1958). This approach has been developed by philosophers as different in orientation as Alasdair MacIntyre and Rosalind Hursthouse.

[19] I.e., if we are not being tortured, starving to death, watching our family die, etc.

palsy lonely for companionship, countless people without health care or clean water. And the more we exercise compassion in one direction – for our family or the wider world, for people or whales or rainforests – the less, we often feel, we must give anyone else: human or not.

There is no solution to this dilemma, except to note, with the Talmud of two thousand years ago, the lesson that "You are not obligated to complete the work, but neither are you free to desist from it."[20] This "solution" is harder to come by now than it was when this lesson was offered because knowledge of the global range of suffering, displacement, and destruction is available on every phone and laptop. Yet here the virtue of acceptance comes into play. This is not a recommendation for passivity, renouncing the world, or adopting some metaphysical belief that it is all part of God's plan or that everything will turn out all right in the end.[21] Rather, it is a hard-headed ability to realize that the grief or anger the world provokes in us do not change the way the world is. It just *is* the fact that the world contains, along with many other things, endless amounts of suffering, human and nonhuman alike.

Despite these limitations, the role of virtue in human happiness and contentment remains. It surely is an argument that we should not cut down the rainforest or continue fracking because people will be injured, and trees have inherent value. And it is *also* an argument to suggest that the form of life that is driving us to these actions is also driving us more than a little crazy. Given the severity of the situation we are in, and the wide diversity in what people will respond to, we need every argument we've got.

[20] *Pirkei Avot:* 2:21.
[21] Or: we are all engaged in some cosmic educational experience, the end of which will be universal connection, love, and bliss.

6

Guilt and Responsibility

1 THE HEART OF THE PROBLEM

Abolitionists didn't own slaves; peace activists don't join the army. A man can only consider himself a feminist if he does his share of the housework, interrupts his friends' sexist jokes, and can accept female authority. It is commonplace that moral inconsistency is often seen as moral hypocrisy and that few things are more ethically repulsive than a person who preaches a moral principle and constantly violates it. That is why, for example, sex abuse from the Catholic Church is particularly disturbing. It is not just the abuse, but the abuse coming from an institution that is constantly proclaiming its ethical stature.

And thus the dilemma faced by the vast majority of environmentalists in the industrialized world, including the author of this book and – I would imagine – virtually everyone who is reading it. If I am so upset about global warming, why is it that I have commuted from my home in Boston to my university – an hour each way – for thirty-five years? My diet has moral drawbacks, as does the food served at almost all environmental conferences, as do the ecological effects of the planes environmental studies professors fly on to get to conferences. We all use power from the same grid, the grid largely dependent on coal and oil and gas, on oil leaks at sea and fracking-caused gas leaks and earthquakes on land. The casual ease with which I switch on my computer to write today's 2000 words for this book is my connection, and in a way my commitment, to a globally destructive energy system.

Environmentalists, no matter how strong their critique of the ways things are, remain enmeshed in the very system we oppose.

For poor villagers whose environment is poisoned by oil extraction, or urban slum dwellers choking on leaded fumes from taxis transporting the rich, such issues don't really apply. Even in the wealthy United States native peoples are afflicted by uranium mining, and African Americans and Hispanics are many times more likely to have lead in their drinking water, pollutants in their air, and toxic facilities in their neighborhoods.[1] All such people are disproportionately bearing the costs of our environmental system, and their own contributions tend to be small.

But many middle-class people who, like me, come from neighborhoods that are not disproportionately polluted, drive cars, take trips by plane, and consume more goods and energy than they really, actually need.

What of us?

2 BETWEEN GUILT AND RESPONSIBILITY?

The moral inconsistencies of most environmentalists, certainly including myself, may help us understand a few features of moral life. Some of these are common to moral life in general, and some, I suspect, have a particularly important place in the context of the environmental crisis.

First, any moral concern exists alongside other moral concerns, practical daily needs, and any given person's level of energy and need for rest and amusement. For example, I do not commute to work out of choice or environmental laziness, but because Esther's care has required that my family stay close to Boston's wealth of medical resources. My obligations to Esther as my daughter come in conflict with my obligation to limit my contributions to global warming. We face a variety of moral ills: domination by race, gender, and ethnicity; violence from religious fanatics and secular states; callous disregard for people with disabilities and the aged. While a serious social theory will often link some of these issues – e.g., in cases like environmental racism, or pollution's role in birth defects – practical action often isolates one concern from another.

Besides moral conflicts, there is also simple human weakness. I like to think I have done my best morally in life, though I certainly have not been a moral example to anyone. Sometimes, however, I am simply

---

[1] Writings on environmental racism/justice are vast. Here is a short summary of some facts: Jasmine Bell, "5 Things to Know about Communities of Color and Environmental Justice." Center for American Progress Website. Accessed January 15, 2018, www.amer icanprogress.org/issues/race/news/2016/04/25/136361/5-things-to-know-about-commu nities-of-color-and-environmental-justice/. The pioneering work of Robert Bullard is a way into the topic: http://drrobertbullard.com/.

self-indulgent and uncaring. As much as we despise modernity's environmental consequences, even some of the most passionate environmentalists
like some of the luxuries and toys it provides: a pleasant drive in a not
particularly fuel-efficient car on a beautiful fall day, fruits from South
America in the winter, air conditioning, meat.

And that is perhaps one source of the dilemma of guilt and responsibility in an age of environmental crisis. Very few of us are moral heroes;
most of us have other moral commitments; not too many are willing to
sacrifice all our free time or freedom (if we were to be jailed for civil
disobedience) for the cause. As well, there are countless occasions when
my moral self takes a back seat to fatigue, a need for distraction, or plain
laziness.[2]

3 GUILT AND RESPONSIBILITY

Consider Diane, a secretary at a major energy company, who commutes
to work in her aging gas guzzler, pays no attention to phantom power in
her home, and eats lots of meat. She is certainly a contributor to environmental problems. Yet as we look closer we see that her salary is low, her
rent is high, she is constantly pushed to work harder, and on weekends
and evenings she frequently helps her aging parents with shopping,
driving to appointments, and daily chores. When the doctor clears her
throat and starts talking about treatments for breast cancer, and Diane
remembers how close she grew up to a plastics processing facility, we see
that besides being a miniscule cause of the environmental crisis, she is *also*
one of its victims.

Contrast Diane with Richard, the boss of her boss's boss, a high-level
executive in the company. His job is to convince the public that fracking
does not pollute groundwater, increase earthquakes, or cancel out its own
climate advantages over coal and oil by the potent climate effects of the
methane that escapes during routine extraction processes. Richard has the
salary (and probably the accumulated wealth) and educational background to live an ecologically responsible life. He could pay for local,

---

[2] There are self-sacrificing heroes of the environmental movement: Ken Sara-Wiwa
(murdered by the Nigerian government for defending the natives of the Ogoni peninsula
from oil development), Chico Mendes, (murdered for defending the Brazilian rainforest),
or the dedicated, mainly female, and often uneducated pioneers of the US toxics
movement.

organic food, and drive an electric car. More important, his actual liveli-hood depends on his active defense of practices he knows are damaging. He is not simply consuming what's out there, as Diane is, he is helping make sure that what's out there stays out there – and that, if anything, there is more of it.

We can make a number of different analogies to describe the morality of Richard's (and comparable people in other industries) effects on the environment. He is like the people who made the trains run on time to take Jews to the gas chambers, or like someone who sets off a bomb in a crowded place but times it to go off 20 years later (cancer being, after all, as deadly as a bomb).

If Diane is, like most of us, *responsible*, then Richard is, as only a small fraction of us are, *guilty*.[3] Whatever justification he offers ("Others do worse things, I work hard and deserve to make a lot of money, I'm not really in charge, I'm just following orders, if I didn't do this someone else would") are morally bankrupt. Given his education and social position, he could find other work. As a highly educated white man, he would neither starve nor become homeless. There is no excuse for what he does. And consider that while it may be hard to connect emotionally to the abstractions of climate change, people like Richard are also responsible for the role of polluting chemicals in the nearly one-third of America's children who suffer from the "new pediatric morbidity" of asthma, autism, cancer, severe allergies, birth defects, mental retardation, cleft palate, and disordered endocrine systems. This modern industrial assault means that a "whole generation of kids has been trashed by causes that are preventable."[4]

Diane, on the other hand, has few employment opportunities and finds herself constantly exhausted from her work, commute, care of her parents, and the cancer diagnosis. She has not been educated and has little knowledge of the effects of modern meat production or the huge energy waste that is standby power.[5]

---

[3] A distinction made by Karl Jaspers and Abraham Joshua Heschel.

[4] Cancer among children alone, which used to be a "medical rarity," has gone up 67 percent between 1950 and 2001. Philip and Alice Shabecoff, *Poisoned for Profit: How Toxins Are Making Our Children Chronically Ill* (White River Junction, VT: Chelsea Green Publishing, 2010), p. 21.

[5] I am always surprised by how few people know about this. Even my students, generally far more technologically knowledgeable than I am, usually have no idea.

There are a whole range of positions between Diane and Richard and some places – poorer in money and social capital, subject to forms of racism or ethnic oppression – in which responsibility is extremely small to nonexistent.

But most of us in developed nations are probably somewhere in the middle, like Diane. For the constraints and limitations of Diane's social position do not release her from her share of moral responsibility – from the reality that as well as being a victim of pollution, she is an agent of it. Like those of us who pay taxes to support a militarily aggressive government, her daily participation in the environmental regime makes her – as well, of course, as it makes me, and in all likelihood you, the reader, as well – an accomplice. We lack significant social power, yet enjoy a lifestyle that is responsible for several times more average greenhouse gases and general pollution than billions of the poor people of the world. What is the moral climate like in this position?

4 WHERE DOES THAT LEAVE US?

Consider Diane again – as well as other comparably situated people. Not starving but certainly not wealthy; a free citizen but a person who lacks political power. Not technically sophisticated, but at least educated enough to read an account of pollution in the daily newspaper or any of the dozens of internet sites that offer information in accessible terms. Diane could be a secretary, a college student, a single mother, a nurse, a tax lawyer, a farmer, a pediatrician, a plumber, a sales clerk, career military, a philosophy professor.

How are any of us to live our ordinary lives in a society that is environmentally destructive?

To begin we should, I think, get used to navigating the thin line between obsessive concern with our current moral status and self-imposed moral blindness. On the one hand, we cannot change the world with our individual behavior. The heart of moral concern in our time is collective, political action (the subject of the next chapter). Yet even though I cannot change the world by becoming vegetarian, driving less, or turning down the air conditioner, such actions are not morally irrelevant. There are, after all, many ways to evaluate the moral meaning of our behavior, and calculating consequences is only one of them. Perhaps in some sense it is the most important, but it is still one among others. Political theorist Paul Wapner suggests that in the face of climate change, moral behavior should be oriented to "principles or deep-seated values of what constitutes the good life in the midst of climate hardship, independent of a consequentialist calculus."[6]

For we do not evaluate actions solely in terms of their measurable outcomes. Sometimes we ask: "What is the right thing to do?" and mean by that: "What kind of person do I want to be, *regardless* of the outcome?" I know what's right, and even if no one else will do it, and it probably won't help, perhaps I should anyway. Perhaps that is part of what means to have a moral sense at all. How deadened to moral life in general will I be if my moral perspective is governed only by an evaluation of effects! Moral reality would then be perpetually displaced into some future time. And a future defined, if we are honest, by often largely speculative accounts of what it will be like. It can be enormously difficult to know what the effects of our actions will be.

By analogy: If ten million innocent people are being murdered, and I only kill one, does the fact that my action is only the tiniest fraction of the slaughter give me license to pull the trigger? Does the wrongness of my action diminish because it is such a miniscule part of the totality of bad actions being committed? Surely this one person had a life that was meaningful to him. Probably he had family or friends who would feel the person's death as a loss. Who knows what creativity, love, or just good humor this person could have brought into the world if they had not been murdered by me? Even if someone would take my place if I turned away, do I want to be a killer of an innocent person? Don't I have an obligation not to harm other people unjustly, even though so many other people are harming, and they might very well be harmed in any case? We might say "An awful lot of people eat meat, waste water, and drive when they could walk, so it doesn't make any difference if I do." But would we ever say, "An awful lot of people sexually abuse children, so it doesn't make any difference if I do"? If we would be horrified at the second, why not the first – which also, though over time and distance – creates unjust suffering?

Also: We should keep in mind that "It won't make any difference" is a factual assessment about a future state of the world. How sure can we be that it is true? Quite often our supposed "knowledge" of the future turns out to be false. When a crucial presidential election in which a 125 million vote is decided by less than 100,000 in a few crucial states, the defense of

---

[6] Paul Wapner, "Ethical Enhancement in an Age of Climate Change," *Ethics and International Affairs* 28, no. 3 (2014): 334.

not voting because "It makes no difference" is shown to be mistaken. It makes a big difference.

But let us assume that we can know that one single negative environmental act will make a near vanishingly small difference. Even so, do I want to pollute or consume unnecessarily?

Consider: You've just finished your coffee on the way home from a late night of work or a study session in the library. Your car is messy enough already; why not just toss the cup out the window? Given the incalculably vast quantity of junk humans have spread around the planet, including the oceans and the surrounding atmosphere,[7] what's one throwaway coffee cup? It is, after all, just one of something like 25 *billion* such cups thrown away each year. If it is paper, it takes "only" one-quarter pound of CO_2 to manufacture[8]: an infinitesimal part of the approximately 33 billion tons of CO_2 produced per year.[9]

Nevertheless, I can still ask myself: Do I want to be part of this enormous waste? Am I *really* too tired, stressed, or preoccupied not to put the cup down, wait until I get home, and toss it in the recycling bin? And because I stop at that coffee place several times a month, is it really not possible for me stick a travel mug in my backpack and stop consuming the throwaway cups at all? And is it too much trouble to check to see if the coffee is organic, shade grown, and fair trade?[10]

This trivial example highlights two facts. First, if we take the environmental crisis seriously our daily behavior can become a matter of intense moral attention. Like the rituals of spiritual discipline – the daily prayers, the restrictions on food choices, or the practice of reading from sacred texts – environmental care in our daily lives can be taken seriously just because our moral self-evaluation requires it. "Won't make a difference. Really, there's nothing to be done." Such justifications for moral sloppiness and personal self-indulgence lose their appeal. Instead, we will seek for a certain level of moral integrity – including harmonizing broad political goals and personal behavior. In a discussion of global warming that can be extended to virtually all environmental problems, a philosopher observes: "A commitment to mitigating climate change should …

---

[7] Approximately 25,000 football or larger sized bits of leftover garbage orbiting the earth from our technologically nifty space efforts.

[8] Carry the Cup Website: www.carryyourcup.org/get-the-facts. Accessed May 25, 2017.

[9] CO@ Earth Website; www.co2.earth/global-co2-emissions. Accessed May 25, 2017.

[10] Coffee that is not is grown in ecologically damaging ways, often employing extremely poorly paid and exploited labor.

entail a commitment to being the kind of person who is thoughtful about her greenhouse gas emissions and makes an effort to reduce them."[11]

Second, that is because just as we evaluate our physical appearance, social status, and career successes, we *also* evaluate whether we are acting rightly. As I roll down the car window and drain the last of the coffee, I may think: even if the roadside is littered with a hundred throwaways already and in a minute, I'd be unable to determine which of the refuse came from my hand, I *still* don't want to be the guy who makes it worse. So, I roll the window back up, sigh over the mess in the car, and try to remember to put the empty cup where it belongs or carry a reusable mug. In doing so I will, as psychologist Eric Ericson put it, be entering a moral adulthood in which my actions are guided by love, care, and wisdom.[12]

In such a situation attention on the future diminishes, and we collapse our awareness into the present. Right *here*, right *now*, we examined the empty cup in our hands and looked out the window at the yard, or city park, or sidewalk where we might have tossed it. One more piece of trash surely wouldn't have "made a difference" – except that it would have made a difference to *me* – for it would have been *my* trash. That is, it would have been an unchangeable fact about who I am as a moral being. As well, such acts need not be *purely* individual. I can casually mention what I did to friends. In conserving energy I might learn something I could share with colleagues. If I ride my bike to work I might inspire others. And it will also be important to affirm that my tiny act connects to countless tiny acts taken by others. Environmental care is a collective enterprise and certain collective enterprises are morally binding on everyone who is part of the collective.[13]

At the very same time we will also be asking: How's my physical health and emotional well-being? What can I do without driving myself nuts? Changing bad environmental habits and avoiding environmental sloppiness takes time, energy, effort, and often money. In a society set up to be environmentally wasteful, being environmentally reasonable is usually going against the grain.[14] How am I to ration my energy among family, community, workplace, and other political causes? For as a moral being

[11] Marion Hourdequin, "Climate, Collective Action, and Individual Ethical Obligations," *Environmental Values* 19 (2010): 451.

[12] Erik H. Erikson, *Insight and Responsibility* (New York: W. W. Norton & Co., 1972), p. 115.

[13] Ryan Darr, "Climate Change and Common-Sense Moral Responsibility," *Environmental Ethics* 39, no 1 (2017), pp. 21–37.

[14] Though sometimes the environmental and the financial go hand in hand.

in a complex, highly interrelated society, in which knowledge of the world's ills can easily be had, my awareness of environmental crisis exists alongside awareness of unjust wars, refugees, sexual violence, starvation, totalitarian repression, and racism (for a start!). If I sacrifice time, energy, money and emotional passions for one, will I still be able to meet the moral demands of others?

You may have noticed how much of the previous several paragraphs are devoted to unanswered questions. And that is because when it comes to issues of guilt and responsibility, in some cases the best a philosophical analysis can offer is a series of queries.

For example, it will do no good to exhaust myself trying to do more than I can. I might have to skip the environmental group meeting, buy cheap nonorganic junk food, drive rather than take my bike. No good will come of draining myself today so that I cannot function, tomorrow. But "Gee I'm just too tired" is only a valid excuse if I really am too tired. We often hear people saying, especially when they've committed a moral lapse, "I'm doing the best that I can." Surely that is a valid excuse – for people can only do what they can do, and we are all finite and fallible. Yet how do I know it's true? How can I be sure that I couldn't do better? For I could be kidding myself, making excuses for laziness or just wanting not to be bothered.

In my own case: Can I be honest with myself about which habits – like eating meat occasionally – can be changed and which (like moving out of Boston and away from Esther's medical support system) I cannot, at least not without a fair amount of collateral damage? In any situation, all of us can ask whether we are being honest about what we can and cannot do, what is or is not reasonably possible for us. And we can also ask whether we are living in a manner that cultivates the ability to answer such questions truthfully. Are we trying to be psychologically self-aware and morally consistent? Can we have frank moral conversations with people who know us? For if we are not at least attempting such things, then we are not "doing the best we can."

In the face of the environmental crisis, any of us can ask: How much avoiding and denying – or, conversely, self-indulgent, passivity inducing environmental despair – do I engage in? E.g., do I avoid looking at the footage from the factory farms? The flooded coastal villages in Bangladesh? The birds literally dropping dead from the trees in Mexico City due to air pollution? Or if I do witness all these, do my pained emotional responses lead to maudlin sympathy combined with political inactivity?

And this question of how much we can do is not limited to personal lifestyle choices (eating, driving, shopping, etc.) or engaged activism, but to crucial issues of work, as well.

Consider Diane again. Clearly, she doesn't have the freedom of action – some might say privilege – of Richard. But is a fossil fuel company the only place she could work? Has she looked for jobs with companies that are benign or even, perhaps, serious about environmental transformation? If she looked a little, could she look more? She is strapped for cash now, no doubt about it. But could she make a little less and still survive reasonably well?

In her everyday work Diane does not directly pollute. What about people who do and who must, or who believe they must, continue to do so to survive economically? For example, consider comparatively small farmers who use pesticides they know – or have been told – are dangerous to the health of their workers, neighbors' fields, animals, and consumers. "I need my chemicals," said one, "I can't afford to let my yields drop even by a few bushels per acre."[15] And this concern is not only about quantity of produce. Large buyers put a premium on the appearance of the crop, appearance that is more likely to come with high amounts of polluting pesticides. The farmer, like Diane, and unlike the giant chemical companies who lobby for lax pesticide regulations or the suppliers who determine food choices, has limited freedom. But how much does he have?

For example: When the farmer says he "can't afford" not to use chemicals, what does he mean? Will he become bankrupt without them or simply lower his income by 10 percent? No longer afford a good vacation and a new car every five years? Or be unable to get medical help for a child with disabilities or a parent with Alzheimer's?

Morally, we are caught in a system we did not design, faced with unpleasant choices we would rather skip over, torn between wanting a little more ease and a nagging conscience that suggests such ease is not worth the moral cost, and sometimes compelled to choose what we would like to think is the least bad of two distressing alternatives.

Self-understanding, therefore, does not simply exist in the realm of personal psychology, but is also an ethical obligation. And this is particularly true because of our culture's unreflective, habitual, socially shaped sense of what is "necessary." We are constantly taught to see each desire

---

[15] Jill Lindsey Harrison, *Pesticide Drift and the Pursuit of Environmental Justice* (Cambridge, MA: MIT Press, 2011), p. 71.

as something to be satisfied, each increase of our collective capacity for technological manipulation as a good thing. Every headache or depression is to be cured by painkiller or SSRI, and not by serious examination of how the way we are living is making us ill.[16] It is, supposedly, our all-important personal taste that fills the drugstores with twenty-three types of shampoo and the media sources with endless different genres of amusement 24/7. The claim that my immediate feelings, impulses, and desires should shape my behavior is the very principle on which a consumerist, endlessly expanding, thoughtless society is built. As Bill McKibben observed, after watching what was on 150 cable television channels over a 24-hour period: "Everything on television tells you ... that you're the most important person, and that people are all that matter."[17] Similarly, I recall the power company ads I used to see, which claimed, in ominous tones, that "In ten years our region will need 17 percent more energy." It was a claim that never asked – and clearly thought it unnecessary to ask – "How much energy do we really need? What do we need it for? How much are we wasting? And could we have better lives and still use a lot less?"

Yet moral self-examination, including the at times seemingly inescapable regret or even guilt we might feel when we fulfill one moral obligation at the expense of others, must coexist with a recognition of how the subject of morality is not just individual persons, but also communities, nations, cultures, even civilizations. Unresolvable moral conflicts that arise in the face of the environmental crisis are surely not just *my* problem. They are not something for which I am in any general sense personally responsible. My freedom may consist in how I respond to the essential facts of the physical and social worlds; but my lack of freedom consists in the way those facts are set by collective forces. If I am put in a situation in which I cannot help but fail to fulfill a moral responsibility because of moral conflicts – e.g., between my responsibilities as a father, a citizen, and an ecological agent – what I am left with is not only the feeling of guilt or regret over what *I* haven't done, but also a sense of the larger context that is, as it were, acting *through* me.

Depending on the situation, and certainly often arising in the face of the environmental crisis, is a kind of collective guilt, or at least collective responsibility, which is very different from smaller, interpersonal

[16] Clearly the holistic health movement stands in contrast to these tendencies. But while much more socially present than in past years, it is still a minority practice.
[17] Bill McKibben, *The Age of Missing Information* (New York: Penguin, 1993), p. 225.

situations that I could have dealt with had I been more moral, intelligent, and caring.[18] Jean-Paul Sartre offers the telling example how, during the Nazi occupation of France in WW II, a man had to choose between staying in his village to protect his aged mother and abandoning his mother to join the resistance. In environmental contexts such conflicts are common and inescapable: between getting to a demonstration by car or not going; between saving this species or that; between letting the feral cats decimate endangered species of birds or killing the cats; between spending time protecting a local ecosystem or helping a mildly green political candidate. Because we care about being moral, we may feel bad for what we don't do, haven't accomplished, or downright ignored. But clearly the actual responsibility is far bigger than we are. This truth may release us from some of our moral regret. But it is also somewhat dismaying to realize how little we can control. And it may in fact create a rather different moral responsibility: to take part in political movements that will alter the general moral conditions we face.

5 BEYOND THE PALE

The Richards of the world – from the knowing polluters to their kept politicians and theoretical apologists – have been the subjects of several different analyses. A study of the Nazi doctors who did horrible experiments on concentration camp inmates suggested that such people performed a kind of psychic "doubling" that allowed them to be vicious sadists at "work" while being normally affectionate and caring to their friends and families.[19] In another book I have suggested that as personal identity becomes dependent on maintaining a public work identity, this psychological attachment can lead a person to knowingly commit immoral acts in the service of that identity.[20] A detailed study of people who design nuclear weapons – and whose lab turned into a Superfund cleanup area because they had been so causal with waste – revealed an

---

[18] Lisa Tessman, *When Doing the Right Thing is Impossible* (New York: Oxford University Press, 2017) examines such difficult situations, but omits serious engagement with this social dimension. Similarly Bernard Williams, who identified the moral "remainders" of guilt and regret that follow on moral obligations unfulfilled due to unsolvable conflicts, fails to adequately recognize how such remainders are often social facts more than personal ones.

[19] Robert Jay Lifton, *The Nazi Doctors: Medical Killing and the Psychology of Genocide* (New York: Basic Books, 2017).

[20] Roger S. Gottlieb, *A Spirituality of Resistance* (New York: Crossroad, 1999), Chapter 3.

arrogance that they were an intellectual elite who could handle this threat better than anyone else.[21]

These are the people who spread disinformation about global warming; military officers who shoot indigenous peoples trying to protect their land from environmental ruin; lobbyists weakening regulations on chemicals they know to be toxic; lumber companies suing environmental organizations to keep them from publicizing the destruction of forests.[22]

How can we morally assess such people? On first examination, we might say that as awful as such behavior is, it is (sadly) all too familiar. Human history is marked by countless examples of people who are cruel, selfish, brutally dishonest, and murderous. Perhaps people who defend a chemical they know to be carcinogenic are not, or not much, different than generals who order the bombing of civilians, terrorists who target mosques or subways, or black marketers who hoard food when their neighbors are starving. What is more depressingly common than a lack of respect for human life and well-being?

I believe this to be true, and that the frequently high economic status of environmental perpetrators – the $2,000 suits, gracious suburban mansions, and seven-figure salaries – hide a moral evil as extreme as that of any drug lord or corrupt politician.

And yet there is a difference, a way in which the guilty are not simply savage sadists, or soulless pursuers of wealth. For, as has often been observed, there is a kind of insanity in poisoning the air and water that you yourself consume and knowingly worsening the climate in which your children and grandchildren will live.

There is a telling moment in the wonderful movie *Erin Brockovitch*, a film centered on how a California electric utility knowingly polluted the water of the surrounding towns. At a lawyers' conference an attorney is defending the utility, denying any responsibility. She is offered ice water from a lovely pitcher – and then, after the water has been poured, told that it comes from a well in the town the utility polluted. With a grimace the lawyer quickly puts the water down and pushes it away.

Of course, the polluters don't want to drink the water they themselves have polluted. Of course, oil company executives don't want their children – whom we must presume they love – to live in a world wracked by huge storms, uncontrollable droughts, an altered ocean, and international

---

[21] Hugh Gusterson, *Nuclear Rites: A Weapons Lab at the End of the Cold War* (Berkeley, CA: University of California Press, 1996).

[22] All these events have happened.

relations of climate refugees and climate-provoked wars. Even if they think their wealth will allow them protected, gated lives, do they really think they can escape the global environmental consequences and social disruption that is coming?

And yet this is the world they are creating. Why?

One answer might be in the way that ruling groups *necessarily* help create the conditions of their own eventual overthrow. Unrestrained capitalism created system-threatening economic depressions. Soviet communism's repressive rule weakened the Soviet economy. Perhaps it is simply inevitable that a ruling class will be blind to the consequences of its actions, consequences that lead to the diminution or elimination of its power. And is its current defense of policies that cause climate change, depletion of fisheries, rampant environmental illness, environmental refugees, and environmental wars, just another instance of the ultimately self-defeating actions by a global elite who cannot fathom the long-term effects of what they do?

The problem with this answer is that over the last eighty years or so[23] segments of the ruling class have learned that crises can be managed by a kind of transformative maintenance of the social order. For example, the introduction of a variety of social welfare programs in the New Deal of the 1930s was a direct response to the threat of communist revolution.[24] In other words: far from endlessly pursuing the most immediate, short-term gains for themselves, the 'one percent' have allowed reforms to get most of the population to believe in the legitimacy of the social order. The result is a society still highly stratified by income; with an interlocking ruling class of corporate power and financially dependent politicians accumulating the vast majority of society's wealth and generally pursuing policies that benefit themselves at the expense of the rest of society. But *also*, a society in which several social programs and financial safety nets blunt the worst excesses of unequal distribution of wealth and power. (Of course, when economic times worsen, those safety nets thin and weaken. And then widening inequality and the suffering of the lower classes is covered with racist appeals and talk of "foreign threats.")

---

[23] I'm starting with the New Deal. Some might go back considerably further: to Bismarck's introduction of social welfare legislation to lessen the appeal of the German Social-Democratic party.

[24] I believe that fear was mistaken. But it was a time of enormous economic hardship and collapse, along with a global movement. I have analyzed this at length in *History and Subjectivity; The Transformation of Marxist Theory*.

Yet such foresight has *not* been exercised, or often not been exercised very well, or at least exercised with great inconsistency, when it comes to environmental problems. When the chemical giant DuPont was aware of the ozone-depleting consequences of the CFC chemicals it sold for air conditioners and refrigeration, its response was to lobby in defense of CFCs, continue to sell them abroad after they had been made illegal in the United States, and then profit by the delay it has helped to cause by cornering the market on its replacements.[25]

Did DuPont's executives, lawyers, lobbyists, and advertising staff not realize that they too were now at a higher risk for skin cancer? That their grandchildren, playing in the sun during school time recess, would also be at risk? Had they been asked if they fully understood the consequences of their defense of CFCs, how would they have responded?[26]

The point of these questions is that while many people profit in money and social power from their role in producing, distributing and advertising carcinogenic pesticides, climate destabilizing fossil fuels and the like, they are *also* hurting themselves. How do we understand them?

We do not have much trouble describing the morality of the thief who steals your wallet. From the Ten Commandments on we know that it is wrong to steal. Insofar as the thief steals, he is immoral, wrong, unjust, unfair, not a good guy. But what about the thief who steals not only your wallet but also a bomb that might go off some years in the future, which he casually leaves lying around his own house?

The immense global folly of the environmental crisis is certainly fueled by the actions of us all, but also certainly shaped in much greater measure by the people who have political, economic, and cultural power. But in what they do they hurt, or at least seriously threaten, themselves and those they care about. And here I am not thinking about the way greed, short-sightedness, unconcern with others, and endless pursuit of wealth and power are ultimately not a very happy way to live. Though I believe that to be the case, I am talking about something much simpler and more direct: a kind of self-destructive, blind, monomaniacal, single-minded compulsion to pursue a course of action that is against their self-interest.

By analogy: toward the end of WW II Germany was struggling with the Russian army on their eastern front. In hopes that the tide could be

[25] John Nance, *What Goes Up: The Global Assault on our Atmosphere* (New York: William Morrow, 1991).
[26] The comparison with the lying executives of tobacco firms has often been made. However one presumes that most of those people did not smoke. Or if they did, they didn't have to.

turned, Hitler's generals kept demanding more troops, for it was clear that if Germany lost in the east, America's presence on the Western front would soon doom the Nazi cause. At the same time, however, Hitler put out a clear directive: military needs took second place to a more important goal – transporting Jews to be slaughtered in concentration camps. The continued murder of innocent, completely nonthreatening people was more important than getting needed support to his soldiers fighting the Soviet army.

In short, Hitler's mad compulsion toward genocide took precedence over the self-interested need to defend his own power.

There are certainly many differences between our own situation and that of the Nazi forces. The point, however, is the one similarity: the way people in power can act irrationally, against their own best "interests," because of a psychological compulsion.

Addiction can serve as a second analogy. Heroin addicts are in the grip of a vicious illness, but while some kind of "dual diagnosis" of mental illness is often at work, the typical addict is not without some awareness of how self-destructive the habit is. They may think that nothing else is possible; they may be unwilling to give up the temporary high, even though it is part of a miserably painful form of life; they may not have the courage to face the extreme physical discomfort that going off heroin entails. So, they do not quit, even as they know they are destroying themselves.

The people most responsible for the environmental crisis, at least in many cases, also know. It is striking that Rex Tillerson, then head of Exxon, kept a secret email account under a different name in which to discuss the reality of global warming, a reality Exxon was committed to denying in public.[27] It is striking that makers of formaldehyde, aware of its negative health effects in use in particle board (home construction) and dry cleaning, nevertheless mounted an active lobbying campaign to defend it. The engineers who created VW engines that would perform one way when tested and pollute five times as much when driven were not ignorant of air pollution. They knew what they are doing. And they chose to do it anyway.

---

[27] Meghan Keneally, "Secretary of State Tillerson used alias account in some climate change emails at Exxon, prosecutors say," ABC News Website. Accessed January 5, 2018, http://abcnews.go.com/Politics/secretary-state-tillerson-alias-account-climate-change-emails/story?id=46117655.

6 WHERE TO?

A kind of madness haunts us all. And the more powerful, influential, rich, and respected, the more the madness is present. This is a difficult claim to make, for typically we identify the crazy person as the one who is out of touch with a reality shared by the majority. The mad person is the one who thinks he is Napoleon, who hears voices that aren't "there," who can't leave the house without washing his hands twenty times. Yet in R. D. Laing's apt analogy: the plane that flies in a different direction from all the others may be "out of formation."[28] But that does not mean it is off course; not, that is, if the rest of the planes are going in the wrong direction.

Sadly, we have sufficient examples from the last hundred years of societies that are afflicted with a kind of madness. Certainly Nazism is one clear example: a supposedly civilized country converted to monstrously false and irrational beliefs about Jews, led to monstrous crimes. The nuclear arms race is another example. Supported by intellectual, scientific and technical elites throughout the world, putting the entire human race on the edge of nuclear annihilation. In smaller settings we have the moral monstrosities of ISIS, with its tortured version of Islam leading to casual violence on a horrific scale. The crimes of Stalinism, Maoism, and the Vietnam War, all of which required the support of powerful social groups, have similar overtones of collective madness.

Is it expecting too much of society's leaders that they resist the madness? Cure themselves of their compulsions and addiction? See the awful consequences for others and, at least potentially, for themselves as well? Can people be forced into sanity? Or out of addiction?

As individuals, perhaps. Every crazy person, every addict, always looked like they would never recover. But some do. Some corporations are claiming to take significant environmental steps, particularly in relation to renewable energy. Apple and Citibank, Walmart and IKEA, Coca-Cola and Facebook and GM are all part of the RE100 group, many significant corporations that claim to be switching to a low-carbon or totally renewable energy footprint.[29] Clearly, they are at odds with the fossil fuel industry, especially with oil and coal. Yet even so, Apple is not taking serious actions about the polluting heavy metals used in their products. Coca-Cola continues to advertise beverages that cause obesity,

---

[28] R. D. Laing, *The Politics of Experience* (London: Penguin, 1967), pp. 118–120.
[29] RE100 Website. Accessed February 3, 2018, http://there100.org/.

diabetes, and malnutrition and deplete water reserves for Indian communities. The overall thrust of capitalist business is, and necessarily is, at odds with environmental sanity somewhere between quite often and all the time.

In the face of such widespread, pervasive, devastating madness, however, what is needed is not psychiatric medications, a personal connection to 12-step programs, a lot of meditation, or a great therapist. What is needed is collective action toward a social reality marked by morality and sanity.

We need, that is, a political movement.

7

Changing the World

A Moral Primer on Environmental Political Activism

I POLITICAL ACTION

The idea of a just and rational society is very old, as is the question of how it is possible to get from where we now find ourselves to such a society. The Torah offers moral maxims to sustain the whole community: Don't hold workers' wages overnight, don't mistreat the disabled, don't favor either the rich or poor in legal judgments, extend help, care, and fairness to the "widow, the orphan, and the stranger." That is, extend fairness to those lacking social power.

Similarly, Greek philosophy in Plato and Aristotle issued detailed warnings about what happens when leaders of a society are not wise, either because they are individually selfish and power-hungry or because as a group they are unable to comprehend the deep structures of human virtue in particular and reality in general.

These efforts, as important they are, do not constitute what I have in mind by "political action." For by that I mean something that is much more recent than ancient Israel or Greece. It is an idea and social reality that emerged in the mid- to late eighteenth century: the creation of a better society not through the edicts of enlightened emperors, prophets, or philosophers, but through collective action of a large, organized, goal-directed segment of society.

This form of politics is perhaps so familiar to us that we take it for granted. How else, we might ask, can any political change take place? Even if God is speaking to a prophet or a philosopher has comprehended The Truth, their insights will mean nothing, we suspect, without a mass of people – a social force – to put them into practice.

And indeed, if we examine some of the crucial political shifts over the last 250 years we can see how a certain pattern of social change is repeated.[1] A social group with common interests wishes to change what they believe is unjust, unfair, and/or irrational. They are opposed by people who benefit from the status quo, who think that society is reasonably acceptable as it is, or who distrust the politically activated group more than they dislike the current state of affairs. In response the group seeking change must do three things. It must organize itself in some way: as a political party, decentralized loosely affiliated groups, mobs in the street, a military force. It must articulate what it wants: democracy over kingship, national or ethnic rights, freedom from slavery, gender equality, the end to animal exploitation or dependence on fossil fuels. Finally, it must choose a way to use its mass power to achieve those goals; i.e., it must decide on how to get what it wants.

This basic structure of political life thus gives rise to three dimensions of political movements. How broad are their political demands? How are they organized? What methods will they use? Let us see how these dimensions unfold in environmental political activism.

2 THE SCOPE OF THE DEMAND

Here is a neighborhood group concerned about mounting trash and noise pollution in the local park. They want restrictions on the folks who ride their motorcycles or try out their drones in this small green area; they want more garbage cans; and they want higher legal fines for littering and park rangers to enforce the new rules. This is a small focused demand, well within the scope of current environmental concern. It is not a fundamental challenge to current social practices or existing social power. It will irritate bikers, drone lovers, and those who like to be casual with trash. But it will probably not arouse too much resistance. Too little is at stake.

Here's another group, deeply concerned over the fate of some particular endangered species. In the United States, it wants the animal to receive "endangered" status, a legal designation from the EPA, which can limit the actions of private property owners and restrain economic activity. Outside the United States the group will attempt to influence other

[1] Clearly this is *not* the case with social changes that happen through actions of elites, and many times with few people intending them. E.g., the growth of capitalism, the computer/cell phone revolution, and the environmental crisis itself.

nations and create transnational agreements. While these goals may challenge particular interests (local building projects, logging, the trade in body parts of endangered animals), they are nevertheless a familiar practice of recent decades; e.g., in campaigns in defense of whales or elephants. People who oppose these campaigns are comparatively limited in numbers and power. Protecting tigers or songbirds does not significantly challenge the socially powerful.

Here are several local groups, perhaps led by mothers who have noticed the amount of cancer and birth defects in their neighborhood, or by long-term residents whose land rights are under attack by huge coal companies. Emboldened by the 1970 government regulation that "ordinary" citizens be consulted on local environmentally significant policies or plans, and the diffuse emphasis on participatory democracy of political movements of that era, these grassroots groups of primarily nontechnically trained people may resist mountaintop removal mining, river pollution, the dumping of toxins in poor and minority neighborhoods, and other environmental assaults. While such actions typically bring them up against powerful corporate interests and government officials sympathetic to those interests, each demand can be accommodated by the existing system. Pollution can be shifted somewhere else; corporations can improve their management of toxins; resource extraction can move to countries with more helpful and repressive governments. Of course, for environmental fairness and responsibility to be achieved throughout society, massive change in ecological behavior – and the social power of different classes and races – would have to occur.[2]

However, what happens when we expand the scope of our environmental demands? We want, let us suppose, a drastic increase in the size of protected wilderness areas in a country, areas in which all mechanized transport, machine uses, logging, mining, and hunting are forbidden. We are asking, say, for an increase of 25, 50, or even 100 percent. Think of the vastly larger number of social interests this challenges: logging companies, loggers, fossil fuel companies, real estate developers, lovers of all-terrain vehicles and mountain bikes. Such people have political power in virtue of their wealth, numbers, and influence over politicians and the media. The result is a persistent political struggle between the

---

[2] Many fine writings on this topic exist. See, e.g., Cody Ferguson, *This Is Our Land: Grassroots Environmentalism in the late Twentieth Century* (New Brunswick, NJ: Rutgers University Press, 2015).

conservationist group and those who wish to extract, develop, and enter the wilderness with machines.

Still, however, there is an established history of conservation. The argument here is over where and how much. There is nothing radically socially transforming about asking for more conserved land.

A great leap upward happens when a fundamental social policy – the use of fossil fuels – comes up for grabs. This is a necessary step to avoid the catastrophes of global warming, or at least mitigate the consequences we are facing already. But this change is a threat to fossil fuel companies, among the most powerful economic, and hence political, institutions in the world. Their power is evident, to take just one example, in the way the coal industry–financed political support and propaganda helped dramatically alter the public policies supported by the Republican Party after 2007.[3] Similar interests shape global politics in petro states like Russia, Saudi Arabia, and Venezuela. Just in the United States the pursuit of a carbon free or carbon lessened economy requires fundamental shifts in foreign relations, tax policy, the design of cities, building codes, public transportation subsidies, the design of automobiles, and agriculture.

The way each of these is being done now benefits some people rather than others, and even without significant economic benefits may often be culturally significant to large numbers of people. Try, for instance, to tell Americans that a lot of individual driving around in a large, fuel-inefficient car is a bad thing. And might be regulated for environmental purposes. Or that, to reflect the actual environmental costs of the massive "production" of cows and chickens, the price of meat might rise by 50 percent.

Finally, even a drastic shift in energy policy is insignificant compared to a challenge to the economic, political, and cultural system. Some will argue, for example, that the concentrated power of corporations to shape production and influence our patterns of consumption is guaranteed to further degrade both humans and the rest of the planet; and that any reform will be insufficient unless corporate power is replaced by democratic socialism.[4] Others will add that American racism (and comparable attitudes in other countries) needs to be deeply changed to lessen

---

[3] Coral Davenport, "How G.O.P. Leaders Came to See Climate Change as Fake Science," *New York Times* Website. Accessed February 15, 2018, www.nytimes.com/2017/06/03/us/politics/republican-leaders-climate-change.html.

[4] For anticapitalist or ecosocialist positions, see, e.g., Joel Kovel, *The Enemy of Nature: The End of Capitalism or the End of the World?* (London: Zed Books, 2nd ed., 2007); the journal *Capitalism, Nature, Socialism* (their online discussion site: www.cnsjournal.org/;

environmental injustice: the disproportionate way in which racial minorities are polluted and (not) defended from polluters. Ecofeminists have argued for a fundamental cultural shift away from patriarchal attitudes that identify women with nature and devalue them both in comparison with men. Patriarchal hierarchy of masculine reason, mind, or soul over the "grossly" mortal, fleshy, and bodily feminine and natural should be replaced by an acceptance that human dignity "just is the dignity of a certain kind of animal"; and that morality and rationality are "thoroughly material and animal."[5] This would be a "revolutionary understanding that we call feminist and ecological, in which we share the world with all creatures and all living things and know that their stories are our own."[6]

Thus at its most extreme environmental politics may seek the overthrow of capitalism, racism, and patriarchy.

3 METHODS

What can we do to achieve our environmental goals? Let's start with the mildest, least threatening and least demanding: writing a book such as this one, along with the associated activities of teaching environmental philosophy and giving public lectures. That is, simply expressing my beliefs as loudly and widely as I can. Note that while I personally support the most extreme of the aforementioned goals, my methods (with occasional exceptions) are quite mild. I simply try make other people's beliefs more like my own. And for the most part I've done so in nonintrusive, easily avoided, ways.

As we move up the scale of activism there are people, supported by membership in large public organizations like Sierra Club or Audubon Society, who try to influence the government. They lobby – argue, present information, offer policy recommendations – to change laws and policies. There are also smaller, more local, less-professionalized groups who testify at hearings, collect information, and demand accountability from elected officials and corporations.

and the more accessible Naomi Klein, *This Changes Everything: Capitalism vs. the Climate* (New York: Simon and Schuster, 2014).

[5] Martha Nussbaum, *Frontiers of Justice: Nationality, Disability, Species Membership* (Cambridge, MA: Harvard University Press 2006), pp. 132–133.

[6] Grace Paley, in Irene Diamond and Gloria Orenstein, eds., *Reweaving the World: The Emergence of Ecofeminism* (San Francisco: Sierra Club Books, 2000), p. iii.

Professional environmentalists, their nonprofessional supporters, and grassroots groups may come together in public demonstrations. Anywhere from a few dozen to hundreds of thousands demanding action on climate change, clean air, and toxins in everyday products. Such demands may be focused in lawsuits, boycotts of offending corporations, and, moving up higher still, in direct action. Greenpeace is known for plugging the outflow pipes of polluting factories and intervening to protect whales from hunters. Other groups go undercover to video the horrors of industrial meat production or try to block the construction of oil pipelines.

Some activists will not be bound by the conventions of private property. They free animals from zoos or labs; "monkey wrench" to protect endangered wilderness by damaging construction equipment; block coal trains by putting a body across the tracks; hang fifty-foot banners from corporate headquarters accusing Monsanto or Office Depot or the like of using products that destroy old-growth forests, contribute to global warming, and devastate indigenous peoples.

And finally, there is direct violence. In several places oil development in particular has wreaked destructive havoc on local communities, poisoning air, water, and earth, making life literally intolerable. When local tribes resisted to protect their homes and lives, they were met with violent repression and, at times, responded in kind.

4 ORGANIZATIONAL DIFFERENCES AND LEARNING FROM THE PAST

Throughout the world environmentalists work in very different ways. There are local, national, and international groups. In some countries, Germany for example, a Green Party runs candidates for government office. In Taiwan and Zimbabwe groups rooted in local religious institutions have had significant effects on recycling, reforestation, and resource use. When in 1992 a Republican congress threatened to dismantle environmental regulations, leading environmental groups (Sierra, Audubon, World Wildlife Fund, National Resource Defense Council, etc.) mobilized members to flood their representatives with protests. Antienvironmental efforts were, if not stopped completely, considerably lessened. In response to President Trump's 2017 withdrawal from the Paris Climate Accords, states, cities, and corporations have both offered vociferous criticism and committed to continuing greenhouse gas reduction.

Can we evaluate this wide variety of strategies, group forms, and range of goals? I believe that how we think about environmental politics now will depend, to some extent at least, on how we think about the history of political movements in general. To do that, we have to decide what parts of political history are relevant and which are not.

Which past political movements can help us know what to do and which can warn us about what to avoid?

Let us compare two very different movements. In the 1930s American industrial workers forced both the government and several major industries (e.g., auto, steel) to recognize their rights to collective bargaining. The AFL-CIO, forged from different industries into a centralized, unified, and powerful force, achieved significant victories for workers' standard of living and other benefits. In the late 1960s and 1970s the women's movement exploded onto the world and the American political stage. It was virtually the direct opposite of the labor movement, being made up of thousands of small to medium-sized local groups: intimate consciousness raising circles, organizations focused on issues (sexual violence, reproductive freedom, creating community or professional spaces for women), and groups with broader, more general agendas such as equal political rights and cultural recognition. And all of these goals existed along a spectrum from the modest request for legal equality to the complete overthrow of every vestige of male domination.

Were these movements successful? If they were, or to the extent that they were, do contemporary environmental activists have anything to learn from them? Do we need a highly organized, hierarchal, single environmental organization or party? Or should we continue with the myriad local, regional, national, international, political, and cultural groups that exist now?

And what about lessons from the civil rights movement, anticolonial struggles, the animal or gay rights movements? Given the severity of the environmental crisis, the life-and-death consequences of pollution and resource extraction, should we also reflect on partisan movements during countries occupied by foreign forces or even uprisings in Nazi concentration camps?

On the other hand, perhaps the environmental crisis is unique – and thus environmental political movements have little or nothing to learn from history. The crisis is, after all, the first fully global political issue. Climate change and pollutants affect everyone. There can be, I suppose, bystanders in the struggle against racism – but not in resistance to environmental problems. You are affected one way or another.

Keeping the differences in mind, what do environmentalists have in common with some of these other struggles? At least four things. First, the need for legal, state action to enforce needed changes. Whatever strides workers, racial minorities, and women have made have depended in great measure on laws: guaranteeing blacks the right to vote in the south, punishing men for sexual violence, opening areas of employment through Affirmative Action. Without government action and enforcement, environmentalism recedes into personal choice, lifestyle, visionary experiences, and historical irrelevance.

Second, however, legal changes and state action in and of themselves both require and reinforce, in a continuing spiral of interaction, broader cultural changes. Without cultural changes broad popular support for political shifts simply won't be there. And the culture is not simply something imposed from without, but also internalized. Women accepted patriarchal values and taught them to their daughters. Similarly, environmentalists themselves have been raised in a culture that privileges human desires above all, and learning to value other species is not an automatic consequence of environmentalist opinions.

Third, we have seen that no success is guaranteed to last. The degree of voter suppression is not likely to reach the pre-Voting Rights Act (1964) levels but attempts to limit black voters have taken place in several states and been identified as such by some federal courts. Women's reproductive freedom is consistently under attack, as restrictions on abortion rights continue to increase, not fade away. A woman may become prime minister of India, but Indian women are routinely sexually harassed in public. The level of sexist invective hurled at Hillary Clinton was appalling. "Slut shaming" and body shaming permeate adolescent culture. The widespread presumption that it is up to women to care for sick and aging family members persists. While there have been many environmental victories, the destructive juggernaut of industrial civilization has not been stopped. In 2017, after leveling off for a few years, global CO_2 emissions rose 2 percent. No one reading this book will see a final, decisive victory over the environmental crisis in their lifetime.

Finally, fourth, and an issue that requires some elaboration: A combination of "intersectionality," emotional immaturity, and careerism can turn what should be a cooperative struggle into a chaotic, sprawling collection of often antagonistic subgroups. "Intersectionality" refers to the way in which members of one socially defined group – African

Americans, women – are simultaneously part of several other groups whose interests may not coincide. A given African American will simultaneously be male or female, an upper-middle-class lawyer or an unemployed high school dropout, heterosexual or homosexual or non-sexual. He may be an activist or socially passive, and if an activist may hold any one of a number of perspectives on how to achieve racial justice and may or may not want to use political activity as a forum in which to attack not only racists but also African Americans who have different views or as a way to get status, power, or money.

The history of political movements is littered with examples of intragroup conflict, leadership shaped by egotism and self-aggrandizement, vicious conflicts over doctrine and strategy, members of the group seeing their own struggles and situation as primary and not seeing, or particularly caring about, those of others. We have had white middle-class feminists not comprehending the situation of black women, the attempted exclusion of lesbians during the early years of the National Organization of Women, the derogation of homosexuals in many black political groups, male-dominated political organizations frequently marginalizing the concerns and participation (except in subordinate positions) of women, and conservation groups privileging elephants and rhinos over the native groups who live near them. Such failures of progressive movements bear no small relation to the partiality and temporary nature of the victories they have won.

The history of the Green Party in Germany – a large, well-organized group with representatives in the German parliament and even a ministerial position in the government – is an instructive (and cautionary) tale about the inability of political leaders to communicate respectfully and compromise over differences. Split by opposing political views between reformist and more radical demands, leaders engaged in vilifying their opponents within the party, and eventually the organization split into two much less powerful and influential parts.

Whatever we can learn from the past, I also believe that there is something distinct about the environmental movement that simply has not been true of other movements. Given the history of the Green Party this is surely not true of all environmental organizations, but it is, I believe, true enough.

It is this: Unlike virtually all other progressive movements, a good deal of environmentalism takes as its object not this or that oppressed group but *all of life*. The Environmental Defense Fund's mission is to "preserve the natural systems on which all life depends." Greenpeace's core value is to "ensure the ability of the earth to nurture life in all its diversity."[7] If this universality of concern has not always been effective; if at times environmentalism has been, for example, dominated by a concern with wilderness to the exclusion of humans, or some "charismatic megafauna" (large cool animals) to the exclusion of, say, lab rats, or of a pristine Arctic or rainforest to the exclusion of the fate of indigenous peoples, these limitations have been pointed out and often the mistakes have been remedied comparatively quickly.

Consider, for example, the way in which US environmental organizations responded to the idea of environmental racism. In 1990, after the publicizing of the United Church of Christ's landmark study on racially unfair pollution, minority environmental activists sent critical letters to major US environmental organizations. These letters diagnosed ignorance of the condition of racial minorities, few or no people of color in management positions, and preference for wilderness concerns over urban pollution or the effects of mining.[8] These were extremely strong criticisms, challenging the self-righteous presumption of virtue that marks most environmental groups. Yet within a year virtually all these organizations responded favorably. Articles on environmental justice appeared in their publications; lists of demands for government action became part of their programs. As time wore on the concepts of environmental racism and justice became common currency throughout United States and then world environmental organizations. Whatever blindness or unconscious racism (as in not noticing or paying attention to poor and nonwhite communities) had been responsible for the omissions and limitations, was overcome.

Was the response perfect? Of course not – so few things in human life are. But compared to *other* political organizations responding to criticism of racial blindness or gender bias, the correction was quick and powerful. And, I am suggesting, this is so because with an ultimate commitment to all of life, environmental organizations have nothing to lose by rectifying a mistaken policy or theoretical lack. Unlike a union movement in which

---

[7] "Our Mission and Values." Environmental Defense Fund Website. Accessed January 16, 2018, www.edf.org/our-mission-and-values. "Our Core Values," Greenpeace International Website. Accessed January 16, 2018, http://m.greenpeace.org/international/en/high/about/our-core-values/.

[8] For an example, here is the letter sent by the Southwest Organizing Committee, see EJNet. org: Web Resources for Environmental Justice Activists. Accessed January 15, 2018, www.ejnet.org/ej/swop.pdf.

racism was common within membership, responding to the needs of African Americans would not reduce their appeal to their supporters. Unlike a middle-class-oriented white women's movement, the inclusion of concern with inner-city pollution would be less likely to be seen as a distraction from "real" issues.

To put it another way: Because injustice and irrationality are always benefitting somebody, all political movements toward justice and reason encounter resistance. As threatening as greenhouse gases are, owners of oil and gas companies benefit from generating them; as do ordinary people who love to drive pickup trucks. Therefore, political challenges to privilege and power inevitably encounter fierce resistance – who, after all, wants to give up their privileges so the world can become more rational and just? In exactly that way political movements typically are *for* some group victimized by the benefits that the dominant group receives. And in this pursuit other needs or struggles can be easily and systematically overlooked.

But an environmental movement that, however imperfectly, takes all of life as its object has no such inherent, built-in limitations. *Have we missed somebody? Been blind? Ignored our privilege in some way? Terribly sorry to have been so short-sighted. Thanks for pointing it out. Let's get moving to include this issue and the part of life that we've ignored, whether it's people, animals, trees, or anything else.*

5 WHAT IS RESISTANCE?

The scope of the environmental crisis is so vast, the needed changes present in virtually every aspect of society, it is not surprising that there is a daunting range of options for environmental activism. As well, issues are technical as well as moral and political. Changes in environmental practices need to be both technologically feasible and socially acceptable. If we simply eliminate sexual harassment and racist jokes, no replacements are needed. But we must provide energy and grow food even as we stop using fossil fuels and carcinogenic pesticides.

This is comparatively easy in the case of replacing throwaway plastic bags with cloth reusable (and biodegradable) ones, but much harder when it comes to replacing single drivers commuting with public transportation. In this latter case a host of changes must be put in place: enough buses, vans, light rail, bikes, bike lanes, and subways to get people where they need to go in a reasonable amount of time; and the attitudinal change that accepts the trade-off from individual to mass transit. As in virtually every other political context, environmental forces will have to mobilize enough social power to overcome the entrenched resistance of those who benefit, or believe they benefit, from the way things are now.

Given the range of environmental politics in final goals, method, and organization, how are we to know what are "good" – effective, meaningful, helpful – ways of going about making serious environmental change? Part of me would like to dismiss this question by simply saying, "Every environmentalist needs every other environmentalist. We are all headed to the same goal. Let a thousand flowers (methods, areas of focus, styles of political engagement) bloom." Sadly, this won't work. I don't support litmus tests of environmental purity, off-the-cuff rejections of those who differ, and hostile dismissals of other groups as wimpy reformists, pie-in-the-sky radicals, or sellouts. But I don't think it's wrong to try to offer some reasoned way of evaluating what makes for good environmental politics and what might be a form of greenwashing; i.e., pretending to support environmental change while trying hard to keep things the way they are. Such greenwashing is evident when corporations spend five times as much money proclaiming their environmental virtue as they do on cleaning up their practices or take credit for environmental improvements they've lobbied against.[9]

I will try to offer a way of thinking about this question that, perhaps surprisingly, refers to the Holocaust.

The Holocaust was the systematic attempt to annihilate all the Jews of Europe – and, if military fortunes had been reversed, probably all Jews everywhere. The most widespread images of the Holocaust are barbed wire, piles of Jewish bodies, wretched inmates of concentration camps, and the endlessly repeated number: six million.

Images that rarely appear are of Jews holding machine guns as members of partisan units in forests, fleeing concentrations camps during an uprising after disabling a crematorium, or risking their lives to smuggle food into horribly overcrowded, disease-ridden ghettos. Comparatively few people are aware that alongside victimization and death, there was a full range of Jewish resistance to the Nazis, resistance that occurred in every ghetto where Jews were concentrated before being taken to the camps, and in each of the camps themselves.[10]

---

[9] See Frances Bowen, *After Greenwashing: Symbolic Corporate Environmentalism and Society* (New York: Cambridge University Press, 2015).

[10] This account explored in Roger S. Gottlieb, "The Concept of Resistance: Jewish Resistance in the Holocaust," *Social Theory and Practice* 9, no. 1 (Spring 1983), pp. 31–49.

There were instances where, without hope in the future and under pressure of unimaginable losses, people resisted. And to do so Jews had to forge a new Jewish identity, a new Jewish culture, in their embrace of violent resistance – because Jewish tradition and social position offered virtually no preparation for military action.

Resistance took place alongside other behavior: submissive acceptance and, sadly, collaboration. The historical question then arises: into which category does an action fit? Some actions – blowing up a Nazi troop train or docilely walking to the trains headed to the gas chambers – are easily categorized. But what of the "Judenrat" – Jewish councils who did the day-to-day administration of the ghettos, often responsible for choosing or helping carry out ordered selections for extermination. When asked, many of the Judenrat said they were protecting their fellow Jews, that if they hadn't given the Nazis "something," much more would have been taken. At the same time, such people were relatively better off than other Jews, typically protected from starvation and deportation to death camps – or at the very least the last to be taken.

Similarly, consider the concentration camp inmate who doesn't help smuggle in bits of ammunition to forge a bomb, but simply manages to stay alive despite starvation, bitter cold, and constant terror. She could have, as many did, simply succumbed to numbing depression and despair, and without the will to live either fall from illness or be "selected" for gassing because in her obviously weakened state she was no longer capable of doing her share of slave labor.

If your actions preserve your life, but simply shift the murderous acts to someone else, have you obstructed the assault in any way, or simply moved it around? If the forces bent on your destruction want nothing more than your death, is simply staying alive a form of resistance? When is an act resistance and when is it something else?

Here is an answer. To be considered resistance requires, first, a context of concerted, systematic action that is vastly unjust and that is causing suffering and loss. Second, an agent who can identify the aggressors, the agents of injustice. Third, an attempt by either a targeted victim or a bystander to obstruct, lessen, or eliminate some part of the assault. Whether or not the attempt is successful is important practically, but not in terms of knowing whether people resisted. Finally, for any given act of resistance, there must be some alternative that is, at least in the immediate future, less difficult, painful, or risky – say, less likely to lead to execution or torture.

Problems do arise with this definition; e.g., if the agent's intention is key to the definition, how are we to be sure of that? Perhaps Jews who cooperated "really to protect" other Jews actually thought they were trying to stop the Nazis, rather than just evade the terror themselves.

But these details are not essential here. The point is that we can learn from the Holocaust some of the alternatives that we face in contemporary environmental politics.

Whether a group of environmental activists are seeking the complete overthrow of capitalism, or simply to protect a particular endangered species or wetland, we need to know: What aspect of the world does this particular environmental practice threaten, and how will this act of resistance lessen that threat? Demonstrations against a toxic facility will do little good, for example, if they simply seek to get the toxic facility moved to somewhere else. Resistance to the facility needs to include resistance to – or at least a refusal to approve of – it being placed *anywhere*. Using nuclear power as a substitute for coal or oil may lessen greenhouse gases but creates enormous risks of plant accidents and faces the unsolved problem of radioactive waste disposal. Any attempt to use nuclear power must address those issues. It's great to protect a wilderness area. But people in the neighborhood who have been using it for food or forage need to be compensated. And if the area is in a poor, developing country, neighbors must stand to benefit from ecotourism rather than simply be arrested for poaching so that the area is kept pristine for wealthy Western tourists guided by foreign-owned firms.[11]

Trade-offs in politics are necessary. As is, at least sometimes, getting financial support from sources that are far less than perfect. So, cooperating with a known polluter – e.g., a chemical company who becomes a major donor to a wildlife protection organization to garner some good publicity – is not in and of itself necessarily a bad thing. *If*, that is, the donor is publicly identified by the recipient organization for what it is. Using one cause – saving the elephants – to justify contributing to another

---

[11] See Raymond Bonner, *At the Hand of Man: Peril and Hope for Africa's Wildlife* (New York: Knopf, 1993) and Mark Dowie, *Conservation Refugees: the Hundred-Year Conflict between Global Conservation and Native Peoples* (Cambridge, MA: MIT Press, 2009). Race and class also sometimes motivate laws on hunting and fishing. See Connie Y. Chiang, "Race and Ethnicity in Environmental History," in Andrew Isenberg, ed., *The Oxford Handbook of Environmental History* (New York: Oxford University Press, 2014).

one, is not resistance to the environmental crisis. It is simply spreading it around to some place with which you are less emotionally connected. "Oh, but what about the elephants saved with the donations from Mega Mega Mining company? After all, that's what our focus is, elephants." Not good enough, I would reply. You don't buy the health of the elephants at the price of greenwashing a company that poisons water and air someplace where there are no elephants – any more than it is resistance to the Nazis to just get them to move to the next village.

6 REFORM OR REVOLUTION

This is one of the most familiar conflicts in progressive politics. In the realm of animal rights it is phrased as the struggle between "welfarists," who seek to gradually improve the conditions of animals in factory farms or labs, and only outlaw the most extreme practices (e.g., testing cosmetics by dripping samples into rabbits' eyes until they go blind); and "abolitionists," who seek to end all human uses of animals whatsoever: meat eating, experimentation, fur, zoos. Welfarists argue that only so much is possible now; that to garner widespread support it is necessary to keep demands within the realm of general acceptability; and that extremist demands (e.g., end all meat eating) and extremist actions (liberating lab animals) will only alienate possible supporters and lead to more, not less, animal suffering. Abolitionists criticize welfarists as comparable to people who wanted to keep slaves better fed rather than freeing them, lacking in boldness and political imagination, and lessening the chances of ultimate victory by limiting their demands to the horrible status quo.

A similar conflict arises over tactics of wilderness protection. The activist group Earth First! – slogan: "No compromise in defense of Mother Earth" – used tactics like destroying bulldozers or spiking trees so they couldn't be used for lumber. They condemned more mild-mannered Sierra Club or Audubon Society policies as sellout accommodations: endless maneuvering by lobbyists that led to few victories and ever-greater losses. In turn, the advocates of main line environmentalism were concerned that the general public would come to think of environmentalists as violent anarchists with no respect for property or people and, therefore, come to reject all pleas for wilderness and biodiversity protection.

Some will argue that an "environmentalism of the rich" simply aims to make life safer and more comfortable for the reasonably prosperous and protect some wild areas while ignoring fundamental structures of consumption, inequality, racism, and colonialism.[12] Others will reply that system challenging reforms have failed and that moderate personal and policy changes are the best we can expect. Therefore, it makes sense to praise polluting, resource-destroying corporations in exchange for financial support and limited environmental improvements.

Some environmentalists argue that the movement has not succeeded because environmental strategies are mistaken: too bold, too moderate, too global, too local, too elitist, too absorbed in distracting issues of race or class, or too concerned with nature and not enough with people. And some offer the bleak assessment that environmentalists are doing the best we can and not succeeding because most people don't care, are in denial, are too short-sighted and too politically powerless, and that the political and economic elites benefitting from fossil fuels, clear cut forests, and toxic chemicals simply have too much power.

In a still larger context, on one side there is the attempt to control corporations, an attempt whose end would be socialism: democratic control over the central engines of economic activity. Investment, production, and consumption (at least in terms of meeting basic needs) all collectively owned and aimed at meeting the common good. The economy would not be private but public: like the army, a public park, or a city hospital. The enormously socialized production of the modern world – the way a given car or computer, say, results from the labor of dozens to hundreds of often geographically separate people – would be matched by the socialization of control.

Without this as at least our final goal, ecosocialists (or eco-Marxists) say, the inherent structural tendencies of capitalism will inevitably continue on a course of environmental destruction. As an economic system, capitalism requires growth, tends to overproduction, and consciously cultivates a popular culture of consumption and distraction. Politically, the enormous power generated by enormous wealth necessarily tilts governmental action in the direction of supporting what's good for corporate investors. The "one percent" have vastly more political influence than the rest of the population. Further, when corporate power is checked, but not eliminated, corporations can move to countries where environmental or financial regulations are limited or simply cut down on investment to increase unemployment and thereby shift public sentiment

---

[12] Peter Dauvergne, *Environmentalism of the Rich* (Cambridge, MA: MIT Press, 2015).

in the direction of relaxing controls of any kind. For all these reasons, the ultimate goal must be some drastic reduction in the private control of what are essentially highly socialized, indeed often global, economic processes.

Reformers will answer with a variety of criticisms of the ecosocialist position. To begin, it is a mistake to believe capitalism cannot be reformed. It has accommodated unions, the social safety net, occupational health and safety regulations, and affirmative action. Environmental care need only be another level of reform – and can be shaped to benefit corporations and the general public alike. As well, certainly in the United States and (ironically) China, anything like socialism is impossible for the simple reason that the vast majority of the population in both countries would not accept it as a political goal. If nothing else, state control of the economy has too dismal a track record. Finally, under the current system there are at least three major social forces – government, corporations, and public. If we combine government and corporate power in a state-controlled economy, the ensuing bureaucracy would be even more immensely powerful than either of them are separately. As limited as they are, government and corporations offer some check on each other. Corporations provide some of the economic efficiency and rationality that government programs can lack; government limits the corporate tendency to run roughshod over public health and community well-being in pursuit of profits. Finally, given the prevalence of political passivity and ignorance of social realities among the general population, it is hard to see how a state-controlled economy would give rise to anything but a powerful, privileged, uncontrolled ruling class of government bureaucrats.

A more extreme version of this last position claims that capitalism is essential to environmental improvement. Progress that has been made already doesn't come from rabid tree huggers or anticonsumerist scolds but is a predictable consequence of higher standards of living generated by capitalist-driven economic development. Only a rich populace can care about the "postmaterial" needs of clean air and protected forests. As well, environmentalists have frightened, depressed, and bored the public with their endless doom and gloom scenarios and their clearly antagonistic attitude toward the actual engines of economic growth; and thus to the resources necessary for environmental improvement. Because capitalism produces economic growth, and such growth is necessary for environmentalism to succeed, the answer is not less capitalism but more – not only in the developed world but also in the underdeveloped world as well. Capitalist ingenuity will provide the technology necessary to clean up the mess, if only depressing environmental forecasters, interest groups holding on to their place in the old economy, and governments more interested in regulation than innovation just get out of the way.[13]

This last point is the most easily disposed of. The idea that environmentalism is only a consequence of capitalist modernity is simply dead wrong. There are environmental themes in indigenous religions and peasant communities, which combine myth, tradition, and community involvement to manage and protect natural resources. There is environmentalism in the third world today: sixty thousand organic farmers in Bangladesh who know that chemicalized agriculture makes people sick; the Sarvodaya movement of Sri Lanka, which has struggled for decades for economic development that serves human interests rather than the GNP; local fisherman warning that mega-trawlers will destroy fish stock; villagers telling highly trained engineers not to build big dams.[14] In many cases it is those without formal training, the "unmodern" types, who have been correct. To ignore the ecological values and environmental activism of the "poor" and "undeveloped" is crude cultural chauvinism.

As well, this defense of capitalism relies on a simple-minded confidence that prosperity once achieved can never go away. The fact that the standard of living of the American working class has been (by various measures) flat or declining since the 1970s, or that a great deal of the globe's post–WWII development may evaporate when cheap oil diminishes, does not figure into calculations of inevitable capitalist prosperity. And neither does the possibility that current third-world immiseration is in some ways caused by global capitalism that destroys subsistence agriculture while propelling hundreds of millions into landless poverty. And it completely ignores the already unfolding catastrophic economic consequences of climate change, oceanic acidification, desertification, and

[13] This position developed by Ted Nordhaus and Michael Shellenberger, *Breakthrough: From the Death of Environmentalism to the Politics of Possibility* (New York: Houghton Mifflin, 2007). For a religiously based endorsement of capitalism – contrary to the usually left-oriented religious environmentalism – see "The Cornwall Declaration on Environmental Stewardship," Cornwall Alliance Website. Accessed January 22, 2018, http://cornwallalliance.org/landmark-documents/the-cornwall-declaration-on-environmental-stewardship/.

[14] On dams, which were in Thailand, see Bruce Rich, *Mortgaging the Earth: The World Bank, Environmental Impoverishment and the Crisis of Development* (Boston: Beacon Press, 1994); organic farmers in Bangladesh (Nayakrishi Andolan), in Bill McKibben, *Deep Economy: The Wealth of Communities and the Durable Future* (New York: St. Martin's, 2007); on Sarvodaya, George D. Bond, *Buddhism at Work* (West Hartford, CT: Kumerian Press, 2003).

species loss. Climate-related disasters cost the United States over 300 billion dollars in 2017, and the vast consequences of drought in Africa have yet to be even calculated.

There are, as well, legitimate questions about the possible scope of free market and capitalist innovation. For example, if increased profit is the motivation for becoming green, then even if production becomes less polluting, the pursuit of greater profits means that the economic tendency will be to increase production. And an endlessly expanding economy will still leave the environment in deep trouble. When a commentator praises a Toyota light truck factory for reducing its carbon footprint, he never asks if the stuff being produced so much more ecologically ought to be produced at all.[15] Do we really need more pickups, more SUVs, more individualized vehicles? Would companies parading their ecological concern ever question the foundation of addictive consumerism that is part of the ecological catastrophe? Ever avoid spreading the gospel of "more and more" to parts of the world not yet at our level of consumption – or suggest that we in the "first world" ought to consume much less and in a radically different way? Or is it that "brand companies such as Nestle, Mattel, and Proctor & Gamble" trumpet "relatively minor reforms as examples of sustainability and corporate responsibility" and then use "savings and feel-good rhetoric to sell even more products"?[16]

Finally, note that while capitalism is truly spectacular at promoting technological innovation, without environmental safeguards such innovation – e.g., in ozone-threatening CFCs and carcinogenic pesticides – can be destructive.

The more general tension between reform and full elimination of capitalism is more complex. While my own sympathies lie with the radical approach, I do believe that the current political and cultural climate makes a truly democratic environmentally oriented socialism at best a distant dream. One can only imagine the fate, for example, of a political movement that advocated no growth, being satisfied with what one has for everyone above the poverty line, and hours of engaged political participation per week. On the other hand, the constant struggle to contain corporate pollution throughout the world, and the way corporations tend to respond to environmental threats only when their

---

[15] Joseph J. Romm, *Cool Companies: How the Best Businesses Boost Profits and Productivity by Cutting Greenhouse Gas Emissions* (Washington, DC: Island Press, 1999).

[16] Peter Dauvergne, *Environmentalism of the Rich* (Cambridge, MA: MIT Press, 2016), p. 114.

own profits might be at risk (as in global warming), does not give much hope for a reformist strategy either.

Do my criteria for evaluating environmental resistance go any way toward clarifying the issue? Perhaps only in this way. However unrealistic the goal of ecosocialism might be, surely any moderate reformist can see the virtue in carefully thought out and consistently enforced laws to limit pollution and the devastation of natural resources, including wilderness areas. On the other hand, radicals can accept that however limited any particular reform (raise fuel efficiency standards, outlaw some particular chemical, punish environmental violations in black neighborhoods as severely as in white ones), surely the consequences of the reform are, in and of themselves, a good thing. Therefore, both in action and in argument, neither reformists nor revolutionaries should act in ways that diminish or obstruct the final goals or limited accomplishments of the other side.

As long, that is, as the valued action is not bought at the expense of some other issue or problem. Again, this does not mean that either side can do everything all at once. Short of a cataclysmic revolution that would sweep away all current environmental practices and replace them with sane ones, environmental organizations of all kinds will be working on this or that campaign, area, or concern. Certain wilderness areas will (hopefully) get protected while others will not; certain chemicals revealed as carcinogenic while others are ignored. There will be enormous focus on greenhouse gases and climate change, and much, much less on the fate of the near 50 percent of lakes and streams in the United States that are unsafe for drinking or swimming.

But this inevitable partiality of attention is not the same as trading one environmental regulation or concern for another. Thus, the standard I am suggesting for environmental political action is just this: Work on whatever project you like, under whatever reformist or revolutionary perspective you might hold. But do not accept environmental damage anywhere, in any form, as a trade-off for what you are working on. If the corporation will only donate to your organization if you stop criticizing its policies, you refuse the donation. If the senator wants your endorsement for his work on climate, and she deserves it, that's fine. But not at the price of ending your criticism of her for accepting lax rules on pesticides.

7 LESSONS FROM THE PAST?

Whether we are extremists or moderates, revolutionaries or reformers, may depend in part on how we view the lessons of the political past.

No matter how different the environmental crisis is from earlier social problems, and therefore how different environmental political activism will necessarily be from other activisms, we will necessarily take both inspiration and some cautionary lessons from what has gone before.

Here are two examples that reveal how environmentalists have thought about the role of the past in helping us comprehend the present.

Some animal rights supporters, for instance, have suggested that the movement resist the tendency toward giving up abolitionist goals by taking lessons from the late eighteenth- and early nineteenth-century attempt to abolish slavery in the British Empire. In the case of slavery, activists faced a centuries-old, globally accepted social practice, one that had extensive intellectual justification, including the blessing of religious authorities. And, perhaps most important, one that involved huge amounts of money in terms of the dollar value of the slaves and the role of their labor in the production of highly valuable agricultural commodities (e.g., cotton, sugar). The idea of abolition was mocked, criticized, or supported as an admirable but distant goal. Abolitionists were verbally attacked for a variety of "crimes" against the economy, the culture, and the well-being of the empire. Extensive propaganda was offered to show that slaves were better off in slavery than they would be in freedom.

All this, some activists argue, should remind us of the current fate of animals: the enormous financial interests, consumption and exploitation and use condoned by secular and religious perspectives alike, their bodies integral to cultural occasions (Thanksgiving, tailgating before a football game, the filet mignon dinner that signifies luxury and success), and their suffering in labs justified based on their moral worthlessness.

Yet the abolition of slavery in the British Empire took place a scant five decades after the first meetings of the Society for the Abolition of the Slave Trade, following a series of reformist efforts, e.g., regulations for conditions on slave ships, outlawing slave trade but not slavery.[17] And that is why, the argument goes, animal abolitionists should not "give up before we've even started" and accept purely welfarist

---

[17] James LaVeck, "Let's Not Give Up Before We Even Get Started," in John Sorenson, ed., *Critical Animal Studies: Thinking the Unthinkable* (Toronto: Canadian Scholars' Press, 2014), pp. 318–332.

approaches to the conditions of animals. The final goal is possible, even if it seems unreachable today.

The struggle for gay rights could be another example of an impossible ideal reached with remarkable speed. It was not very long ago that the idea of gay marriage, gay relationships thoughtfully explored in popular culture, openly gay politicians, and wildly successful gay entertainers would have seemed incomprehensible, let along politically possible. And yet that has all happened.[18]

Are there crucial differences between the current animal rights movement and the abolition of slavery? The financial interest in animal exploitation is incomparably larger and the cultural dimension significantly more entrenched. You can deny that a black man is fully human, but when he asks you to justify your position it is rather difficult to do so. Nothing comparable can be achieved with animals. Similarly, while the cultural resistance to gay marriage was profound – and remains so in many places – gay liberation poses little threat to entrenched economic interests and dovetails significantly with women's liberation to offer a set of ready-made allies.

The point, therefore, cannot be that current environmental struggles are "just like" these earlier movements. But, rather, that just as those activists probably had little hope of success, carried on only for the possible benefit of many generations in the future, and had miraculous outcome, so we too should carry on despite how dismal it often seems – whether for the moral atrocity of our treatment of animals or our moral atrocities to earth, air, water, and our own bloodstreams.

Conversely, consider what it means to act not when future success is at best distant, but when there are no grounds for hope at all. Jewish resistance during the Holocaust faced hopelessly overwhelming odds. Its goal was often something other than success or victory.[19] To a modern culture that celebrates pragmatism, getting things done, moving on with your life, "let the healing begin," and such, the idea of acting without chance of success may seem nonsensical, or at least very hard to fathom.

Can we learn something from how the resistors understood themselves?

In one instance we find a group trying to decide whether to stay in the ghetto and be killed by occupying armies, or retreat to the forests as

---

[18] By February 2018 gay marriage was legal in 26 countries.
[19] I say "often" because, especially toward the end of the war, Jews were part of partisan groups that had some real impact on occupying Nazi forces.

partisans, and almost certainly die in armed actions or of starvation.[20] We are doomed either way, they agree. But nevertheless, we have to do *something*, "or else Jews in the future will see that we didn't act, and they will be depressed." In other cases, we find people on the edge of death celebrating the sheer existential fact of, at least at that moment, being alive and resisting the onslaught. "I am happy," said Mordechai Anieliewtiz, commander of the Jewish uprising in the Warsaw Ghetto, "to have been one of the first Jewish fighters." "During my time in the Ghetto," recounts survivor Selma Urbach, "I was never more alive."[21]

Under the enormous pressure of mass deportations and starvation, casual murder of Jews without the slightest pretext and the threat of complete annihilation by the most powerful country in Europe, thoughts of future success or failure, of "how to do this so that we will win," are diminished. The pressure produces a clarity of concentration on the present only. We can think only of what to do today, next week, at most next month, to somehow signal to the world and each other that we still want to live.

While there are many ways in which the Holocaust and the environmental crisis are very different, they also have some similarities. The crisis is not centrally commanded by a single nation and political party; people involved with the crisis have not set out to create environmental chaos. They are (though this was also used as an excuse for actions that supported genocide) "just doing their jobs." Yet the Holocaust and the environmental crisis do share an enormity of the threat. The first a genocide; the present, an ecocide. Also, as the Holocaust was literally unthinkable before it happened, so it has taken decades to face the scope of the ecological damage we've been causing. Finally, as technological and bureaucratic rationality were essential to the Holocaust (the design of gas chambers, keeping detailed records), so contemporary ecocide combines ever more sophisticated means with ever more disastrous effects.[22]

And so an environmental activist knowledgeable of the full scope of climate change, dying species, and babies born with pollution-caused birth defects might well look to Holocaust resistors for a lesson not of

[20] They did not mention, though it was a danger: being killed by anti-German partisans who were also highly anti-Semitic.

[21] See Gottlieb, "The Concept of Resistance"; and "Remembrance and Resistance," *Social Theory and Practice* 14, no. 1 (1988): 25–40.

[22] See Roger S. Gottlieb, "Some Implications of the Holocaust for Ethics and Social Philosophy," in *Political and Spiritual: Essays on Religion, Environment, Disability and Justice* (Lanham, MD: Rowman and Littlefield, 2014).

strategy or of hope, but of the capacity simply to do the right thing despite the seeming impossibility of a good outcome. An example not of hope but of courage. We will try to save one wetland, one species of fish, one overpolluted African-American neighborhood. And even if we fail, future generations will know that some of us tried.[23] As a US senator put it about his efforts to deal with climate change: He didn't want his grandchildren to chastise him in the future and say: "What did you do about it when you had an opportunity?"[24]

8 VIOLENCE

Comparison with the Holocaust raises the critical question of the role of violence. If the environmental crisis is like an ongoing genocide, only so global in scope that it is better described as ecocide, then perhaps it is appropriate (right, justified, sensible) to resist it with violence.

Views on political violence are highly varied and often opposed. We are frequently told that political violence is a terrible thing, leading to unjustified suffering, generating backlash, discrediting the cause for which violence is committed. And we are told that social change can only come in a meaningful, lasting way if it is pursued through advocacy, public support, and voting for representatives who support it.

At the same time, the United States celebrates its Independence Day, the beginning of a violent struggle to change its political relations with England. And we tend (at least in the north) to view the Civil War as regrettable but ultimately necessary violence to free the slaves. Very few people look back at World War II and say we should not have fought. And, moving into a more interpersonal realm, very few would deny a woman the right to fight back, as violently as she can, against a rapist.

Are environmentalists' political goals like changing the minimum wage or making health insurance more accessible? Like increasing the social safety net or creating stringent regulations on banks? Or are they like a colonized country seeking its freedom? A battered woman resisting her abuser? A victimized racial group arming itself to resist lynching or police brutality? Inmates of a concentration camp trying save a few of their number from genocide by killing guards and escaping? When are we

[23] Presupposing that there will be future generations and that they will be able to remember.
[24] Senator Thomas Carper, quoted in Juliet Eilperin, "Lawmakers on Hill Seek Consensus on Warming." *Washington Post* Website. Accessed February 7, 2018, www.washington post.com/wp-dyn/content/article/2007/01/29/AR2007012901426.html.

talking about a movement aimed at legal political change and when simply a desperate attempt at survival?

To begin, note that "environmentalists' political goals" encompass an enormous range, differences among them so vast that comparisons between them and the examples in the previous paragraph can only be meaningful if the general category is replaced by more concrete examples. On this spectrum there are cases where the idea of violence makes little or no sense. Whom, after all, would you kill to improve automobile fuel efficiency standards? The CEO of Ford? Ford's lobbyists? An EPA staffer? The chair of the House of Representatives' environmental affairs committee? While auto emissions are surely a part of global warming, they are not the most important sector, and in any case improved standards, while a help, would only be a small part of the vast changes that are required. There are countless comparable examples: allocation of research funds, sharing innovation on clean technology with other countries, converting to organic agriculture. In each case progress toward the goal requires long-term advocacy, education, and voting for an environmentally responsible government. The force of violence would not only be questionable, as all violence is, because of its effects on particular people; it would also be just plain irrelevant to the political goal. And this is so despite the fact that global warming is in many places in the world already responsible for immediate loss of life. Melting glaciers mean less water throughout the year, which dries up rivers, which helps create starvation. Increased lightning in forests dried out by increased heat mean more death from more frequent forest fires. Air pollution in general may cause seven *million* premature deaths a year.[25]

Some cases are perhaps morally clearer. Consider the continued poisoning of a community, in a context where immediate illness and death are already occurring and where nonviolent resistance is met with brutal, violent repression. Are the villagers of the Ogoni region justified in fighting back? What about, as in the movie of environmental sabotage *The East*, striking at a drug company that is knowingly promoting a drug that has disastrous health effects – by "poisoning" the heads of the company with their own drug?

Clear answers to these dilemmas are hard to come by partly because environmental threats are often both widely diffuse and have

---

[25] "7 million premature deaths annually linked to air pollution," World Health Organization Website. Accessed February 14, 2018, www.who.int/mediacentre/news/releases/2014/air-pollution/en/.

consequences measured by increased likelihood of bad effects on an extremely broad population. There is generally no one-to-one correlation of murderous intent or culpable negligence and victims. There is a certainty that there will be victims, but no way of knowing who among that afflicted group will be among them. At the same time, environmental effects can be devastating: death; extreme illness; crippling birth defects; polluted food, water, and air. But even so there is no desire to hurt the victims, just a lack of concern of whether they are being hurt. Greenhouse gases build up over decades, no single storm can be tied to any country, industry, or corporation. Yet the droughts and storms, dying coral reefs and wildfires from increased lightning and the social instability all these lead to have already killed millions. The role of global warming–caused drought in the Syrian civil war – a conflict responsible for millions of deaths – is one depressing example.

So unless one believes that violence is *never* justified – not to resist genocide or stop a rape or remove a murderous tyrant – then, yes, violence to resist at least certain forms of environmental assault is morally permissible. If this assertion is met with the oft-heard claim that "violence only leads to more violence – violence never makes anything better," I would like to know if the person making this assertion has studied *all* the cases where violence was employed and was able to trace *all* the effects that ensued. It is not hard to see situations where nonviolence worked much better than violence. But is it also possible to see situations in which violence had, at least in the short run, positive results: revolts by slave and concentration camp inmates, the Warsaw Ghetto uprising, defeating ISIS. And even if the actions were *unsuccessful* – for example, in many slave revolts – that does not mean they were *unjustified*.

However, for the most part I personally doubt that violence will be of much help in environmental struggles. As devastating as the present and future of environmental problems are, the causes are simply too diffuse for the application of violence to have significant effect. To continue with analogies: A woman surely has the right to fight off a rapist. But does she have the right to shoot the editor of a pornographic magazine whose images may have glorified male sexual domination? Or men uttering sexist banalities that reflect and reinforce rape culture? What would such violence do to change the basic cultural norm of misogyny? Of course, if women everywhere were trained in self-defense from, say, age 5–20 and could respond violently to male assaults, that surely would make a difference. But such a vast change would only be possible after a very long period of nonviolent advocacy for such training.

Similarly, violence applied to one corporate criminal – e.g., the head of a polluting chemical company – leaves all the other polluters untouched. And would simply make room for a subordinate to become the next man in charge. Rather than frightening the company to change its ways, it would likely simply invest more in security and pressure the government to crack down on environmentalists of all kinds. During the George W. Bush administration, environmentalists were listed by the FBI as "domestic terrorist threats" because of comparatively mild-mannered actions like freeing lab animals and doing undercover videos of factory farms.

As Martin Luther King Jr. said when the Black Panthers talked about armed self-defense: White people have the police, the National Guard, the FBI, and the Army. We are only 10 percent of the population. If you start an armed conflict, who do you think will win?[26] Until environmentalists are the majority, or at least have far more support than we do now, violence can be at best an extremely rare and limited option, which will in turn probably have only the most limited and immediate benefits. The other side is simply far too powerful. As much as I might admire the brave souls who do what they can to stop the wanton slaughter of wolves or whales, if such defense turned violent, how long would it be until the armed might of the government came down upon the defenders?

In short, except in the most immediate and extreme cases, environmental politics must be nonviolent: careful outreach, thoughtful policies, the constant attempt to improve action by governments, businesses, local communities, and institutions – from the local church and school to wider organizations like trade and professional associations. Each social group can be urged to clean up its own act and to use whatever political leverage it has to move the government in a rational direction. This urging can take the form of civil disobedience, but that under the traditional form: well-advertised, nonviolent acts for which people are willing to take legal penalties.

And so this is yet another unresolvable feature of moral life under environmental crisis. We face a series of critical, often lethal, and for a good deal of humanity perhaps even existential threats. But our responses must be patient, nonviolent, perceived as reasonable, and oriented to the long-term solution of generating profound changes in people's attitudes

[26] Martin Luther King, Jr., "Where do we go from Here?" in James M. Washington, ed., *I Have a Dream: Writings and Speeches That Changed the World* (New York: HarperCollins, 1992), p. 175.

and social structures. It is not surprising that "feeling overwhelmed" is a common condition among environmentalists.

9 SPIRITUAL VIRTUES IN POLITICAL LIFE

Despite the well-known examples of Gandhi and Martin Luther King, there is still a commonly shared presupposition that politics is one thing and spirituality another. Activists often view self-described "spiritual" people as politically passive narcissists, and spiritual types see the politicos as angry, verbally (or actually) violent, emotionally out of touch, arrogant egotists. As inaccurate as these generalizations are, they also have some truth. There are countless examples of spiritually oriented people turning their backs on social issues and of political movements' self-defeating and personally painful internal conflicts rooted in emotional immaturity, intolerance of different views, and ego-tripping leaders. Too often the reigning culture of male power, domination, and inability to listen is reproduced in political circles that claim to be reformist or revolutionary.

Here I want to suggest that the central spiritual virtues of awareness, acceptance, gratitude, compassion, and love – celebrated in both traditional religions and in eclectic, nonreligious "spiritual but not religious" teachings – can be enormously helpful in political life.[27] And this is especially true because of the specific difficulties that confront morality and political activism in an age of environmental crisis.

We can begin with *awareness*: a willingness to experience, identify, and express the powerful emotions that are common to the stress and challenge of activism.[28] Without an ability to tolerate painful feelings, negative consequences are likely to arise. For example, as the coal magnates fight for more coal-fired power plants, the chemical companies lobby against regulations, and the meat merchants make it illegal to film slaughterhouses, there is a good chance we will get angry, at times very angry. If the energy of anger fuels our activism and political courage, that's all to the good. But what happens when no matter what we do, the change we

---

[27] The much longer version of this view is in Roger S. Gottlieb, *Spirituality: What It Is and Why It Matters* (New York: Oxford University Press, 2013).

[28] Miriam Greenspan, *Healing through the Dark Emotions: The Wisdom of Grief, Fear, and Despair* (Boston: Shambhala, 2002) for a general perspective on experiencing difficult emotions. She does not address anger.

seek doesn't happen? Will the anger then convert to resentment of other environmentalists whose strategy (we are sure) is not as good as ours? Or hatred of the mass of people who are environmentally ignorant, environmentally passive, or who think environmentalism is just a hobby for elitist liberals?

What political good does it do, after all, to express our thinly veiled (and much more evident than we realize) contempt for people who eat meat, toss plastic bags out of their cars, want to defund the EPA, hunt for recreation, or think pesticides in fruits are perfectly safe? Imagine such a person who, despite being somewhat in denial, somewhat culturally anti-environmental, is also interested in some aspect of what we are doing or has some initial sympathy to a few of our ideas. How will we get her to join the cause if we refer to anyone who shares any of her beliefs as "deplorable," "out of touch," "hopelessly ignorant" – or worse. How long would such a person's initial inquiry last before she decided that this was a movement that despised her? When environmentalists not only critiqued existing patterns of resource extraction and animal agriculture in the Yellowstone region, but also laid on blanket moral condemnations of traditional residents and a complete rejection of residents' cherished symbols and practices, of course the response of people they sought to organize was antagonism, resentment, and rejection.[29]

Mindful awareness of our emotional state requires a basic kind of *acceptance*, for often the greatest damage of powerful emotions like anger, grief, or despair is not the feelings themselves, but our fear or denial of them. To do so in the context of environmentalism often requires, I think, that we take in that the world includes extremely powerful forces making things worse, people who are ignorant or uncaring, and other activists who see particular problems in very different ways.

If activists do not fully accept these realities, then despair and desperation will lead to either political burnout or unnecessary internal conflict rooted in the suppressed expectation that "if only people agreed with me things would get so much better." Acceptance here does not mean approval, passive toleration, or some fantasy of guaranteed success. It just means taking in the full scope of what we face and being able to function despite the magnitude of the crisis.

---

[29] Well described in Justin Farrell, *The Battle for Yellowstone: Morality and the Sacred Roots of Environmental Conflict* (Princeton, NJ: Princeton University Press, 2015).

Paradoxically, *gratitude* is another spiritual virtue that will help us face how bad things are. This might seem a wildly inappropriate response to oil spills, plastic-clogged oceans, and the dying bats and bees; and these are, of course, nothing to be grateful for. Yet even if nine out of ten trees are dying from acid rain, we can still be grateful for the one that is not. Even if our email is overflowing with the latest catastrophes and outrages, we can still celebrate the last sunset we've seen and our ability to see it. If there are still some birds left where we live, we can take joy in their ability to move from earth to heaven, the way they are at home in the grass by our feet and the top of a nearby telephone pole. It is to be expected that people will wonder how we can tolerate a world in which a species is being rendered extinct every eleven minutes. It is less common, but surely as reasonable, to fully experience the wonder that we got to be alive on a planet with all this teeming, struggling, flying, swimming, shrieking, crawling, burrowing, crawling, talking and listening, killing and being killed life at all. If we despair over the polluters, we can also celebrate the environmental heroes and quiet, unsung activists.

Awareness, acceptance, and gratitude, in turn, can support attitudes of compassion and love in political work. Compassion for the weakness of people who cannot face the truth and who hide in denial of what are now well-established facts, will be supported by awareness of our own tendency to hide from the truth at times; acceptance of our own limitations may help us accept those of others; and gratitude for the goodness of life can keep us from rage or bitterness. Or, at least, keep our rage and bitterness from shaping how we treat other environmentalists or bystanders we hope to have join us.

10 CODA

It might be asked: *What is the most important issue? What kind of group should I join? What's the best way to do this?* My answer is simple: I don't know, and more important, I doubt if anyone else does either.

In the end, I suspect, virtually every environmental issue is connected, however tenuously, to every other one. If you are undecided between global warming, species loss, pesticides in food, lead in drinking water, factory farming, or the threat of reckless genetic engineering – don't worry, they all reflect the same fundamental problems. In every case we have the socially powerful, the cultural distortions of political passivity, consumerism, and techno-coma, the nonhuman species and disadvantaged human groups being afflicted.

So, in the words of Holocaust survivor and Nobel Peace prize laureate Elie Wiesel: "Where should you start? Start anywhere."[30] Someplace about which you care, for which you are willing to study, work, and join with others so that the effects of your labors can be magnified. As moral beings, that's the best we can do.

---

[30] Address at a conference at National Conference for Holocaust Education, Greenburg, PA, 1991.

8

Dilemmas of Reason

Outside of the most immediate face-to-face relationships – and often even then – being moral requires that we act carefully, reasonably, sensibly, judiciously: in short, rationally. There may be passionate moments of courage or sacrifice, but even these need some careful thought if they are not to be misdirected or even destructive. Especially in moral contexts that are as complex, far-reaching, and technical as the environmental crisis, rationality is an essential ingredient. Like other aspects of moral life in our world, this is not easy. In this chapter I will explore some reasons why.

I A FEW THINGS RATIONALITY IS NOT

Reason is often identified with a kind of objectivity – with an absence of prejudice, emotion, or partiality of view rooted in self-interest. To be rational, we often suppose, is to think of whatever situation we face *not* in terms of what we specifically want or our own limited experience or what we feel, but rather in terms of what has been called a "view from nowhere."[1] Only an objectivity detached from the particularities of our "personal" (individual or particular group) emotions, needs, and views will systematically increase our likelihood of knowing the truth. While being rational will help us get what we want, it should not be shaped by our desires. We must be neutral, detached, open to whatever evidence and conclusions arise, "value free."

[1] Thomas Nagel, *The View from Nowhere* (New York: Oxford University Press, 1989).

An opposing position claims that knowledge is impossible without certain interests. For example, it has been argued that scientific knowledge, and hence rational thinking about the physical world, is impossible without a basic interest in controlling nature.[2] However, in this view the interest in question is "transcendental," i.e., universal, inescapable, and not shaped by the characteristics of an individual or social group. To understand physical existence, to do science, just *is* to engage in reflection and action motivated, at bottom, by our need to predict and control our physical surroundings.

How do these contrasting views relate to our current situation?

Here are two analogies. Think of a historian studying anti-Semitism in 1936 Berlin, investigating the hatred of Jews in German culture, the role of contemporary political and economic factors, and Nazi propaganda. Then add in the condition that the historian is Jew. What would reason considered as impersonal objectivity mean for such a person? Isn't her research project deeply connected to her personal identity? Is she supposed to be unmoved by what she finds? Perhaps her intense personal connection to the subject matter would drive her to search more intensely and think more deeply than someone whose concern was merely intellectual, merely "academic." Or think of a mechanical engineer investigating the tensile strength of metals, their ability to withstand shock while moving (say) through water – and then imagine that this study is undertaken while the engineer is sailing on the *Titanic*. Could the threat to his life provide a passion for the truth lacking in someone casually hired to do mechanical engineering for a bridge that will be under construction for six years?

What kind of sense would it make for the Jewish historian or the engineer on the luxury liner to abstract from the fact that it is *their* lives that are deeply threatened? Can they be rational if rationality *means* impartiality, detachment, and neutrality? At the very least, wouldn't they echo C. Wright Mills's distinction: "I try to be objective; I do not claim to be detached"?[3]

Bring these examples into the present subject. Can we think about ongoing ecological catastrophes without being rooted in our own situation as beings essentially dependent on the biosphere? That is, could we do so without sinking into a kind of dissociative insanity?

---

[2] Jürgen Habermas, *Knowledge and Human Interests* (Boston: Beacon Press, 1968).
[3] C. Wright Mills, *The Marxists* (New York: Dell, 1962), p. 10.

The opposite view on knowledge and interests – that scientific knowledge requires the permanent, inescapable, and universal human interest in the control of nature – is challenged by the reality of the consequences of this view. If control of nature is the defining aspect of our rational (scientific) relation to nature, how can we rationally think ourselves out of a situation where both nature and people are dying from the consequences of our endless attempts to control? When rationality equals control, what happens when – as in the present contours of the environmental crisis – we are so in control that we are out of control? If interests are essential to rationality in general and science in particular, can we find other interests that might not produce the technologically based destruction we are experiencing now?

Clearly these points are simply the beginning of a long discussion. No matter how desperate the engineer is, it will do him no good to make an assessment of the hole in the *Titanic*'s hull shaped by panic rather than careful observation. And even if we turn to care and empathy for nature, rather than domination and anthropocentric separation, we will still want to heat our homes and grow food – and even use a control-oriented science to help clean up all the messes we've made. The ecofeminist critique of dominating, (supposedly) emotionally detached, culturally male reason coexists with the ecofeminist critic's desire for food, shelter, medicine, transportation, and culture.

As well, notice two other realities.

First, recent neurological research suggests that rational thought – calculation, taking in information, comparing results of tests, executive function – is literally impossible without emotional input. When the emotional centers of people's brains are severely damaged, so is what we conventionally think of as their rational capacities. Without caring about ourselves and the world, we cannot think clearly about either.[4]

Similarly, emotion can be an essential element in certain kinds of assertions or claims. Anger necessarily involves the belief that something is unfair, unjust, or morally wrong. Grief signals not just loss, but the loss of something of value. If we expel emotions from "rational" discussion, how would oppressed people register their "rational" resistance to

---

[4] When the emotional centers of the brain are damaged, for instance, it can become virtually impossible to make a decision. See, for example, Anthony Damasio, *Descartes' Error: Emotion, Reason and the Human Brain* (New York: Penguin, 2005).

oppression, or survivors of genocide signal the depth of the crime that has been committed against their group?[5]

Second, rationality should never be defined in terms of an absence of presuppositions, premises, or points of view. The condition of any learning is believing something already, e.g., that your senses are reliable, that other scientists are not lying about their results, that the textbook you're reading was written by an expert. Therefore, objectivity cannot mean neutrality about what is true, openness to any belief whatsoever, or a lack of assumptions. If we find out later that we were dead wrong about what we took for granted, that is not a reason to doubt the necessity of taking some things for granted now. Our beliefs are "absolute" just in that they are the basis for the rest of our inquiries and for our actions now – not in the sense of being immune to change.

2 VERSIONS OF RATIONALITY?

Let us return to the baseline, default meaning of nature as an object to be controlled for our benefit. In pursuit of this control we have for centuries accepted that scientific reduction of the natural world to controllable bits and pieces (bodies to cells, cells to molecules, behavior to DNA and brain neurology, forests to lumber) is the only way to truly understand the world. The license to do virtually anything to the nonhuman in this pursuit rests in the assumed rationality of the belief that nature has no moral value.

By contrast: If a person believes all of life is sacred, or that the natural world is essential to their identity (the "all my relations" standpoint of indigenous peoples) these are seen as religious, philosophical, or spiritual views that the individual is certainly entitled to hold but which should have little public place in a modern, secular, scientifically based society. Communing with the spirits of the forest is irrational or nonrational. Working long hours to produce a new version of the iPhone every nine months – or to be able to afford one – is normal, sensible, rational. Similarly, it is generally considered rational

---

[5] This role of emotion as central to morality and epistemology is developed by many feminist philosophers; e.g., Alison Jagger, Victoria Spelman, Marilyn Frye, and the womanist thinker Audre Lorde. And in the now classic Carol Gilligan, *In a Different Voice: Psychological Theory and Women's Development* (Cambridge, MA: Harvard University Press, 1982).

to pursue self-interest as the primary goal of one's life, with that self-interest often interpreted in economic terms.

Is this understanding of rationality... rational? What standard could we use to answer this question that would not beg the question by utilizing one or another concept of reason? On what basis could we possibly evaluate different fundamental concepts of rationality? As Max Horkheimer and Theodor Adorno observed, modern European thought since the eighteenth century tended to dismiss the idea that "reason" could be applied to fundamental frameworks of meaning or value. With the downgrading of religion as a source of truth, we were left with just "instrumental reason" – which could only evaluate how well a body of knowledge, a technology, or a practical strategy helped us fulfill our goals. The goals themselves, the overarching sense of what was good, valuable, wise, or right, could be only a matter of choice or taste. We were left with a "single stranded reality of industrial calculation"[6] in which science was the only real form of knowledge, and everything outside science was "written off as literature"[7]; that is, as art, personal values, or purely "subjective," private preferences.

One consequence of the cultural diversity and lessening of trust in traditional religions is that modernity has many comprehensive beliefs about how nature should be treated and what is the best life for human beings – and that the groups that hold these beliefs all believe them to be rational. The problem, contra Horkheimer and Adorno, is not that these don't exist, but that there are so many conflicting versions of them – and that we lack any shared method of resolving the conflicts. Alasdair MacIntyre described modern moral discourse as characterized by interminable moral disagreements and later posed the question: *Whose Justice? Which Rationality?*[8] With so many opposed versions, and so little sense of how to evaluate them against each other, we are left with no single dominating sense of reason. While everyone wants their cars,

[6] Ernest Gellner, *Plough, Sword and Book* (Chicago: University of Chicago Press, 1988), pp. 64–65.

[7] "To the Enlightenment, that which does not reduce to numbers, and ultimately to the one, becomes illusion; modern positivism writes it off as literature." Max Horkheimer and Theodor Adorno, *Dialectic of Enlightenment* (New York: Seabury, 1974), p. 7.

[8] Alasdair MacIntyre, *After Virtue* (Notre Dame, IN: University of Notre Dame Press, 1981). He gave as examples abortion, welfare policy, just war theory, and capital punishment. He did neglect to mention areas where some agreement had generally been reached, e.g., slavery. *Whose Justice? Which Rationality?* (Notre Dame, IN: University of Notre Dame Press, 1989).

airplanes, heart surgeries, and machine guns to work, these technological concerns arise in broader perspectives of secularism or fundamentalism, globalism or nationalism, cultural conservatism or intense multiculturalism, animal rights or no animal rights, respect for nature or pure anthropocentrism. And frequently the perspectives themselves possess significant inner contradictions. Religion rejecting secular people worship at the altars of power, money, or fame. Fundamentalists who reject evolution and climate change communicate with cell phones and utilize modern medications. In an ironic image, a third-world Christian theologian suggests that global capitalism "has its God: profit and money… its high priests: GATT, WTO, IMF-WB… its doctrines and dogmas: import liberalization, deregulation … its temples: the super megamalls. It has its victims on the altar of sacrifice: the majority of the world – the excluded and marginalized poor."[9]

These differences reflect fundamental differences about how the world works, what human nature is, and what form of life is reasonable. The secularist and the fundamentalist dismiss each other's priorities as out of touch with the essential realities of the cosmos. Meat-eaters think vegans just make no sense or are trying to impose "unreasonable" demands. Vegans think meat-eaters are hopelessly self-contradictory (generally considered a failing of reason) when they love their beagles and eat chickens.

The only solution I have for this dilemma is to point out that we cannot establish the ultimate morality or rationality of any given position, but we *can* point to their consequences – or at least to what we think are their consequences. Take nature almost exclusively as an object of domination, and you get the environmental crisis. Have no feelings about dying species, and you are severed from an emotionally sustaining connection to nature. Don't care about the unequal distribution of environmental damage, and you get a society marked by inequality that is virtually impossible to justify. Care only about the bottom line of your corporation's profits for this quarter, and effects of climate change might wreck the economy. Rest in confidence that God will solve these problems, and you will find that – just as in the past – God will not keep us from hurting ourselves. Imagine that technological management can replace the complex structure of nature in everything from pollination by bees to wild salmon's need of living rivers, and you will suffer vast losses in

---

[9] Mary John Mananzan, "Globalization and the Perennial Question of Justice," in Mary Hembrow Snyder, ed., *Spiritual Question for the Twenty-First Century* (Maryknoll, NY: Orbis Books, 2001), p. 157.

biodiversity, ecosystem services, and human well-being.[10] Thus despite their widespread acceptance, we can still ask whether "science is reason" and "self-interest should guide behavior" *are* truly rational – or perhaps just another unjustifiable faith.

Justifying a view of rationality solely based on consequences is a strategy many will reject. For one thing, there are significantly different ways to interpret the relation between a world view and its effects. Does the environmental crisis stem from too much technology or too little? Too much capitalism or not enough? Too much science and too little meditation – or the reverse? Some will hold out for a guaranteed rational method, justified by the essential structure of knowledge and logical consistency.[11] Others may discount my environmental ravings because they are sure that a cosmic apocalypse or technological fixes are just around the corner, or that environmental problems are fictions created to justify governmental intrusion. Such folks might see me as out of touch with reality, perhaps a little nuts. And I might feel the same way about them. In many cases a fruitful exchange will not be possible.

This lack of a resolution about reason is clearly a bedrock feature of modern culture, but it might also be a permanent feature of human culture generally. The ancient Israelites had little success convincing the Egyptians that there was only one God. Twenty-three hundred years ago Buddhism split into two significantly different branches. Catholics and Protestants are no closer to agreement than they were when the latter originated. Why should differences between ecocentric and anthropocentric values, or between a vision of science rooted in control and one in partnership, be any easier to settle?

Finally, besides looking at the consequences of our environmental practices and values, we can also ask: Who benefits when the common thrust of so much of our society is obedience to authority and conformity in the pursuit of personal financial advancement, technological gadgetry, military power, or group hatred? One need only see how unequally the

[10] The example of salmon is particularly interesting. While they are being devastated by global warming presently, for seventy-five years there was an attempt to replace natural supports with artificial, human-constructed, propagation. The results were disastrous. See Jim Lichatowich, *Salmon without Rivers: A History of the Pacific Salmon Crisis* (Washington, DC: Island Press, 1999).

[11] Countless philosophical critiques of this model have been offered from John Dewey to Jacques Derrida, from pragmatism to varieties of post-modernism, from Thomas Kuhn to criticisms of racial, gender, and cultural biases in scientific research.

benefits of these priorities are distributed to begin to suspect that they are not so "rational" – universally beneficial, for example – at all.

3 REASON, SCIENCE, VALUES[12]

There is a widespread tendency to distinguish between two clusters of concepts and social practices: between fact, truth, science, and technology, on the one hand, and religion, culture, morality, and personal taste or choice on the other. I do not deny the significant differences that exist among these. But, as suggested already, connections between the two realms are present as well.

Here is one: What causes, or at least makes possible, an area of scientific research? What – or who – determines which scientific questions are asked? How do we know what is worth our time, energy, and money? Out of the myriad scientific or technological investigations we might be doing, why are we doing *these*?

Does a modern society require so much variety in toothpaste, makeup, and shampoos? Ever-increasing energy consumption? No restriction whatsoever on medical intervention at the end of life? Food from thousands of miles away throughout the year? Why is so much more money being spent on finding the cure for cancer than on prevention? Why are so many trillions being spent on weapons and so little on dealing with the world's simultaneous (and surely not unrelated) epidemics of opiate addiction and depression?[13]

The reasons for these priorities are not hard to find. For example, cures for cancer can be sold at a profit, while investigation of causes might threaten enormously powerful, polluting corporations. Breakthrough cures might lead to a researcher's Nobel Prize while commonsense prevention measures surely will not. Weapons keep political elites in power, while the suffering of the depressed and addicted doesn't carry much weight in the circles of people who set research agendas (except, again, for research for a sellable, potentially profitable medication).[14] Unceasing

---

[12] Long on examples and short on pretentious vagueness, an excellent overview is Kevin C. Elliot, *A Tapestry of Values: An Introduction to Values in Science* (New York: Oxford University Press, 2016),

[13] Ten to fifteen million opiate addicts worldwide; 350 million depressed worldwide. World Health Organization Website. Accessed January 2018, www.who.int/substance_abuse/facts/opiates/en/depression.

[14] On cancer: Robert Proctor, *Cancer Wars* (New York: Basic Books, 1995). Samuel Epstein, *The Politics of Cancer Revisited* (East Ridge, MN: East Ridge Press, 1998).

trivial changes (improvements?) in consumer goods are the stuff of relentless advertising campaigns and continued profits.

The general point is this: to the extent that scientific research reflects the priorities of those who fund and undertake it, to at least the extent that all scientific research is shaped by "values" – in the broad sense of priorities, desires, and goals; and surely these values reflect not just personal choices but the encompassing economic, political, and cultural framework as well. It is not that the conclusions of this research are necessarily false or tainted, but that we have *these* conclusions rather than other ones. We know *what* we know not just because it is true, but because social forces lead us to this knowledge rather than other knowledge, to these truths rather than other ones.

Without values (in this sense) science itself would be impossible, for we would not know where to look, what to think about, or what experiments to conduct. And this also applies to what are more benign human values that can motivate scientific research, such as wonder, curiosity, and awe.[15]

It is also true that the day-to-day conduct of science would be impossible without certain key ethical values. If researchers are not honest, if dissenting voices are forbidden, if competent people are excluded because of prejudice, the truth will continually be obscured or lost.

If we then oppose rationality (or science, or facts) to "values" where could "rational" knowledge come from? It would seem to be impossible.

Defined in this way, the problem cannot be settled. Rationality will be impossible, and we will be left, as philosophers from Nietzsche to a constellation of post-modernists, theorists of identity politics, and nihilists have suggested, with only a struggle of conflicting wills, desires, preferences, and goals.[16] There is, and there will always be, science in the interest of the ruling class, science shaped by gender or racial privilege, science conditioned by one culture or another. The people who see things one way will do their science; and the people who want something else will do theirs. Understanding of knowledge in general and particular scientific claims in particular will bear the stamp of socially defined interests. Race, gender, class, and ethnicity will create biases and limitations that are typically unacknowledged. Many times basic principles or particular empirical results will overlap. But in many cases different sets

---

[15] Thanks to David Kidner for this last point.
[16] Foucault comes to mind. As does the tendency in feminist and multicultural studies to make all knowledge relative to various forms of social identity.

of information will arise, different problems will be approached for solution. Given the power of environmentally destructive corporate and governmental forces, the general drift will be in that direction. To the extent that countervailing forces exist, or that corporate and government forces recognize that they too face environmental threats, significant knowledge will be achieved based on the principle of the value of humanity – and perhaps even life on earth.

Could there be a solution to this dilemma of endlessly opposed "rationalities" in the perspective offered by Habermas already described: that the rationality of science is privileged not because of the absence of human interests but because it reflects an interest in controlling nature that is "transcendental?" That is, an interest that is universally shared, necessary for survival, and integral to virtually every other human desire or goal. We might adapt Habermas's position and say that the environmental crisis leads to a comparably universal interest. We all want to avoid getting polluted, having our children live on a much less habitable planet, or eliminating the ecosystem services of bats, bees, and wetlands. This is an interest that transcends culture or gender, race or religion, class or moral framework. And it is an interest that might support a vision of rationality in which cooperation with rather than domination over nature is the basic presupposition of scientific research and technological innovation.

Yet this solution has its limits. To return to earlier analogies: We might say the heroin addict violates his real, true, authentic, long-term, healthy self-interest in continuing to score and get high. But the heroin addict, at least by his actions, disagrees. Similarly, there are a wide variety of ways in which people can deny the importance of ecological health. They may be committed to short-term profit or power, believe in an afterlife, have faith that technology will cure all the problems, or prefer human comfort and convenience to the well-being of every other species. They may so discount the future as compared to the present that what happens in twenty years means nothing, and even five years away dwindles into insignificance compared to next month, next week, or this afternoon. They may be so culturally committed to endless consumption, endless driving, endless meat eating, and war that environmental consequences simply do not motivate them; or at least, do not motivate them very much. Racial or male privilege may be so crucial to their identity that seriously reckoning with the racial consequences of environmental practices or acknowledging their own vulnerability and naturalness – which they relegate to women and nature – are too great a strain to be undertaken.

4 TRUTH?[17]

The immediate goal of rationality is truth. What then becomes of reason when contemporary social life in general and politics seem to be dispensing with truth? This process did not start recently. It culminates a long historical process, including the lies that accompany various forms of oppression (racism, sexism, anti-Semitism, etc.); extreme forms of mass propaganda from fascism, communism, and liberal capitalism; and television's neurological colonization of the psyche through advertising. Yet what is happening now has reached, I believe, a whole new level.

Public language is first shot through with lies, distortions, concealments, and emotional manipulation via affecting phrases, images, and music and then progressively ceases to have a significant connection to reality at all. I doubt that people "believe" advertising. Rather, what the word *would* means is simply an emotional stimulus to fear, greed, lust, and escapist fantasy. The words and images make us feel something because *if* they were true (if *x* were a danger to our health, if *y* would make our families happy), then an emotional response of, say, fear or desire would make sense. However, we simultaneously know that the ads are not true and also have an emotional reaction as if they were. They constitute, as it were, a pornography of desire. As a result, statements parading as fact are now experienced as having the same relation to truth as the dragons in *Game of Thrones*: they excite us, frighten us, and perhaps lead us to cheer them on – even as we know they are not real.

For example: Do supporters of Donald Trump really believe his obvious lies and phony promises? E.g., "I'll sue the *Times*" "Nobody respects women more than I." "I had record-breaking numbers at my inauguration"? I suspect not. However, there is a kind of visceral excitement in seeing a public figure brag without shame, threaten a media outlet you hate, and (for misogynist and racists) heap scorn on women and racial/ethnic minorities. Constrained by a stagnant economy, disoriented by cultural change and loss of privilege, threatened by social catastrophes far beyond their understanding (the 2007 economic meltdown, ISIS, global warming) there is a deep pleasure in identifying with a man who offers simple answers to vastly complex questions, flouts "political

---

[17] An earlier version of some of this section appeared as "Truth, Environment, Trump," in Miguel A. De La Torre, ed., *Faith and Resistance in the Age of Trump* (Maryknoll, NY: Orbis Books, 2017).

correctness" and mocks established institutions that have left the typical Trump supporter awash in economic and social insecurity.

True? Who knows? But we don't ask if a warm bath is true, or a pleasing song, or an ice cream sundae. We just enjoy the way they make us feel. Truth? Perhaps. Or maybe just a few moments of pleasure from the feelings the lies arouse. And because everyone else is lying – the conventional politicians, the news sources, the ads – we might as well go with the lies that are amusing, reassuring, exciting, or just plain fun to watch. As Hannah Arendt, brilliantly reflecting on the rise of totalitarianism, observed seventy years ago:

In an ever-changing, incomprehensible world the masses had reached the point where they would, at the same time, believe everything and nothing, think that everything was possible and nothing was true ... The totalitarian mass leaders based their propaganda on the correct psychological assumption that, under such conditions, one could make people believe the most fantastic statements one day, and trust that if the next day they were given irrefutable proof of their falsehood, they would take refuge in cynicism; instead of deserting the leaders who had lied to them, they would protest that they had known all along that the statement was a lie and would admire the leaders for their superior tactical cleverness.

The result of a consistent and total substitution of lies for factual truth is not that the lie will now be accepted as truth and truth be defamed as a lie, but that the sense by which we take our bearings in the real world – and the category of truth versus falsehood is among the mental means to this end – is being destroyed.[18]

The erasure of truth is furthered by the internet, including the websites designed to spread lies for advertising revenue or political purposes. More generally, it is surely a good thing that the internet takes "publishing" out of the hands of the wealthy. For a pittance I can make my ideas available around the world – millions for a printing press or TV station not required. At the same time, however, the internet also makes possible a kind of democratization of ignorance and delusion. No editorial boards, peer reviews, or community discussions are necessary.[19] As an isolated, atomized individual, without connection to possible correction, awareness of other positions, or fact-checking, the web (and thus the world) is my oyster. Like the isolated act of voting, the isolated internet voice does not reflect self-conscious, mediated, relational, communal intelligence,

---

[18] Hannah Arendt, *The Origins of Totalitarianism* (New York: Harcourt, 1973), p. 382.

[19] The "mainstream" media clearly have always been shaped by the political interests of those who control. In a trivial way I saw that when an interview I gave to the *New York Times* was distorted in print. But I think past ideological biases in the press pale before the kinds of lies and systematic distortions found on the internet.

but far too often simply the prejudices and slanted ignorance of an individual or a parochial, narrow-minded, intellectually insular community. Speaking of the press, but in a telling phrase that applies so much more to communication in the age of the internet, Kierkegaard warned that "Here men are demoralized in the shortest possible time, on the largest possible scale, at the cheapest possible price."[20]

Years ago Habermas warned of a future society divided into two groups: the social engineers and the inmates of closed institutions.[21] The more truth is removed from ordinary political discourse and ethical interaction, the more we are closed into institutions of fantasy, illusion, emotional manipulation, and domination by corporate and political elites and group hatreds.

What does this mean for environmental rationality? It means an EPA head who denies both climate change and the well-known negative health effects of fracking; a Republican congress that proposes allowing fossil fuel extraction in forty National Parks, while denying that this is a threat to everything the parks are. It means environmental regulations in the care of lobbyists for the chemical industry. Countless other examples have arisen and will continue to arise.

But, it might be argued, everyone needs the truth. And while the reality of some things might be indeterminate (Jack is handsome, Coke is it), in other contexts it is not (that bridge will support the morning commute, the water doesn't have lead in it). Even the Bad Guys need the truth because they live in the real world. If they commit distortions, denials, delusions, and Big Lies, it will negatively affect their ability to function. And these consequences will ultimately lead to their defeat.

However, the scope of modern technology and communicative connection makes the truth very hard to ascertain. I can see with my own eyes that plants that usually bloom at the end of April are coming up in mid-March. I know that I've been wearing a fall jacket in much of this year's January. But I have no immediate access to climate change as a *global* crisis: melting glaciers, droughts in Central Africa, or the acidification of the oceans. I can know such realities only through reports from media, experts, or local observers. Which ones do I believe? My neighbor's cancer can be clearly known, but not which of the thousands of chemicals he's been exposed to help cause it. If the bridge collapses, which of these

[20] Howard V. Hong and Edna H. Hong, eds., *Soren Kierkegaard's Journal and Papers*, Vol. 2 no. 2171 (Bloomington: Indiana University Press), p. 489.

[21] Jürgen Habermas, *Theory and Practice* (Boston: Beacon Press, 1971), p. 282.

am I to blame: faulty construction, bad initial plans, limited government funds for inspections, bad economic policies leading to lower government revenue to pay for inspections, heavier than usual rains caused by climate change? And given the rate of dishonesty among scientific researchers themselves, how am I to know what's scientifically real and what' made up?[22]

If the media are biased. If fake news abounds. If everyone has "an agenda." If anything beyond my immediate experience is filtered by one side's experts or the other's, how am I to sift through all this information and find the truth – or know it when I find it?

A few years ago, because of a rupture in a pipeline not unlike the one planned for Keystone XL, a West Virginia town was flooded with oil.[23] So the good citizens of West Virginia saw the truth up close: that pipelines are dangerous and promises of "our safety measures are so sophisticated you don't have to worry" are empty. Similarly, and ironically, while the resistors of Keystone at Standing Rock (North Dakota) were being reassured of the safety of pipeline they were fighting, a similar accident happened around 150 miles away.[24]

But outside of the people immediately affected by these spills, how many people were influenced? How many residents of West Virginia or North Dakota were given full information – or paid attention to it if it was offered? How many wrote it off as regrettable, but surely not worth lessening anyone's access to fossil fuels. For after all, it is well known "fact" (a "truth") that environmentalists seek to destroy our nation's economy and that they exaggerate environmental threats to increase their funding and attack the ordinary consumer's freedoms. Further, while such accidents are surely regrettable, how often do they happen? And won't what we learn from the incident make us even safer in the future? Anyway, life is full of risk, right?

---

[22] Daniele, Fanelli, "How Many Scientists Fabricate and Falsify Research?" PLOS One Website. Accessed March 4, 2018, http://journals.plos.org/plosone/article?id=10.1371/journal.pone.0005738.

[23] Gabriel Trip, "Thousands without Water after Spill in West Virginia," *New York Times*, January 10, 2014.

[24] Michael Mcloughlin, "North Dakota Oil Pipeline Spills an Estimated 176,000 Gallons," Huffington Post Website. Accessed January 5, 2018, www.huffingtonpost.com/entry/north-dakota-pipeline-spills-estimated-176000-gallons_us_584f2375e4b0e05aded56896.

West Virginia and North Dakota voted overwhelmingly not for the at least somewhat environmentally careful Hillary Clinton, but for the fossil fuel and pipeline lover, Donald J. Trump.[25]

These reflections suggest, as W. V. O. Quine argued, that beliefs do not connect to the world in a one-to-one fashion.[26] Rather, we have a *system* of beliefs that are more like a web than a series of individual bricks tied to individual facts. When something unexpected happens, when something contradicts what we thought was true, there are countless different ways in which the system can accommodate the new reality.

If you are committed to fossil fuels, you can deny the severity of the accidents or climate change disasters, attribute them to other causes, and blame something else (immigrants, liberals, coastal elites) for economic issues that arise from climate change. A government can refuse to keep accurate records of droughts and floods; or refuse to make the records public. People who tell the country what is going on can be fired. The population can be distracted by a series of spectacles. While we have reports, year after year, of "Hottest year on record!" the White House removes climate change from its Website and the Department of the Interior erases climate change as a goal in favor of "energy dominance." In the meantime, the media dither on about the latest absurd, and soon to be forgotten, presidential tweet. Or the World Series. Or somebody's opinion about something.

In the long run, I suspect (and hope), the room for epistemological maneuvering will get progressively smaller. After a while the Catholic Church had to believe that Galileo was right; male supremacists (at least in parts of the world) had to stop claiming that women were incapable of politics, technology, or corporate authority. And in the long run, at least with regard to climate change and some of the more gross forms of pollution (e.g., the Pacific Garbage Patch) excuses, denials, avoidances, and blame shifting will get harder and harder. If things get much worse with climate, denial will start to seem completely mad.

Yet in the long run, as John Maynard Keynes observed, we will all be dead. By the time the long run comes around, it may be too late not to have a changed climate that will take the lives and livelihood of millions,

[25] Clinton had many environmental failings, including service to the US fracking industry. But there was a difference, and a serious one, between her and Trump.

[26] W, V. O. Quine, "Two Dogmas of Empiricism," *The Philosophical Review* 60 (1951): 20–43.

perhaps tens or hundreds of millions, of human lives, and untold numbers of other living beings as well.

5 NOT JUST WHAT – BUT ALSO WHO

Most discussions of rationality focus on presuppositions, methods, and outcomes. It is as if somewhere there might be clearly written rule book – like instructions on how to use an app or how to change the oil in your car – which, if followed, guarantee your rationality.

But claims about rationality are also privileged because of who is making them. For centuries it has been supposed, for example, that scientists are rational and religious believers are not. And this is crucial because we never, after all, directly encounter science, but only the claims of scientists supposedly reporting on what "science" tells us.[27]

And this is a problem. For while the methods of science and the accomplishments of technology may in some sense be rational, the behavior of scientists and engineers frequently is not. Considering the many dimensions of the environmental crisis, we might well wonder: *Who* made it possible? Who designed and implemented ozone-destroying CFCs without asking, seriously, what would happen when they were released at ground level?[28] Who produced and cavalierly reassured us that pesticides and genetic engineering would revolutionize agriculture with no pernicious consequences? Who was willing to take the chance that the entire atmosphere would catch on fire when the first atomic bomb was tested? Who designs cars that will test for emissions one way and pollute ten times as much when driven? And who designs the enormous factory fishing ships that decimate the world's fisheries? Now that smart phones are ever present, which of the initial creators asked questions about their effects on the eyesight or emotional life of children – among whom there are now dramatically rising rates of nearsightedness and depression?[29] The modern environmental crisis is hardly the product of axes or forest fires set with flint and steel. Virtually every single problem required

---

[27] Is this like having religious authorities tell us what God is and wants?

[28] John Nance, *What Goes Up: The Global Assault on Our Atmosphere* (New York: Morrow, 1991).

[29] Peter Jaret, "Are Mobile Devices Ruining our Eyes," Berkeley Wellness Website. Accessed January 5, 2018, www.berkeleywellness.com/self-care/preventive-care/article/are-mobile-devices-ruining-our-eyes. Lulu Garcia-Navarro, "The Risk of Teen Depression and Suicide Is Linked to Smartphone Use, Study Says," NPR Website. Accessed January 5, 2018, www.npr.org/2017/12/17/571443683/the-call-in-teens-and-depression.

sophisticated scientific knowledge embodied in sophisticated technology. How could it have gone wrong in all these ways?

It might be replied: This is not the fault of science, but of the *misuse* of science. It's not the technology that is bad, but this or that application of it, or this or that group of unscrupulous people driven by greed.

Perhaps, but then I would want to see examples of science and technology that do *not* arise in the context of the pursuit of power, wealth, privilege, and professional success. Where are the scientists and – perhaps more important – the funders of their research who are not motivated in these ways? As Herbert Marcuse suggested: if the effects of science are used as proof of its rationality, then the consequences of practicing science to dominate nature and in the service of corporate profit, governmental/military power, and personal advancement should lead us to the opposite conclusion. That is, scientists can be as fundamentally irrational as violent religious fundamentalists, racial bigots, or celebrity worshipers.

It was a hallmark of perhaps the most important single book in the history of modern environmentalism – Rachel Carson's *Silent Spring* – to critique not just the damaging effects of pesticides, but also the taken for granted moral and intellectual status of scientists. Carson argued forcefully that scientists could be mistaken, could distort the results of their research, adapt their findings and public statements to the interests of their employers, and be so focused on the short-term effects of some technological innovation that they give very short shrift to long-term consequences.[30] In all these ways, Carson claimed, rationality requires public information and public political power to make crucial decisions about scientific research and technological implementation.

But Carson's critique of science and demand for democratic transparency in scientific policy raises an issue that keeps returning: given the highly technical quality of many environmental debates, how will the public decide? While most people will see close ties to a particular industry as casting doubts on objectivity, clearly there is no one who lacks a point of view, a political "agenda," a vision of the role of science in general or at least how best to organize some particular area of social life: e.g., agriculture, health, the treatment of animals, or genetic engineering. We may have relevant information translated into nontechnical form, there may be "full disclosure" – but whose disclosing should we

---

[30] Sarah L. Thomas, "A Call to Action: *Silent Spring*, Public Disclosure, and the Rise of Modern Environmentalism," in Michael Egan and Jeff Crane, eds., *Natural Protest* (New York: Routledge, 2009).

trust? Will the public be any more, but rather probably less, able to form rational assessments of disagreements in scientific–technical matters, than they can in economic or foreign policy? Aren't all the fields in which modern, mass, technically dependent societies operate subject to severe technical and therefore moral disagreements opaque to the public?

So, the socially based limitations of science – from who funds to the culturally racist or sexist presuppositions that guide theory formation – cannot be erased by moving "rationality" from scientists to a democratically activist public. The point, rather, is that a guaranteed source of rationality simply does not exist. At best, we can try for transparency of funding and political orientation, get as many reasonable points of view and sources of information as we can, try to keep track of what approaches have worked and which have failed, and move dramatically away from the cavalier and often desperate pursuit of ever more short-term control.

Against the background of this rather bleak picture, here are two points that might give hope.

First, there is the reality of distinct communities with very different ways of thinking and standards of rationality reaching out to each other to face the environmental crisis. This has happened in the emerging alliances between leading scientists and highly placed religious leaders. The impoverished moral vocabulary of science and its inherent difficulty in identifying morally based social priorities led scientists to approach religious leaders in 1991 and ask for cooperation in drawing attention to environmental problems. Since then there have been joint meetings, letters to political leaders, and combined press conferences. Since then, as well, dozens of formal religious statements on the environment from theologians and religious authorities have begun with extensive quotations from scientific literature detailing the extent and severity of ecological problems. For just one example, consider this statement from a 2005 resolution by the National Council of Churches: "Prominent scientists and major, respected scientific bodies are in agreement that the Earth is warming because of human-induced carbon emissions."[31] Distinguished religious ethicists such as Larry Rasmussen may begin several hundred pages of

[31] "Resolution in Global Warming," National Council of Churches Website. Accessed January 7, 2018, http://nationalcouncilofchurches.us/common-witness/2006/global-warming.php.

moral argument centered on environmental issues by using scientific sources to illuminate the human condition.[32]

The result is a sense of mutual need: from scientists, an account of what is going wrong. From "religion" (which ultimate includes nonreligious ethical voices, through clearly environmental philosophers have vastly less social sway than religious leaders) a more detailed, in-depth, and morally resonant account of just what that "wrongness" involves.

Similarly, there are several concrete situations where people of quite distinct, often perhaps at times violently opposed, worldviews come together to act for ecological health. Examples include Palestinians and Israelis cooperating to protect water resources and culturally radical environmentalists cooperating with "old west" ranchers and miners to protect areas near Yellowstone National Park from oil drilling.[33]

And this leads to the second insight into a specifically environmental rationality. What is it, after all, that distinguishes environmentally oriented scientists *or* laypeople from those whose work helped cause the crisis? Was it better instruments? Better knowledge of the structure of chemical compounds or the long-terms effects of certain farming practices? Do environmental scientists have special intelligence or access to resources that those working for Monsanto or Exxon lack? What led to a recognition that it wasn't just chemicals that make a person sick all at once that are dangerous, but ones that build up in tiny amounts over time?[34]

What is typically at work, I suspect, is a fundamentally different underlying premise or overarching purpose: not the profit of an employer or professional advancement, but the long-term health of the ecosphere; not the domination of humans over nature for wealth, comfort, and violence – but mutual engagement, reciprocity, and coexistence with the rest of life, including humanity.

This underlying commitment, this "interest," can be found among nontechnically trained people as well. Consider the contributions to

---

[32] Larry Rasmussen, *Earth Honoring Faith: Religious Ethics in a New Key* (New York: Oxford University Press, 2013).

[33] For Israeli-Palestinian efforts, see EcoPeace Website. Accessed March 4, 2018, http://ecopeaceme.org/. For Yellowstone, see Justin Farrell, *The Battle for Yellowstone: Morality and the Sacred Roots of Environmental Conflict* (Princeton, NJ: Princeton University Press, 2015).

[34] Nancy Langston, "New Chemical Bodies: Synthetic Chemicals, Regulation, and Human Health," in Andrew Isenberg, ed., *The Oxford Handbook of Environmental History* (New York: Oxford University Press, 2014).

environmental knowledge of the toxics movement – decentered, community oriented groups of nonscientists who initiate inquiries into local pollution because of personal experience with severe health problems.[35] In several critical cases, despite condescension and dismissal by industry "experts" and politicians, ordinary people persisted, found technically trained allies, and were proven correct. Like the broader commitments of environmental scientists, these communities had a very distinct engagement with the reality around them: the health and well-being of their families, friends, and neighbors.

Such commitments do not guarantee truth or success. Inevitably there will be disagreements on how to handle problems. But if rationality is ultimately about the support of long-term human fulfillment, and human fulfillment is seen as necessarily including that of the rest of life, then we see at least the possibility of a fundamentally different orientation to what we know and how we act.

6 ENVIRONMENTAL AMNESIA AND ENVIRONMENTAL ADD

"Generational, environmental amnesia" is an imposing phrase that refers to a simple and frightening phenomenon: the way each generation will take the environmental norm to be what it has experienced.

At seventy I can sense the changes in the climate – how much earlier flowers bloom in spring, how much later in the year I can still see moths gathered around porch lights, and how much rain now falls in a short time.

But for people in their teens or twenties or, at this point, their thirties, this is just "the way things are." They cannot sense a loss they have not experienced. They can read about the past, chat with their elders, and examine photographs or movies. But these are all relics. Unless they are among the few people for whom the past has a vibrant personal reality, all they can encounter are stories of another time. Similarly, when I first encountered the few surviving giants at the tiny Muir Woods conservation area near San Francisco, I could imagine the original vast stretches of redwood trees. But it was only that – imagination. The reality of what the forests used to be – countless huge trunks that created a canopy for hundreds of miles – was only a thought in my head.

---

[35] Many books study this movement. E.g., Phil Brown, *No Safe Place: Toxic Waste, Leukemia, and Community Action* (Berkeley, CA: University of California Press, 1997).

As I had to make my peace with the remnants of the redwoods, so today's young folks will take a rapidly destabilizing climate less as a threatening exception and more as a norm. And the climate takes its place alongside the threats of toxins in the drinking water, the many days when the air is unsafe, the fewer songbirds, and dying coral reefs. With so many species extinguished or on the brink, the world just *is*, for a generation who know only environmental crisis, this scarcity of other forms of life.

Connected to the loss of *actual* biological diversity, is a corresponding lack of *experience* of biological diversity. A diminished immediate environment creates a consciousness in which the past richness of life does not appear. Lacking a sense of loss, there is nothing to fight to preserve. Who, after all, will find it rational to protect that about which they know so little, which they have known only at second or third hand, that is simply the stuff of history books or their grandparents' melancholy nostalgia?

Anthony Weston describes this pattern as "self-validating reduction": motivated by anthropocentrism, economic competition, greed, or militarism, we discount nature's value.[36] The consequence is a devalued nature: fewer species, millions of dead or dying trees, oceans covered in poisonous algae or jellyfish, a falling human sperm count, and an increase in infertility. Such a nature is less beautiful, less spiritually powerful, less a refuge from the onslaughts of modernity. And in a continuous downward spiral, the negative feedback loop continues: The less it benefits us, or seems to have value in itself, the less it seems worthy of respecting or defending. And because humans are essentially connected to what is around us, our own suffering from environmental causes increases as well.

The flip side of environmental amnesia and self-validating reduction is environmental attention deficit disorder (ADD): the inability to focus on the present very long or to remember what has happened in one's own life. The imposing power of social media creates a consciousness that is overwhelmed by a fragmented, ever-receding present. Significant problems – devastating hurricanes or wildfires, threats of war, climate refugees dying on the way to Europe or creating civil war in Syria – get tweet storms, YouTube videos, Facebook postings, obsessed newscasters. To keep from cognitively drowning and emotional overload, most citizens

---

[36] Anthony Weston, "Self-Validating Reduction: Toward a Theory of the Devaluation of Nature," *Environmental Ethics* 18 (1996), pp. 115–132.

must believe that someone else will take care of all this.[37] Or that there is nothing to be done anyway, and therefore the only response is to continue the pursuit of pleasure, distraction, or individual "success."

Further, nature tends for the most part to be slow and unexciting. The occasional tornado, tsunami, or owl picking off a mouse notwithstanding, plants grow, predators wait for prey, and the seasons shift not in a stunning eruption fit for a TV "nature special" but in ways that require quiet, long-term attention to understand and appreciate. The difficulty in encountering charismatic megafauna causes many nature videos to be filmed with captive or trained animals and "nature safaris" to require extensive preparation by guides to ensure that the ecotourists get the desired views. For more than fifty years time-lapse photography has allowed people to see nature drastically speeded up – and to be bored by real-time growth. Just as the ubiquity of pornography has led, paradoxically, to a diminishing of actual, live sexual encounters, so the hyper-reality of media in general and the representation of nature in particular leads to a diminished capacity to attend to an actual tree, this particular lake, the way ducks swim or seagulls drift in the wind.

And so, the world that we've lost through our limited memories and excitement-addicted attention spans becomes ever more diminished.

These reflections are relevant to rationality because it is very hard to think deeply and clearly about that which we do not care. And we cannot care about something the reality of which is lost – either because we never knew it, we can't remember it, or it doesn't command our attention long enough for us to get to know it. If we have not experienced something, or if our experience is fleeting, unprocessed, and unreflected upon, intellectual insight and political activism will be hard to come by. Ultimately, the knowledge that is essential for an effective response to the environmental crisis requires not emotional neutrality or detachment, but a personal connection. Amnesia and ADD dangerously erode that connection.

7 IS PARTIALITY IRRATIONAL? ARE LOST CAUSES CRAZY?

As we've seen, people may be devoted to their pets and ignore animals slaughtered for food, hunted to extinction, or enslaved for amusement and profit. Some zealously defend a particular place or a particular species but do not notice – or are actively destructive toward – other places or

[37] See the discussion of the "dominated self" in Roger S. Gottlieb, *History and Subjectivity* (Philadelphia: Temple University Press, 1987).

species: people dedicated to bird preservation who are avid fishermen, or who volunteer months or years of their time to protect "authentic" American bison and who love barbecue, or who are part of preservation campaigns that require extensive traveling and fossil fuel consumption.

Earlier I used such situations to explore issues of moral inconsistency. Here I am concerned with the degree to which they may be examples of irrationality. Does it "make no sense" (a common phrase denoting irrationality) to expend all the energy I do on my daughter? Or to have dozens of people dressed up in costumes to resemble adult birds, leading flocks of whooping cranes on new migration routes in ultralight airplanes? Is it "silly" (another code) to put so much effort into saving an ecosystem – trucking in tons of sand to save a beach, fighting off invasive species so that the favored plant of a nearly extinct butterfly has the one place they will lay eggs? Given the scope of environmental damage underway, can we offer a solid justification for so much devotion to *this* place or *that* species?[38]

If justification necessarily means proving that these species or places have a right to our protection while others do not; or that action in their defense will have a particularly decisive benefit to the overall environmental crisis, we cannot. But does the lack of such proof make these expressions of care *irrational*? I don't think so. When I love Esther I express an enormous preference for her *because she is my daughter and I love her*. And that is all the reason I need. I do not have to limit my love so that every person with rights gets the same amount, nor do I have to believe that the world in general will be a better place because I care for her. She is my daughter, and I love her, and that is enough. Similarly, if Joe loves bison, or Jill Lang's metalmark butterfly, or Sami the barrier islands of Louisiana, their actions in defense of them are understandable and reasonable. If they are not *particularly* rational, they are not particularly *irrational* either.

Note that the fact of Esther being my "blood relation" is not a deciding factor here. It would not be irrational for me to be devoted to Esther if I had adopted her rather than being her biological father. What Joe and Jill and Sami have done is, in a sense, to adopt a particular place or species – to consider them as part of their family. Brenda Peterson, who grow up in a National Forest, remembers: "Because the trees were older and taller than the grownups, and because all of us – from snake to

---

[38] See the accounts of these campaigns in Jon Mooallem, *Wild Ones* (New York: Penguin, 2013).

squirrel to people – were obviously related, I assumed the trees were our ancestors."[39] This way of talking is commonplace among indigenous groups.

Equal rights do function as a restraint on behavior, but only in very limited ways. I do not have to love, respect, or care for everyone the same – I just must, for instance, allow them all to vote, get fair jury trials, and speak their mind in public. I can devote a great deal of my time and energy to Esther, but I cannot steal money or kill someone to do so. We can try to save this or that species, but not at the expense of eradicating others. Though in some cases I might have to kill representatives of a species that is not endangered to preserve one that is. There is, as I've argued before, no justification for creating serious ecological problems to solve other serious ones.

It will often be fruitless to say to people devoted to particular species or places: "Look at the larger context. Wouldn't it be more effective, 'make more sense' (i.e., be more rational) to give all that energy to encompassing problems like pollution and climate change?" Perhaps it would. Yet perhaps the larger problems are so large, and the time so late, and the consequences of this or that campaign on behalf of these issues no more certain than those on behalf of one species or place, that our efforts are as well spent simply trying to do our best for one place or species. In situations this complex it is virtually impossible to be certain about the effects of our actions.

Further, I suspect it is a mistake about human action to suppose that we could always be motivated by some impersonal calculation of the long-term, overall consequences of what we are doing. Ultimately, for good or ill, we are moved by love as much as anything else. And if for whatever reason Joe or Jill or Sami love *this* particular bit of the world, it is no more irrational for them to try to protect it than it is for me to love Esther or for you, the reader, to express your love to the very particular people, animals, trees, places, or species who are fortunate enough to receive it.

[39] Brenda Peterson, "Killing our Elders," in Peter Sauer, ed., *Finding Home* (Boston: Beacon Press, 1992), p. 56.

9

Despair

It takes moral courage to grieve; it takes religious courage to be joyful.
Soren Kierkegaard[1]

Several years ago, at a small interdisciplinary conference on the environmental crisis, an internationally respected expert on the oceans confided to us all, in a bleak tone: "Everything I've studied to get my big deal reputation, everything: It's all dead or dying." He hadn't stopped working, he told us, because he didn't know what else to do with his life. But he had no hope that anything, or at least very much, could be done about the destructive mix of climate change, industrial pollution, overfishing, encroachment by development, and noise pollution (which affects sea mammals). This man was afflicted, and with good reason, by environmental despair.

"Despair" is often defined as the loss or absence of hope, but I think it is a deeper and more complex state of mind that can arise in all of us who take the environmental crisis seriously. Psychologist Miriam Greenspan defines despair as a disruption of the relationship between what we thought the world was and what we find it to be and a corresponding loss of meaning that stems from the fact that our beliefs and actions no longer seem to connect, to make sense, to what the world actually is.[2]

---

[1] Bruce Kirmmse, ed., *Kierkegaard's Journals and Notebooks* (Princeton, NJ: Princeton University Press, 2008), Vol. 2, p. 120.
[2] Miriam Greenspan, *Healing through the Dark Emotions: The Wisdom of Grief, Fear, and Despair* (Boston: Shambhala, 2002). Joanna Macy was, of course, a pioneer in this area.

Environmental despair can take many forms. For example: Why take part in a modern industrial system whose technological brilliance is so often devoted to violence, distraction, and degradation? How can we seek to love and protect a world where so many species are being extinguished so quickly? If people are this crazy, and this much is already irrevocably lost, why continue to inform myself and demand change that won't come? Why care about the future of humanity when people seem so motivated by short-term pleasures, profits, and power rather than long-term ecosystem – and human – health? What happens to our sense of life in the present when we realize how many other species we are killing? If every landscape has its own integrity, and the organisms within it have their own inherent life, which we could "read" if we were serious and attentive, what happens when the only landscape is built; when what is built is poisonous and destructive; when we only read it for commodification, celebration of cultural stupidity (e.g., sports stadiums), wasteful and brutalizing amusement (road racing); or a sense of self-aggrandizing beautification that only serves the rich (decorative gardens in exclusive suburbs whose wealth stems from toxic industries)?[3]

Our despair can arise not only because of what happens to us personally: a nearby river polluted, favorite forests clear cut, our children poisoned by pesticides. We are also affected by what psychologist Kaethe Weingarten calls "common shock": media driven exposure to violence and suffering happening to other people, in other places.[4]

As we look at responses to environmental calamities, we might well agree with philosopher Dale Jamieson: "Our failure to prevent or even to respond significantly to climate change reflects the impoverishment of our systems of practical reason, the paralysis of our politics, and the limits of our cognitive and affective capacities. None of this is likely to change soon."[5]

We have public acknowledgment of genocides, war, and traumatic events (e.g., 9–11). There are funerals for family members attended by loved ones, friends, even acquaintances. But what are we to do with our grief at the loss of a single species – or a thousand? Or of places only seen from afar – the rainforest, the coral reefs, the Colorado River? There is

---

[3] On "reading" landscape see Anne Whiston Spirn, *The Language of Landscape* (New Haven, CT: Yale University Press, 1998).

[4] Kaethe Weingarten, *Common Shock: Witnessing Violence Every Day* (New York: Dutton, 2003).

[5] Dale Jamieson, *Reason in a Dark Time: Why the Struggle against Climate Change Failed – and What It Means for Our Future* (New York: Oxford University Press, 2014), p. 8.

some recognition of deep sadness at the death of a cherished pet, but few people outside the environmentalist orbit would understand deep sadness over the extinction of some wild animal or meadow community.[6]

Emotionally, despair is a painful place. It can easily slip into depression or rage or a deadened numbness. Yet it is an appropriate response to learning the details of the environmental crisis. If you come from a place of ingrained confidence in the moral goodness and rationality of the human species, and of faith in the continuity of the beauties and miracles of nature, the facts, added up one by one by one, are a deep shock.

An overwhelming despair can drastically diminish moral life. Why think about virtue, moral obligation, even love, if what we do will have no good effect? If it's "all dead or dying"?

Here are a few lines of thought, lines that I have turned to for help in dealing with my own environmental despair. Sometimes they give me comfort. At others, they seem like whistling in the dark. Despair, I suspect, will for the indefinite future be a permanent part of an awakened consciousness. But perhaps it need not be the whole story.

I REALITY AND LOSS

In fall, 2017, environmental journalist Robert Hunziker warned of eco-system breakdown:

The evidence is too prevalent to ignore. For example, when (1) abundance of insects plummets by 75%, and (2) tropical rainforests mysteriously emit CO_2, and (3) Mt Everest's snow is too toxic to pass EPA drinking water standards, and (4) squid at 5,000 feet below the surface carry toxic furniture protection chemicals, and (5) ocean oxygen production plummets ... something is wrong, horribly, horribly, horribly wrong.[7]

How much more do we need to know?

Yet it is not any fact or group of facts that lead to environmental despair, but the steady accumulation of loss and the growing sense this will continue indefinitely. The polar bears cannibalizing their young

---

[6] See Lisa Kretz, "Emotional Solidarity: Ecological Emotional Outlaws Mourning Environmental Loss and Empowering Positive Chante," in Ashlee Cunsolo and Karen Landman, eds., *Mourning Nature: Hope at the Heart of Ecological Loss and Grief* (Montreal: McGill-Queens University Press, 2017). This collection has many fine essays on this theme.

[7] Robert Hunziker, "The Ecosystem Is Breaking Down," Counterpunch Website. Accessed November 7, 2017. www.counterpunch.org/2017/11/06/the-ecosystem-is-breaking-down/.

because global warming makes it impossible for them to hunt from the vanishing sea ice; the millions of deaths each year from air pollution; the slow, steady deterioration of the health of the soil and the consequent desertification; the slow and steady deterioration of human fertility (which is, doubtless, good news for the medically assisted fertility business); the pretentions of meat purveyors who act as if their "locally, humanely raised" animals are all too happy to donate their flesh to our chic "farm-to-table" eateries. The continuously proclaimed notion that every human desire must be satisfied, every human need met – while the rest of life is savagely used and discarded.

Some reassure us that it isn't all that bad; that several other times in earth history there have been cataclysmic geological, climatic, and biological shifts. Fred Pearce and Emma Marris tell us that change just *is* the norm of nature, and that damaged landscapes and extinguished species will recover and/or be replaced. Others remind us that in any case, eventually the sun will explode and all life on earth will perish.

These reflections may comfort some, but I wonder: What does it say about *us, here, now* that *we* are the cause of so much damage and death? Is pleasure at the prospect of new species taking the place of the ones we've killed all that different from saying: "Well, the Holocaust wasn't great, but look – new people are now living in the houses where Jews used to live"?

If people were systematically blowing up museums, destroying the last copies of the music of Bach and Beethoven, burning the last copies of Shakespeare, the Bible, and Dostoyevsky; if they were knowingly pursuing policies that would contribute to the deaths of millions, tens of millions, potentially hundreds of millions of people – would we not despair for the human species? And would we not despair even if we knew that other books would be written and music composed and people born?

Despair here is a function of our connection to other people and to the rest of life as an essential part of our identity. The loss of a species can be felt as *our* loss. The shame and guilt for what people everywhere are doing is felt as a depressing fact about ourselves. As Samuel Scheffler observes, the idea of the death of everyone on earth, or even some collectivity such as our extended family or community, is for most of us more frightening and dispiriting than our own, individual death.[8] And this is because our

---

[8] Samuel Scheffler, *Death and the Afterlife* (New York: Oxford University Press, 2013).

sense of our essential identity, of who we are, while deeply *personal*, is not *individual*. And this aspect of identity, I believe, is moral as well as psychological or emotional. It is not just that other species and other people are dying, it is that *we* are partly to blame. We feel a sense of responsibility, of ethical pain, for what we as a species are doing – and even more so because we are all too likely to be contributing as individuals.

2 KNOWLEDGE?

It is perhaps a measure of how bad the environmental crisis can make us feel that we might turn for solace to the simple fact of human ignorance. As much as we think we know what the future will hold, we really don't. It might, indeed, be much worse than we imagine. Rather than climate change and ecosystem breakdown killing millions of people, it might kill a billion or more. Modern civilization, rather than "just" being made more difficult in countless ways, might completely collapse. Ecosystems, rather than losing keystone species and diminishing in biodiversity might simply be erased: deserts replacing forests, wetlands, and meadows; the ocean reduced to jellyfish and algae blooms.

At the same time, things might get considerably better. As long as human creativity and the capacity to learn from the past persists, social changes might arise that we, from our vantage point, simply cannot envision. In my own lifetime I have seen what are to me progressive, beneficial changes take place that I not only wouldn't have believed were possible, but also couldn't even have conceived of. A half century ago, who would have believed that some of the most significant positions in academia, medicine, or government would be occupied by women: presidencies of half the Ivy League, directors of major hospitals, Secretaries of State? Or that a series of revelations of sexual abuse would shatter the careers of men in entertainment, politics, and media.

The general point is that no matter how bad things look – and they certainly do look bad – we cannot be sure what they will be like in the future. Emotionally, this means that while grief, fear, and anger are perfectly rational, the despair that stems from a sense of certainty about the future is not.

I am not suggesting that things will work out or that progress is inevitable. Such beliefs are easily refuted by even a casual awareness of humanity's cruelties and irrationalities. Rather, I am proposing that it is possible to live in the present without certainty about the future: either about how awful it's going to be or about how, somehow, we will learn to do better. Such certainty is virtually always a mistake, at least when applied to large social transformations. Despite how attractive either may be, neither hope nor hopelessness are epistemologically appropriate.

However, hopelessness and unjustified hope do share the advantage of both attenuating deep anxiety about the future. If we are certain about what is coming we need no longer be anxious. We can remain confident no matter how bleak it all looks; or we can rest in despair rather than be tortured by continually dashed hopes.

Given the limitations on what we can know about the future, such anxiety, I believe, just is a permanent feature of the situation we are in. What is called for, then, is perhaps neither hope nor hopelessness – but courage to live with the fear.

Where could that be found?

3 IN THE HOSPITAL

Let us imagine (God forbid) that someone you dearly love, say, your mother, is terribly ill. Confined to a hospital bed, perhaps hooked up to a breathing machine or simply extremely weakened. Confused and dispirited by pain and increasing disability, her future is completely in doubt. There is a good chance that she will die. Yet recovery is still possible. Certainty either way is impossible, both because of the nature of the illness and because of the many times when medical prognosis has been dead wrong.

What do you do? Would you sink into a passive, unmoving despair because things look so bad; even worse after one of the nurses confided to you that there really wasn't any hope for your mother and you'd better "make all the necessary arrangements"? Would you rest in a kind of exaggerated certainty that "Of *course* Mom will get better; she just has to!"

How much of your emotional energy would you want to devote to the future, to the outcome, to what things will be like when the anxiety over the future is over?

Is that where you would want to spend your mental time? Is that what you would want to dominate your consciousness?

Not, I don't think, if you really loved dear old mom. Not if connection to her in the present is more important – personally, morally – than whatever the future will bring. I think you would spend as much time in the hospital as you could: making her as comfortable as possible, conferring with doctors, perhaps reading and singing to her, or just holding her hand. You would want do what you could, for as long as you could, to express your love; and to be in her presence while she was still alive.

What this has to do with environmental despair is simply this: The illnesses and damage with which humans are afflicting nature, and themselves, have no certain future. But to the extent that we feel connected to trees and birds and our relatives and neighbors and perhaps just life in general, wouldn't we want to embody that connection in love and care *whatever* the future holds? As we would want to comfort dear old mom even if she will be dead in three days, so wouldn't we want – knowing that the future is in doubt and nothing is forever – to try to make a carcinogenic pesticide illegal, clean up a polluted stream, liberate some dogs from labs, or keep snowmobiles out of a wilderness area?

Perhaps we don't need to know what the future holds to express our love *now*.

What is that love made of? In part, if you have a reasonably good relationship with your mother, a deep sense of appreciation for who she is and the part she has played in your life. The precise contours of her face, the unique sound of her voice, her laugh, even the sound she makes walking across a room. Whatever the future may hold, these have been real, deeply important, and treasured – even if now her breathing is labored or she has cancerous tumors on her forehead.

And despite the many dimensions of the environmental crisis, comparable things are true of our natural environment. It too can be appreciated for the part it has played in your life. It too has been essential to your being alive at all. "Mother Nature" might be a cheap cliché, but, considered from another perspective, it is a simple truth. What else, after all, gave birth to us?

Thus the future – and along with the future our hope or hopelessness about it – can recede just because of what you *can* be certain about: the value of the beings who are suffering; how you feel about them; what you want to do to ease their pain and, just maybe, make a brighter future for a few of them.

4 IT'S ENOUGH THAT IT EVER WAS

A complete and unshakable despair over the present and the future is only possible if we forget our gratitude for the present. Reality can be reduced to *only* an unmitigated horror if the delights and gifts that we have *already* experienced are treated as commonplace, ordinary, not very important, and – above all – taken for granted.

"Of course I have had a, b, c, and d, and still have e, f, and g ... but what's really important, what's crucial, what will occupy all my mental and emotional energy, is that h, j, and k have died, and in the future x, y, and, worst of all, z, will happen."

Now I am certainly not denying that x, y, and z terrible environmental realities may very well unfold. Or that countless such realities have occurred already. What I am suggesting is that mental and emotional energy is finite. We can only think about so much at a time.

Why spend it all on the terrible future, especially because that future, while likely, is not certain? Why not reserve some energy, from time to time, for the miracle of life that has already existed, and that despite everything continues to exist in the present? Why not celebrate that we ourselves have been alive, and that so have maple trees, dolphins, and butterflies – as well as all the fungi and bacteria who liberate nutrients from dead bodies.

Is the existence of the universe itself something that we can "rationally" regard as just something to be expected, a matter of course, as in "Of course there is a universe, now let's pay attention to all the ways in in which it isn't what I want it to be." While it might be a widespread psychological tendency to notice, over and over again, what's lacking, is it a sensible way to respond to life?

It's no secret, and there are growing number of psychological theorists who have been exploring what is commonplace among the world's spiritual traditions, that gratitude is an essential component of happiness. As I explored in Chapter 2, gratitude for its existence can be an important aspect of our moral concern for nature. I believe it can also be an important psychological – or, if you will, spiritual – element in enabling us to carry on with a modicum of contentment and even joy despite what we are doing to nature, including our fellow humans.

Gratitude is often a choice. Among the possible objects of consciousness there are, for any reasonably informed, empathic person, a host of things to feel miserable about – and with good reason. But there are, I am suggesting, a least some things to feel good about as well. We can decide that gratitude is possible, that it makes sense, and that we want it to be part of our lives. And then we will need to use techniques ranging from prayer and meditation, to writing or music or petting our dogs or looking carefully at ducks on a pond or leaves on a tree to make it a reality.

Choosing such a response to the environmental crisis depends on our believing that we are entitled to a modicum of happiness and content-ment – *even* if the world is going to hell, and there is widespread misery among human beings from environmental as well as many other causes.

We might think: By what right do we celebrate some tree in our backyard or a nearby park while rainforests are being cut down to make grazing land for beef cattle, and the pine trees of the American west are being devoured by climate change–increased beetles?

The answer is: no right at all, for contentment is not a matter of right and wrong, but of a fundamental disposition toward reality. For we do not save one tree or sparrow by being unhappy. Our despair does not take a single toxic chemical out of the air or improve the life of one animal trapped in a lab. If we take nature as our inspiration, note that a tree will not waste its energy in anxiety over the future or bitterness for its fate, even as the chain saws approach. It will simply give all of its being to life until its life expires or is taken from it.

Can we do the same?

Along with our reasonable and deeply felt fear and grief, can we appreciate, just as deeply, that the universe has existed and that we got to be alive?

As we grieve all the losses that have been, and all the ones that are coming, can we say: *It's enough that it ever was – and that we got to be part of it.*

If we can, then despair will be real and potent, but will not dominate. If we can, then the miracle of the universe and life on earth will be just as true as the waste and destruction.

It's enough that it ever was. Enough for what? For the creation of life, in itself a strange and unlikely wonder. And for us to continue, for as long as we have, to both celebrate and protect it.

Moral life in an age of environmental crisis can count on little else. But if it has this, it will be enough.

10

Futures[1]

*I have set before you life and death, blessings and curses. Now choose life,
so that you and your children may live.*

Deuteronomy 30:19

I ADAM AND GRANDPA

Adam:

I haven't been outside for 2 days, and I'm getting pretty hungry. But the
wind just won't let up. Every time Grandpa shuffles up what's left of the
stairs and pokes his head out, I can hear it – howling, whining, pulling at
everything it touches, trying to get in here. So he just slams the hatch door
shut, and shakes his head, reaches over to pat me on the shoulder. "Soon
Adam, soon. Then we'll go out and see if the berries have ripened; and
maybe some kind of fish is in the flood plain. I know it's hard here, but it
could be worse. There are places where the wind is as bad, but it just
stopped raining. People are stuck inside without water when the blows
come hard." He's right, I know. We have jugs and jars and old plastic
containers full of water. And we sprout old seeds, the ones that aren't too
moldy, and that's mainly what we eat when we can't get out. But I also see
what he doesn't think I can see – that look in his eyes. It's pretty bad, not
as bad as the look I saw in a dog once, that we caught and chased down
because it had lost a leg, just before we killed it. We roasted it slow over a
fire, that last time the wind stopped for a whole week. Grandpa's eyes

[1] An earlier version of this chapter appeared in *Interdisciplinary Journal of Partnership
Studies* 4, no. 3 (2017). https://pubs.lib.umn.edu/index.php/ijps.

look like that dog's – fighting till he couldn't go on anymore, but knowing it was hopeless.

Grandpa:

If it wasn't for the boy I would have killed myself years ago. He's lucky, he doesn't remember what it was like before … It had been happening for years. But the stuff before seems like nothing – a few tornadoes, hurricanes, long droughts in Oklahoma and Texas, typhoons in Bangladesh, heat waves in Moscow. A few hundred deaths here, a few thousand there. Maybe, if it was a really bad heat wave or typhoon, as many as 50,000; and maybe a few million homeless. We thought that was bad. We didn't know. Or we knew and we didn't care.

How many of us are left in the U.S.? The world? No way to know. The planes, the grid, the cloud, the cell phone towers, the Internet – all gone. Everything we believed in, from local hospitals, to supermarkets where we bought all that food, to the police smiling and helpful on the corner, to the gas stations – Ahh, all those gas stations, and how we loved to say, "Fill 'er up" and whip out the smooth plastic card that made it all happen.

How did it start? With the first car or the first train? The first time some scientist said "Global warming? We'll just float white Styrofoam on the ocean to reflect sunlight." The first time there was an "oil crisis" and we just went back to business as usual afterwards. With every stupid empty phrase: Drill baby drill, energy security, American way of life, job creation, gross national product, economic growth, standard of living, protect the middle class. We didn't know we were just whistling in the wind, dreaming of a future that was about as real as some little girl's fantasy of marrying a prince.

But me, I think it started with the bees. And the bats. Global warming, climate change, all that – most people couldn't get their minds around it. The earth is too big, other people's weather was just a lot of headlines; and if it was in the third world, well, we were always used to those brown, yellow, and black people dying like flies anyway. If something went wrong here – a hurricane in Vermont, twisters in Alabama – there'd be headlines and hysterical newscasters and interviews with blown-out families.

But then things would calm down, more or less, after a while, and we'd all think about the next election or the Big Game, the new American Idol or some idiot on reality TV. But when the bats and the bees started to die – a fungus for the bats, a pesticide for the bees – that cut into the food supply. Fruits and vegetables started to skyrocket in price – well, there it was, right in front of us. We'd made some changes in the food chain, in the air and water, in the bugs and microorganisms. And now those changes were going to change us. But lots of things were right in front of us and we didn't look at them. A hundred thousand pine trees in the Rocky Mountains were falling every day because some beetle really, really liked the warmer weather and could eat trees for an extra few months every year. Breast cancer was an epidemic. Spring was coming weeks earlier and the ski resorts were going out of business almost as fast as the pine trees in Colorado. There was a stew of plastic junk in the Eastern Pacific that was as big as fucking Texas, some said as big as the U.S.

We knew all this. At least some of us did, and tried to tell the rest. But we didn't listen. We thought we'd ride it out. That someone else would take care of it. Worst of all: we didn't realize all this was kid stuff, like rolling down a little hill. And that we were about to fall off a cliff.

Adam:

The wind is slowing down. Grandpa says we'll go up soon. We'll try to find something safe to eat. Grandpa says there used to be lots of good things – something called bread, which he tells me about but I can't quite understand. He even showed me a picture in an old magazine. But I've never seen anything like it and I can't really imagine. I only know this world. And there was fruit, all kinds of fruit, all year round, and so many different vegetables besides the seeds. And none of it was moldy; and you didn't have to fight the rats or the roaches for it.

Grandpa:

Did we understand how easy we had it? How much we had? Couldn't we have made do with a little less, just to protect Adam and all the others? Moot point now, too late. We wanted food without sweat, so we kept playing around with the genes and the earth and insects; and we wanted to make a lot of money off it, so we gave the power to agribusiness. When the viruses came, the ones the monocultures couldn't handle, and they hit the rice, the wheat and the barley, and something else had already begun to wipe out the bees and the bats so the pollination was way down, and then they tried something to kill the viruses, and that spread to the vegetable fields in California and what they used to deal with that spread to the wheat and corn in the Midwest and the fruit in Mexico and Brazil.

And all of a sudden the global marketplace was a series of shuttered windows and locked gates protected by armed men. Every country got more and more afraid that what we had would spread to them. They shut us out. After a few months, while we lived on that processed crap in the supermarkets, all the shelves were empty. In six months there was nothing to feed the cows and the pigs and the chickens so they died off. In the big cities, in the suburbs, people were starving. The little isolated organic farms were o.k. But even if we couldn't eat, we still had guns, lots of them. No one with a little farm could hold it for long.

So the government declared martial law and nationalized all the farms, everywhere. Which worked for a while, at least it got food for the people in power. But then they couldn't feed the soldiers, who turned their guns on the great and powerful, and took the little that was left. We begged the rest of the world for help. But no help arrived. Because each country closed its doors to everyone else, not just us. But it turned out all the technology depended on trade. When things started to break down, they had to choose between fixing the machines and taking the chance that all the food would be ruined.

And when whole nations started to suffer, they would take their weapons and do just what people here did with the farms. Take for themselves. And then the weather really turned bad. Nothing we'd built, almost nothing anyway, was made for this. Cars picked up and tossed around, we'd all seen that before. But trucks, trailer homes, bulldozers? After a storm it wasn't twenty or thirty power poles down, but hundreds, thousands. And it wasn't just the little poles on the little streets, it was the big metal things that carried the main lines. Even if they could stand the wind, they couldn't stand the trees that smashed into the wires. There just wasn't any power you could depend on, not with the wind like this. Cell phone towers? A joke.

Adam:

So we went above, and for a whole day the wind was down. There were no 'nadoes and we didn't have to fight off any of the wild dogs. There aren't too many of them left, Grandpa says, because they can't get enough to eat. But when they do come, I get really frightened. Out on the road there are lots of cars, lots. They used to move around, really fast, I've heard. But then something ran out, or we couldn't get any more of it, and there wasn't any way to use anything else. So people walk everywhere now. Some folks have horses that they ride, but it's hard to get food for them. And when the winds come, sometimes they go a little crazy and we can't control them and they run away and get eaten by the dogs.

Grandpa:

When the oil stopped, that was the worst of it. No cars, no planes, no ships, no fertilizer. Suddenly we realized we'd been living on a dream, a dream of oil forever. Even most of the alternative sources – wind, sun, hydro – depended on spare parts and machines and stuff that came by truck, or car, or were dependent on other stuff that came that way. Or the people that made it or fixed it needed some medicine for their asthma or their diabetes that came that way. We could get power off the grid, but we couldn't live off it, not enough of us anyway.

And the same thing that happened with the organic farms happened with everyone who had solar or wind. People tried to take it, and then the government took it, and then the soldiers took it for themselves or their families, and then it broke or ran out and there was no way to get it back. I heard there are some places where they still have some oil. Venezuela maybe, or somewhere in Africa. But they don't have the machines to get it out, refine it, make it do anything. Or if they do, they don't have any spare parts, or enough engineers to make it work. They always left that sort of thing to us. And even if they did, people would come to take it away, and there would be fighting. Someone told me they heard a last desperate message from some radio station in Saudi Arabia, before all contact was lost. They had a secret reservoir of oil, a fair amount of it, at least what had become a fair amount after the major wells ran dry. And they were offering to trade it, straight up, gallon for gallon, for water.

They had all this oil, you see, but they couldn't get their machines to run because all the spare parts had stopped coming, and there hadn't been rain in three years, and all the other countries around them had dissolved into chaos and no one would help. They were dying of thirst, finally realizing that you can't drink oil. I remember, when I was a teenager, some kind of storm hit New Orleans and people got very upset. Thirty years ago we had four of them in a month, and the last two just went up the eastern seaboard – Miami, Charleston, D.C., Baltimore, New York, Boston, Portland – water in the city center, coastal homes taken down, subways ruined, roads washed out. No electricity for months, no way to get food to kids, to evacuate hospitals or old age homes, dead dogs and cats and homeless people rotting in the streets when the waters went down.

And then a week later the real tornadoes hit the Midwest, from Chicago and St. Louis to Lincoln and Ames and all the rest. And three nuclear power plants on the rivers got overrun with water and there was no electricity to work the pumps, so the waters turned radioactive. Millions of people without a place to go, no power, bridges destroyed so fuel deliveries were stopped, cars left on the road. And then what we used to call a freak snowstorm took out train tracks and highways from California east – and the food deliveries stopped. How many died just from starvation – and then from the gunfights for food – we never knew.

That's when martial law came in, and never left – not until the government just dissolved because there was no power and no food in

D.C., or most state capitals either. Who knows, maybe the president and the other big guys are still in some undisclosed location, waiting for things to clear up. But in those other places, inland, it's worse. There's just no rain, no water. Whatever oil they have left they use to truck in water, or to pump it in. But they can never get enough, and then their storms kick up and smash the roads, or the machinery, or the pipeline. We never did figure out how to desalinate ocean water – too busy building smart phones and tablet computers, I guess. All we've got now is hundreds of millions dead, refugees from storms, and drought, and famine roaming the land hoping to find something better. And when they do, there are too many of them and then in a few years, or months, that's gone too.

Adam:

I guess this is just what it is. I'll never understand what happened, what there used to be. Grandpa says all the broken trees used to be something called a forest, that in some places you could swim in lakes, they weren't all choked with green slime; that there were things called beaches where people went into the water, which wasn't all filled with jellyfish and old plastic. All those things that used to be. Where did they go?

2 EVE AND AMANDA

Eve:

I love to go out into the garden before anyone else. It's cold, but I put on two sweaters and Amanda doesn't mind. The vegetables in their beds are just coming in now. If I push my fingers down just a little I can feel the carrots, and the lettuce just glistens (Oh I love that word) with the dew on it when the sun comes over the hillside. Of course I wouldn't do more than look, and touch them a little, and say a blessing over each carrot I see and all the vegetables, thanking the Goddess for plants, and sun, and water. There are new flowers on the apple trees. The fruit won't be in until the fall, but I bless them for their colors and their smell. So many beings to bless. So many. Of course I know I have to be back in the tree house before the sun really comes out. It's too hot later, and if I get caught in the sun in the middle of the day, Amanda says, something bad could happen to my skin. But I bless the sun anyway, because without it nothing would grow. It's not us who make the food, says Amanda, it's all these others. We just help out a little, and they help us out a lot.

Amanda:

Eve is a good girl, and so precious after all those miscarriages. God knows what was in the food and water for her mother, even after The

Change, and what it did to her. I'm very lucky to have made it to my age – not many do. But I'm still concerned that something will start to show in her. If I go, well, it will be my time. And others will take care of Eve. That's what we do now. Death we will always have, but at least we have stopped poisoning ourselves and the others. We eat what comes from the Goddess, we don't add and don't subtract. And thank Her for everything we have. And if there's a bad year with bugs or storms, we eat less and thank Her for helping us understand our limits. Even if that means some of us die.

Eve:

Some months, even one whole year a while ago, can be pretty bad. Nothing grows right, there isn't enough rain, and we don't eat much. But Amanda says that is just the rhythm of life. The Goddess blesses us with food, and then with hunger: to teach us to appreciate every day, every moment, every song we sing and breath we take.

Amanda:

How did we get here? I'll tell you, I don't know. All I can say is about the part I played, me and a few others I know. The rest of the world had to do it their way. There were some storms, big ones. And there was hardly any winter that year – it only went below freezing a few times and the river, which had always frozen solid for at least a few weeks, ran all through January and February. Then a thaw, which wasn't really a thaw because nothing had frozen, came in mid-March, and the May flowers were out before the first week of April was over. And it was hot, t-shirt and shorts and still sweating hot, in April when you usually needed a sweater and jacket both.

Other stuff was going on too, and getting worse. People diagnosed with cancer, scared about water quality, bats and bees were dying, a rash of frogs with horrible deformities. Coral reefs off Florida bleaching white from the warming, and a bigger than usual dead zone in the Gulf of Mexico from the chemical agriculture, and the Asian carp had gotten past all the barriers and were ravaging fishing in the Great Lakes. It was all going to hell and no one was doing anything about it.

Oh, the EPA was making its usual noises, and the environmental groups were trying to raise consciousness, but the people with the real power, from the networks to the politicians to the CEOs, were doing business as usual. Talking about economic growth and more buildings and more computers and more cars and more and more and more, God forbid we should just be satisfied with what we had right now, or double God forbid we should ever have less.

I couldn't stand it. Neither could my friends. We said, "It can't go on," and "Why don't they do something?" and, most of all, we saw that our parents and aunts and uncles, and the priests and ministers and rabbis and school teachers and rock stars and really, really pretty girls in movies and on the magazine covers and the team that won the Super Bowl – that they weren't going to do anything for us. That the people who ran everything and owned everything, well they sure weren't going to do anything. So if anything was going to happen, it would have to be us. And you know, it was easier that anyone dreamed. And it happened so much faster, too.

Eve:

At night sometimes I get up and leave the tree house oh so quiet and climb down and walk to the meadow. Amanda doesn't know, because I hardly breathe when I pass her sleeping pallet, and my bare feet don't make a sound on the path. And I sit in the little space between the garden and the wild, and I just listen. I can hear things – insects and small animals and bats in the night. And even more. I can hear the earth breathing, and the sky humming along being the night sky. And sometimes, when it's perfectly clear, I think, I just think, I can hear the stars.

Amanda:

It was on the parkway, one morning going to school, which was a few miles away from my house, but of course no one would walk or bike. I was driving, all by myself, and my friends Sue and Rachel were up ahead. The traffic was horrible, we were barely moving, just inching along, so we were texting about, I don't know, some nonsense or other. To think of how much time I wasted with that ridiculous phone of mine – when there were all these others to listen to, and look at, and care for. Oh, but that's just silly. We were what we were, and we're different now. And better.

Eve:

I am so glad I am alive. And that Life is here to provide for me. Every breath, Amanda tells me, every breath shows how I'm connected to everything else in Life. After all, no breath, no connection . . . no life!

Amanda:

So all of a sudden Rachel's texts get a little crazy. There's a guy in the car in front of her. He gets out. He stands on the hood of the car. He starts to yell so that people can hear him over their stereos and car TVs and iPhones. "This is no way to live. Don't we all know it? This is crazy; this is suicide. We have to find something else. NO MORE CARS, NO MORE HEATING UP THE EARTH AND POISONING OURSELVES. We must

tell them it has to change. We must be the change. NOW!" And crazy as
crazy as it sounds, he just leaves his car and starts to walk.

Where? Who knows? Maybe to the state capital building, which don't
you know was about four miles away. Well the craziest thing is, people
started to follow him. They knew what he was talking about, and the
word spread to the other cars of people who hadn't heard him. They
understood. We all understood. We'd just been too scared and too
wrapped up in all the cars and phones and computers and handy little
gadgets and meat to barbecue and orange juice that got shipped here from
Brazil to do anything about it. And we'd all gotten so damn lazy at the
same time that we were so wrapped up in the crap that we were all the
time exhausted. We didn't sleep, we just passed out when we couldn't
stand being online any more.

So I got out of my car. Just walked away, and joined up with Rachel
and Sue and we started to walk too. What were we going to do? We didn't
know! Isn't it wonderful? We didn't know – we just knew something had
to change, and it was going to start right now, right here, with us. Yeah,
with us – a bunch of dopey high school girls who didn't know their asses
from their elbows, as my father would have said, but just one thing, one
thing we did know. The way we were all living was crazy.

Eve:

I learned to read two years ago. Amanda and I had to walk for two
days to the library. There was an old man there, real friendly, but I swear
even the million creases on his face had creases, and his hair was whiter
than the big clouds that build up in summer. But he just kneeled
down, and smiled at me, and said that I was beginning a very exciting
journey, and I was lucky to have such a wonderful guide. He let us have
ten books, and said he would send more with a courier in two months.
That wasn't soon enough for me. But Amanda taught me not just to read,
but to savor (Isn't that a great word? It's like you're eating something with
your mind.) each word, each thought.

Amanda:

So we walked together, more and more of us. And then it spread.
People called their friends and texted their parents and their grown kids,
and their colleagues at work; and all of sudden, all across the country
people were just walking off the job, out of their cars, out of their houses
and into the streets. They went to the big office buildings where the oil
companies were, and to the banks and the police stations and the mayor's
offices and every federal building.

Well the People in Charge got terrified. They called us communists and terrorists and whispered that we worked for Russia or Al-Qaeda or were all on drugs. But it didn't work because there were just too many of us. Too many people who'd lost their mothers to breast cancer. Too many people freaked out about the weather, about their kids with asthma, about the strange, scary color of the sky on a hot day in August. They sent the police after us, but they just smiled and asked us please not to break any windows. They sent in the National Guard, and then the Army, but they just put down their weapons and lined up right beside us.

Easy? No, it wasn't easy. A lot of people died because we were all so dependent on The Machine. The hospitals didn't work as well, and there was a lot less food. And it got really cold and really hot and a lot of the time we were uncomfortable, or hungry, and things were harder than they'd been. People had to walk miles and miles and miles. We'd try to make exceptions for the old and the sick and women with babies.

But pretty soon it just became a kind of common sense. Don't ride when you can walk; don't burn something that doesn't absolutely need to be burned. Don't use anything you don't absolutely need. But we all knew this was what we had to do to change. And we hooked up to people who knew how to do things locally and grow food without chemicals and get power from the sun. Suddenly everything that was healthy and real became precious, and all the stuff we'd had before – everything that distracted us from what was really going on – just seemed empty and a waste of time. And we started to accept that being alive meant that sometimes you're hungry or cold and we were all going to die, so it was better to live sane than crazy. And if a lot of people had to die ... well, people were dying already: for war, for poisons in the food, for nothing. At least these people were dying for something.

Eve:

We don't go to the city too often. People bring us what we need – food and blankets, wool to make clothes, the news of what's going on. Amanda says even though the cities are so much smaller, and so much cleaner than they used to be, if she is going to do her work, she needs to be out here – with just the garden for the special herbs she uses, and the forest nearby, and the animals, and the fish in the river. She is so good at being a healer that people walk or ride their bikes, or if they are really sick, the special cars for that will bring people to her. And that's how we get the stuff we can't grow ourselves.

Amanda:

The change came when we realized that oil wasn't the enemy, wasn't evil, wasn't the source of some horrible poison that was destroying the earth by making the climate change. No! Oil is sacred; it holds the life force of billions of living beings that can give us heat and movement and so much else. The problem wasn't oil, it was us – treating oil like some cheap throwaway junk, wasting it, my God, how we wasted it. As if the life force bound up in it had no meaning. And that was true of everything else – food and water, even air, that we polluted as if there was an infinite supply, when really there is just this thin shell around the earth, and the rest of the universe probably doesn't have a single molecule.

We finally figured out – or was it that we finally remembered? – how we should treat the things that are the most important: air, water, food, sources of energy like oil and wood, old people who need company more than a lot of medicines, kids who need love and attention. We learned that the sacred is not some God in heaven, some afterlife, or some words in a book. It's the living beings and the sources of life. That's all. And that's enough.

Eve:

I'm really glad I'm alive. Each morning I get up, and say my prayers to life. And I mean them, 'cos where we would be without life? But Amanda tells me that life means death, just like death means life. That we come in one form, for a while, and then become something else. I hope I become a butterfly, or a cardinal, I love their calls in spring. Of course I know I won't be me when I'm something else. I'll just be something else! But in a way, I'll still be me – not the me that says words and walks on two feet and wears clothes, but the me that breathes, and has a body, and lives on the earth. That's enough, I think.

Index

male domination, 22, 165
Maras, Emma, 53
Marcuse, Herbert, 206
Marris, Emma, 217
McDaniel, Jay, 80
McKibben, Bill, 151
meat, 22, 45–46, 83, 102–104, 107–111,
    114–115, 119, 137, 143–144, 146,
    149, 162, 164, 173, 186–187, 195,
    199, 217, 231
Meister Eckhart, 46
Menominee Tribe, 83
Merchant, Carolyn, 34
methane, 25, 143
Midgely, Mary, 85
Mill, John Stuart, 23, 37
miracles, 51
Monsanto, 14
moral community, 78, 116
moral concern, 41–43, 47
moral conflict, 118
moral consideration, 37, 45, 47, 131
moral inconsistency, 212
moral intuitions, 33, 103
moral philosophy, 70
moral reality, 146
moral responsibility, 17, 152
    of ordinary people, 145
moral significance, 39
moral value, 35, 39–40, 48–49, 66, 85, 91,
    193
morality, 22
    and consequences, 213
    conflicts within, 142
    denial of, 59
    dilemmas of, 109
    and hierarchy, 125–127
    and inconsistency, 126
    and knowledge, 128
    and personal choice, 146–149
    and privilege, 130
    and restraint, 131
    and self-knowledge, 148
    and social system, 150
Mother Nature, 220

Naess, Arne, 34
National Council of Churches:, 207
national parks, 26, 35
National Parks, 202

native peoples. *See* indigenous peoples
nature, 11, 22
    and change, 53
    compassion for, 137
    concept of, 32
    connection to, 27
    control of, 44, 58
    as egalitarian, 56
    experience of, 70
    and gratitude, 43
    and humanity, 32
    human similarities, 72
    intimate connection with, 95
    knowledge of, 26, 72
    knowlege of, 74
    and mora significance, 79
    as marvel, 48
    moral status of, 36
    moral value of, 60
    need for, 48
    relationship with, 42
    and selfhood, 68
    separation from, 25
    as slow, 211
    as social construction, 88
    as spiritual teacher, 56
    and spirituality, 66
Nazi doctors, 152
Nazism, 18, 157
neoliberal, 16
New Deal, 154
Nhat Hanh, Thich, 12, 40
Nollman, Jim, 74, 81
nuclear power, 25
nuclear weapons, 20, 152

objectivity, 190
Ogoni, 183
Ojibwa, 73
ozone layer, 13, 16, 21, 38, 44, 79, 108

Pacific garbage patch, 33
Paris Climate Accords, 164
patriarchy, 44, 71, 163
Pearce, Fred, 53, 217
People First, 103, 105, 109
pesticide, 14, 27, 150, 220, 224
pesticides, 14, 17, 21, 44, 75–76, 79, 82, 92,
    120, 150, 155, 169, 177–178,
    187–188, 205–206, 215